Praise for the Tarot Re

"For anyone who is looking at understanding life, they need to understand their place in it. The Tarot helps to unlock some of the doors to the vast Universe we all coexist in. Sandy hands you the keys in this book."

— John Edward, Psychic Medium

"At one time or another we are all beginners at the things we do. During these time periods we often times seek out the advice, opinions, and help of a guide or mentor that can lead us through our struggling beginnings and bring us to a point of comfort and certainty. Sandy Anastasi's Beginners Tarot is a profound book with which no beginning Tarot student should be without. It takes the novice and experienced reader alike on a journey of learning not just what each individual card means, but on a road of discovery into how to actually read the cards with accuracy. No prior reading or psychic experience is necessary. In fact, if you follow the book and the techniques presented within, you undoubtedly will learn to become not just a basic reader, but will have a foundation built that can actually take you to that of an expert reading level. It is a source book and guide that, like me, you'll find yourself coming back to over and over again and seeing and understanding just a bit more with each viewing. Even more impressive, it's in an easy to understand format that anyone can pickup and start using immediately."

— John Culbertson, Owner of Starchild: A New Atlantis Rising Company

"This Tarot book is one of the best investments I have ever made! Sandy has provided wonderful tools for both the beginner and professional card reader in an easy to read, easy to understand format. My overall impression of this book is FANTASTIC! This material has given me the confidence through knowledge, to go out and do what I love doing!

I highly recommend this as a 'must have' book to both friends and colleagues who want to learn the Tarot for themselves, or who plan on taking it to that next level of professional reading."

— Lisa Freeman, Professional Psychic Tarot Reader and Psychic Medium

Books by Sandy Anastasi

The Anastasi System Psychic Development Series:

Level 1: The Fundamentals

Level 2: Energy Work and Auras

Level 3: Toys and Tools

Level 4: An Introduction to Channeling and Spirit Communication

Level 5: Developing the Energy and Skill in Spirit Communication

Level 6: Healing in Spirit Communication (to be released)

Astrology:

Astrology: Art and Science

Intermediate Astrology

Tarot:

Tarot Reader's Workbook: A Comprehensive Guide from Beginner to Master

Kabbala:

Pathworking the Kabbala

TAROT READER'S WORKBOOK
A Comprehensive Guide from Beginner to Master

The Future

The Next Six Months

Present
Information

The Last Six Months

The Foundation

Notices

Tarot Reader's Workbook — A Comprehensive Guide from Beginner to Master

Copyright © 2009 Sandy Anastasi

ISBN: 978-0-578-01562-0

Acknowledgements

Many thanks to all of the people who helped this present version of The Tarot Reader's Workbook to come into being. Too numerous to mention individually are those countless thousands of students and clients over the years whose life experience, shared with me, helped these pages take shape. You all know who you are, and you have my thanks. I must single out some very important people for special mention though. First, my friend and long-term client Don Morrison, who after 28 years is still a loyal client. He probably knows more about the Tarot by now than most professional readers do! Thanks go to the now deceased Mr. Campbell who showed me so much about how to read death and illness and give the right counsel. Thanks to John Maerz and the Astrological Institute, which published the earliest versions of this book – many of which still reside on dusty shelves. Special thanks of course go to my life-long friend John Edward. Little did either of us know those many years ago when my classes first took shape where his life would take him! Even the Tarot doesn't tell everything. It is wonderful to see where his early studies ultimately led him, and to be aware of the many millions of people his work has helped. Thanks go to my go-to person, Lisa Freeman, to Rick Rajter, my computer magician and graphics whiz, and to his lady Emily Jack for her excellent editing and proofreading. And last, but never least, thanks and a gold star for my husband, Ron Tourville, whose special talents helped to bring all of the people together to make this current work a reality. To all of you, my most sincere gratitude and love.

Table of Contents

Foreword

Students of the Tarot are found all over the world, due to the phenomenal interest in the archetypes of the psyche that unfold in the various decks. The beautiful art, the esoteric meanings, and the rich symbolism of the cards are intriguing, and stir the imagination of the seeker.

Many inquiring minds found their way to my former business, Planet Earth Book Center in Fort Myers, Florida, where we offered classes in Astrology, Palmistry, Tarot and related subjects. We were happy indeed when Sandy Anastasi relocated from New York and came to the center to join our staff. Sandy began reading and teaching for us in 1989. From the beginning, her classes were well attended, and as the students spread the word, her classes grew. She connected so well with her students, they remained loyal even as they went on to practices of their own. Sandy imparted her own enthusiasm to her students; her adaptation and understanding of the Tarot guided them through their development and their individual quests. From these classes, she honed her Tarot instructions into the remarkable book you hold in your hands.

Sandy Anastasi now brings her knowledge of the Tarot to the awaiting world. She has garnered the teachings of the ancients, the secrets of the masters, and her understanding of the Tarot – all that a student needs to learn – and has created a book that is a wonderful teaching and learning tool. It is a guide for students and seekers alike. Now they may share the immense wealth of her knowledge of the Tarot.

Congratulations, Sandy! Thank you for your contribution.

Mary Alice Warren
Preeminent Tarot Reader
Former Owner: *Planet Earth Book Center*

Author's Foreword

Many people have asked me how I first came to be a student of the Tarot myself. (For even now I consider myself a student, and the Tarot is my eternal teacher.) The fact is, my study of the Tarot was totally unintentional, as was my initial involvement in the entire field of metaphysics, which has been my life for the past 30 years.

I was an engineer and a student of astrology when I first became interested in the Tarot. My scientific mind was able to accept that astrology, being a science itself, might have some accuracy, but I was hard pressed to accept the Tarot as anything other than a party game. I learned the simple card meanings quickly and easily, and began doing them for my friends just for fun.

The 'fun' lasted only a short time. My friends began coming back for more. They wanted to know what happened next. I told them it was only a game. I was only telling stories created by drawing together the simple card meanings I had learned. I was not psychic. But they told me the things I predicted were happening. My friends were getting pregnant, divorced, losing or changing jobs, traveling – and I had predicted all of these things. This made no sense to me. I knew I was not using any psychic ability. I was only reading the face meanings of the cards. So how was I predicting the future? I was hooked. I wanted to know more.

In time I realized that the Tarot works on its own, independent of psychic ability, and that it helps readers to develop their own psychic abilities and a strong connection to their higher self and their guides. The Tarot becomes a teacher to the person who reads with it. This book you hold in your hands will get you started, but the Tarot itself will lead you along your path to self discovery and personal excellence.

Today I still continue to read the Tarot. In my own work I have combined it with both astrology and my ability to channel. I still study the Tarot as I read for people. I have read many clients multiple times over the years and am able to see how through use of a psychic Tarot reader people can take control of their lives, are able to know where their probable future is going, and are able to alter the events they do not wish to occur.

The Tarot is a valuable tool for helping yourself (by working with it) and others (by reading for them). It can lead you toward enlightenment if you allow it to. I hope your journey of self discovery is as wonderful and enriching as mine has been.

Chapter 1

An Introduction to Tarot

The Tarot cards have become increasingly popular as we move deeper into the last decade of the Twentieth Century. Many of us are striving to find that life purpose our innermost selves tell us we have, and in our search we turn to the study of belief systems of all kinds, from traditional religions to metaphysics. Inevitably, our study of metaphysics and New Age philosophy leads us to a study of the Tarot, whose ancient symbols speak directly to our subconscious mind, helping us to find both purpose and direction. The system of Tarot is in itself an age-old philosophy that not only still works, but also can help to bring enlightenment. Try meditating on a Tarot card, or sleeping with one under your pillow, and you'll be amazed at the new ideas and answers to old questions that will fill your mind! As a matter of fact, many experienced readers agree that this is a wonderful way to learn the Tarot!

Some people face our turbulent times with trepidation and fear and seek Tarot readers, or learn to read the Tarot themselves, only for its oracular power to predict the future. For these people, Tarot becomes ever more popular as the uncertainty of life in our times increases. A brief warning to members of this group – it is not wise to read the Tarot for yourself when you're using it as an oracle, or predictive tool. It is far too easy to read what you want to see, or what you fear, instead of reality, when your emotions are involved. Unfortunately, most of us are only really interested in knowing what's going to happen when we're emotionally involved! It's also a danger that people reading their own cards during times of emotional crisis may develop a dependency on the cards that approaches addiction. Needless to say, this is very unhealthy.

I suggest you go to an experienced Tarot reader for Tarot predictions concerning yourself. After all, is there anyone who can remain emotionally uninvolved when he or she is the subject of conversation? Save your own 'predictive' readings for other people. And do remember, the closer you are emotionally to the other person, the more likely you are to become involved, and the less accurate your readings will be. Use Tarot for yourself to gain insight into issues, to answer direct, unemotional questions, to get a better handle on what you need to work on, and to learn and grow.

Some other people approach the Tarot from a magical perspective, using the Tarot cards to tap into universal energies and combining them into magic rituals of various kinds to achieve changes either in themselves, or the world around them. This is possible because the Tarot cards are truly universal in their symbology, as you will soon be learning.

And of course, there are still other people who have become fascinated by the beauty of the Tarot cards themselves, and seek only to collect them, and to look at them. And perhaps, in looking at the cards, these people, too, will gain something special, as the cards impress themselves on their unconscious minds.

But these are not the only ways that people come to study the Tarot. Some people get a reading for the fun of it and become 'hooked.' Some people get invited to a Tarot class by a friend, and discover they love Tarot. Some people, like me, learn the Tarot, thinking it a party game, and discover a new world within the cards.

My educational background is scientific. Initially, I had no interest in metaphysics, but agreed to take an astrology class with a friend because I could relate to it as a science. My Astrology teacher recommended a one-night workshop on Tarot, which I attended for fun. The instructor did not put a great deal of information into his descriptions of the cards, and so it was easy with my quick memory to recall one meaning per card by the end of the workshop. I immediately started doing predictive readings for my friends and colleagues at work, for the fun of it. I did not believe in the possibility that cards could actually be a predictive tool at the time. Imagine my surprise when people began coming back to me, wanting to know what would happen next. I told them they were letting their imaginations run away with them, that no one could predict the future. But it's hard to keep asserting that, when one after another my predictions of specific things panned out and the proof was being delivered to me in black and white!

Gradually, I gave in and came to agree that the cards were accurately predicting events. I considered that I had nothing to do with this. Remember, I was working only with the meanings of the cards I had learned in the workshop, along with my innate logical ability, which allowed me to combine their meanings into a scenario for each person I read.

That means, that the cards alone, and without any psychic aid, can accurately predict events! Essentially I was saying, "This card means a trip; it falls in the position that means in the next two weeks. So, you're going to take a trip in the next two weeks!" And the interpretation would be correct. What a surprise to me! Today, some 15 years later, I am a believer, as well as a full-time reader and teacher.

When I first accepted that the cards, with no help from a psychic, could accurately predict events, as well as give incomparable insight into those events, I decided to find out how they could do this. I also am not a fatalist, and so was profoundly disturbed at this evidence that the future can be predicted. I had no desire to spend the rest of my life telling people about upcoming situations they had to live through and could not change. I decided to investigate the phenomenon of prediction itself. This is what I found:

First, let's focus on how the cards work. This is conjecture, but it's the best possibility I've come across to date. Consider that the patterns, ideas, even people in our lives, can be represented in terms of symbols that we will call *universal archetypes*. These symbols exist in all of our subconscious minds (called by Carl Jung the Collective Unconscious). These symbols, or archetypes, are depicted on the Tarot cards. When a client shuffles the cards, his (or her) unconscious, which understands and recognizes these symbols, has no difficulty arranging the symbols into the patterns evident in his life. The reader, through study and meditation on the cards, has brought knowledge of these archetypes to conscious awareness, and so is able to interpret them for the client. The reader needs no innate psychic ability to do this – only a knowledge of the cards!

Now, recognizing that there was indeed some scientific method (albeit beyond our current science's understanding) behind the capability of the Tarot cards to predict events, I began to investigate the process of prediction itself.

It seems that all prediction is based upon a complete understanding of the present situation and past patterns. If, for example, I know that whenever you've been faced with a crisis in the past you have run away from dealing with it, and I also know that many of your crises have involved being pushed into situations wherein you felt obligated, I can safely predict that you will run away from your current relationship with a woman who has six children and is pushing marriage.

So you see, the more deeply I can understand your past patterns and experiences, the more accurately I can predict your future actions that will arise out of current events.

Somehow the Tarot cards, which speak directly from and to the unconscious, manage to absorb the needed information from the client and present the current situation and predictions relative to past patterns of which the reader may not even be aware.

The important factor here is that the future arises out of the past. Santayana said, "Those who do not remember the past shall be forced to repeat it." And from your point of view, as a reader-to-be, it gives you a very important insight. Your predictions will only be accurate for people who are following their own unconscious patterns of behavior. As soon as someone wakes up and begins to take conscious control in his or her life by deciding the action to take instead of automatically taking it, he or she becomes very difficult to predict for.

As a reader, I find that my relationship with each of my clients matures over time as I continue to read them. Initially, most people tend to see the immediate events in their life as overwhelming, and they do not recognize their own control over those events. They are reacting to circumstance and therefore are easy to predict. But as time goes on, through gentle prodding and recognition of their own patterns, they gradually take control of the situations in their lives. They become harder to predict for. Eventually, they come to me only for confirmation of what they already know will happen in their lives as a result of their current actions because through their actions and awareness they are now controlling their own futures!

Now I don't feel so uncomfortable with the art of prediction. I know that here, too, we have choice. I am still not a fatalist, and I still feel that the most important reason to get a Tarot reading is not so that you know what's going to happen, but so that you know what to change!

A History of the Tarot

By now you are probably wondering where the Tarot came from, who developed it, and where. Well, you are going to be wondering for a long time, along with the rest of us, because no one really knows where these wonderful symbols came from.

Of course, the name Tarot is French. But we know the Tarot cards were not developed in France. Many authorities assert that they were developed in the Middle East, but by and for whom, as well as when, seems to vary from authority to authority. The oldest Tarot designs currently in existence can be dated back to about 1390, so many modern day Tarot authors point to their development as being around 1200 A.D. There is also some evidence that the original designs were initially carried throughout Europe by Gypsies, until they became popular with the various crown heads of the land, and each member of royalty had to have a deck designed for them. However, once many variations on the design appeared, the 'original' symbols, whatever they were, were lost. Incidentally, it is during this time that playing cards, as we know them now, were born. The 52 cards of the typical playing card deck are the *Minor Arcana* (minus the four Pages) of the Tarot deck.

I feel the Tarot is much older than current authorities assert. Here is my version of where they came from:

I believe that the Tarot symbols were developed in the Mystery Schools of ancient Egypt and Mesopotamia as a training tool for initiates. I know first-hand from working with the Tarot cards, meditating upon them, and sleeping on them, that working with the Tarot symbols stimulate the unconscious, psychic portion of the mind, opening it, to higher vibrations. Working with the cards stimulates and develops psychic ability, aids dream recall, gives insight into past lives, and opens the mind to greater insight and understanding. Perhaps some latter day occult fraternity pooled its knowledge and developed these marvelous universal symbols, but I think not. In my opinion, the knowledge required to design something so profound came from an earlier, far more spiritually advanced culture than our own. I have also had many dreams in which I was reading with a mysterious deck of cards, that in my waking hours I have yet to find. Might that have been the original deck?

I believe (certainly with no tangible proof) that the God-Kings of very ancient Egypt were descendants of survivors of an earlier, more advanced culture – perhaps Atlantis. Initially, the God-Kings of Egypt were separated from the populace by what appeared to be miraculous powers of healing and telepathy. Over time, as the 'old blood' thinned out, these powers turned up less and less frequently in the royal line. Ultimately, powers of church and state were separated, and those with special abilities became Priests in what would later develop into the Mystery Schools. Still later, as these special abilities became buried, special tools needed to be developed to bring them out. My belief is that the Tarot was developed then.

Eventually, the Mystery Schools began to disappear, yet they possessed knowledge, which had been handed down from that earlier, more spiritually advanced culture. What better way to preserve some of that knowledge than to entrust it to the Gypsy tribes that we know passed through Egypt at one time. The Gypsies may have used the Tarot only as a divination tool for forecasting the future, but they did preserve them so that they could find their way into use in our society today.

Although I certainly can prove none of this, the fact that the Tarot cards contain so many Kabbalistic symbols supports my theory. The Jews, who passed through this area around the same time as the gypsy tribes, preserved the knowledge of the Kabbala in their wanderings for almost 3,000 years. Could the Kabbala and the Tarot have the same roots?

Note, as I stated above, that after around 1400 A.D., many different Tarot symbols began to appear. Today there are hundreds of different Tarot decks; some have similar symbols to each other, some are purely artist's conceptions, and some are carefully researched and designed.

Choosing a Tarot Deck

Obviously, the new student of Tarot when setting out to purchase a deck of cards faces a dilemma. Among all of these decks, how do you choose one?

First of all, if your intention is to actually use the cards, not just collect them, I suggest you stay away from the decks that are purely an artist's conception. The artist, with no real background in Tarot reading or metaphysical philosophy, is merely recording his or her feeling about a card in pictorial form. Unfortunately, when you read with such a deck, instead of tapping into universal symbology, you will psychically tap into the artist himself. Since the artist is not necessarily an enlightened being, you have little to gain by doing this, and possibly a lot to lose, especially if the artist was or is an unbalanced person.

Decks like the Crowley Tarot Deck, the Enochian Tarot, the Mythic Tarot, the Barbara Walker Tarot and the Herbal Tarot, which were carefully researched and designed over many years, do tap into that universal symbology and make good reading decks, but are so unique to themselves that a reader learning to read with these may be trapped into using that deck alone. If you choose one of these decks, you must study the material written specifically for that deck. I have found that some decks, such as the Medicine Cards and the Karma Cards, make wonderful oracles for self-insight by acting somewhat similar to the I Ching. Each card refers to a written description you are meant to contemplate in order to gain your insight. Of course these particular decks are not true Tarot decks at all since they have a variation in the number of cards from the traditional deck. You may wish to keep one of these as a second deck just for your own use. Students of Tarot who are also astrologers will be particularly interested in the Karma Cards.

Usually, when new students ask me what deck they should start with, I encourage them to begin with the Rider-Waite deck, or one of its many clones. Apparently, when this deck was designed, the designs were configured by pulling out the common denominators from many existing decks, in an attempt to recapture the original symbolism. Whether it's for this reason, or just because this deck became so popular, it's a fact that most available decks seem to either base their symbols on Rider-Waite, or have enough in common with that deck that if you can read with Rider-Waite, you can read with most of the other currently available decks. Some of the more popular Rider-Waite clones include the Aquarian Tarot, the Morgan Greer Tarot, the Hanson-Roberts Tarot, the Connolly Tarot, and the Robin Wood Tarot, to name just a few.

Some of my students prefer to read with older, more traditional decks such as the Tarot of Marseilles, or the Swiss Tarot, or the Visconti-Sforza Tarot. I do not generally recommend these for the beginner, since not all of the cards are illustrated, and it is much harder, initially, to remember the meaning of a card when you're only looking at a number and a suit.

When looking for a Tarot Deck you should by no means confine yourself to the decks I have mentioned. It is very important that you are not only drawn to the particular deck you will use by its attractive color and design, but also that you feel totally comfortable with it. Take your time looking for a deck that suits you, and choose carefully. Over time your Tarot cards will become like a close friend to you – of course, you should choose them as carefully as you do your friends!

Some Tarot readers assert that for luck your Tarot deck should be given to you by a friend. Although I don't really think there is anything wrong with this, provided your friend knows what deck you want and has the ability to tune in to your vibration to make sure they pick just the right one for you, I prefer that you choose your own. If your superstition is that you must receive them as a gift, ask a friend to buy you the ones you've picked out.

One bit of advice about antique or inherited Tarot decks: Don't read with them! That's right. Even though your Great Aunt Sue was a fabulous Tarot reader, and when you use her cards you always get your best readings, you should not use the deck she left to you. The reason you get such good readings with her cards is because through them you are tapping into her skill and knowledge as a reader. That may be just fine. But unfortunately, you can't tap into her skills alone – you also tap into her character. Before long you may begin to speak like her, act like her, look like her; no matter how much you liked Great Aunt Sue, you like being yourself better. DON'T USE SOMEONE ELSE'S CARDS! Buy your cards new, and preferably sealed.

Caring for Your Tarot Deck

Now that you have your cards, what do you do with them? To begin with, initially the cards contain only the energy of the universal symbol on them, and perhaps the vibrations of the store in which you bought them. I suggest that when you first get them you dust your hands with some pure salt (kosher, rock salt, or sea salt with no chemicals added) and shuffle them several times to clear any unwanted vibration they may have picked up at the store or in transit. You may also simply lay the deck on a bed of salt over night, which has the same clearing affect.

Once you have cleared your cards, you're ready to begin to establish a special bond between yourself and your cards by 'charging' them with your energy. To do this, it is important that you keep your cards close to you (within your aura) for at least the first several months. That means that you will carry them with you by day, and keep them under your pillow or on your night table by night. Under no circumstances should you allow other people to use them. It's your energy you're interested in charging the cards with, not your friends' energy. Letting your friends or clients shuffle the deck for readings will charge the deck temporarily with their vibration, so that you can do a reading for them, but the cards will return to your vibration as soon as you pick them up and shuffle them at the end of the reading. I also urge extreme caution in letting your children, nieces, or nephews handle your cards. Children have such a powerful, and yet scattered vibration, that, in my experience, several minutes in the hands of a child can render the most serviceable Tarot deck unusable.

When you are not using your cards, they should be stored in a pouch or box made of natural, dark colored materials – natural, because synthetic materials do not hold vibration well, and dark because dark colors do hold vibration well. A particularly good storage bag could be made from dark blue, purple, or black silk, for example. Today, ready-made pouches are available from most metaphysical book stores, but if you can't find one and don't sew, don't panic – a former student of mine used a black cotton sock, which worked just fine.

If you habitually wear a certain perfume, rub some of it on your hands and then shuffle the cards, to increase your link to them. If you do another form of divination already, such as I Ching or Pendulum Dowsing, store your tools in the pouch with the cards – the cards will pick up the link you already have to the other tool. Some readers like to store a favorite piece of jewelry, well worn, in the pouch with the cards. Again, this strengthens your link to the cards because the jewelry already feels like you! Putting a bit of silver, the most receptive metal, into the pouch can increase the cards' receptivity to you, as well as to the clients you will read. If you carry a lucky piece with you, or crystals, by all means store them in your Tarot pouch. Particular crystals that might enhance the psychic attunement between you and your cards are lapis lazuli, jade, emerald, or pearl. If you like herbs, there are also some herbs that can be added to your Tarot pouch to enhance the psychic bond: try cinnamon, rose, wormwood, yarrow, or peppermint.

If you would like to further charge your deck with universal energy, you can leave them on your windowsill under a full moon. But be sure you retrieve them before sunlight hits the window sill – Tarot reading, like all forms of divination, is a Lunar activity, as opposed to a Solar activity.

This seems like a lot of work to go to just to establish a bond between you and your new deck, but it's well worth the effort. Eventually, you will become so attuned to your deck that even though you aren't carrying it anymore, you can sense when someone at home touches it or moves it. And as your bond to the cards increases, your readings will become progressively more psychic, as the cards lead you, unknowingly, beyond the limitations of logic and into the realms of perception. A nice little side effect will be that no one else will be able to have any permanent affect on the vibration of the cards. No matter who does what to them, they will always bounce back to your energy pattern once that pattern is firmly established.

One last note about your storage and care of your cards: As a practicing psychic, I have learned that all objects retain a memory of everything and everyone with whom they have come in contact. When psychics read the vibrations on an object (this is called psychometry), they are actually reading these memories. Your cards retain these memories extremely well. Remember, you are training them to be a totally receptive tool. When I read a client, I am aware, through the cards, of the client's current situation, where it is going, and what the client may need in the way of immediate help and advice. But this is only a portion of what the cards themselves absorb from him. While the client is shuffling the cards, they are learning all about him. As a matter of fact, by the time he has stopped shuffling, they know everything he knows! This means that when I'm reading a different client sometime in the future, who needs some information that I don't know, but my past client did, that information can suddenly become available to me to pass on to my new client, as the cards deliver it up to me.

For this reason, I do not believe in switching to new Tarot decks all the time, as many readers do. In fact, I am still using my original deck today. By now, after having read so many hundreds of people, the cards do not even feel like paper anymore. They have come to feel alive, and very, very old and wise. When my cards eventually wear out, I will replace them card by card, as individual cards deteriorate. I will keep the old cards with the new, until their knowledge has been passed on. By now my cards are one of my best friends, as yours will soon be to you.

Chapter 2

An Overview of the Major and Minor Arcana

The traditional Tarot deck, and the one I will be discussing, has a total of 78 cards. These 78 cards are divided into two sections: the Major Arcana, which consists of 22 cards, and the Minor Arcana, which contains 56 cards. In many decks, the Major Arcana are numbered in roman numerals, with the titles printed on them. The Major Arcana include the Fool, the Magician, the High Priestess, the Empress, the Emperor, the Hierophant, the Lovers, the Chariot, Strength, the Hermit, the Wheel of Fortune, Balance, the Hanged Man, Death, Temperance, the Devil, the Tower, the Star, the Moon, the Sun, Judgement, and the World.

The 56 cards of the Minor Arcana are reminiscent of present day playing card decks, which are derived from them. In fact, once you learn to read the Tarot, your knowledge of the Minor Arcana (if you are careful to learn them by number and suit and not just by the pictures) can be transferred to regular playing cards for those few of your clients who are 'afraid' of Tarot.

The four suits of the Minor Arcana are divided into Wands (clubs), Cups (hearts), Pentacles (diamonds), and Swords (spades). Each of the suits, similar to playing cards, contains Ace (1) through 10, and four Court cards, as opposed to the three Court cards of the playing card deck. The Tarot Court cards are the King, the Queen, the Knight (or Jack, as he's known in the playing card deck), and the Page, who has no playing card equivalent.

Obviously, since some readers simply read a playing card deck, it's possible to read with only the Minor Arcana. But it's also possible to read with just the Major Arcana. Some decks for sale today consist of only a Minor, or only a Major Arcana. Since we will be learning to read with both, make sure that the deck you purchase has 78 cards.

The Major Arcana cards cover life's major events, turning points, issues, insights, and karmic patterns. In fact, the Tarot cards see life as a continuous cycle, with no real beginning and no real end, just revolutions of patterns and cycles within an eternal whole. One can look at those patterns and cycles as they relate to the events and circumstances of a single life, or even as they move through successive lives. It is in the Major Arcana cards that these major patterns and issues can be seen most clearly.

The Minor Arcana cards cover the more minor issues that we deal with on a day to day basis. In fact, if you think of one Major Arcana card as being the equivalent of all four of the suits of the Minor Arcana equivalent to its number, you have an accurate picture. That means that the Magician, Key I in the Major Arcana, is the equivalent of all four Aces from the Minor Arcana suits. Understand all four Aces, combine their meanings, and the Magician will be understood.

How to Learn the Tarot

There are many methods for learning the Tarot, and none of them are wrong. In the introductory pages I mentioned that one way to learn the cards is by meditating on them. This is a preferred method for some people, especially people who are seeking to read the cards totally intuitively. This method of course can be combined to good effect with any other method. I do not recommend that people who are natively very psychic use this technique exclusively because there will be a tendency to open too much too soon, which could lead the student into some potentially dangerous psychic situations.

Most techniques of learning the Tarot involve learning the meanings of the cards, and using your growing skills in logic to combine the various card meanings into a total picture. This method is perfectly safe for all people to learn by, as your intuitive skills will develop at a pace equivalent to your natural and growing ability to protect yourself psychically. This is the technique that I will be using in the following pages.

Eventually, you will be able to feel a bond form between you and your client as you lay the cards out. This bond enables you to tap into the client psychically so that you may read them this way, as well as through the pictures on the cards. The bond also acts as a shield surrounding you and your client while the reading is in progress, protecting you both from outside influences. The forming of this bond is a natural outgrowth of working with the Tarot cards. When you pick the cards up at the end of a reading, the bond, and its protection, is broken.

Some readers also like to leave a full glass of water on the table during a reading to absorb any negative energy that may be released during the reading; the glass is emptied down the drain after the reading, breaking any bond that has formed between the reader and the client, and eliminating any residual negativity. I find this is rarely necessary, unless you are reading for someone you probably really shouldn't be. Remember that someone in the throes of emotion probably would benefit more from a counseling session than a psychic reading that his or her strong emotional discharges would likely render inaccurate anyway!

Still other readers like to ring a bell at the end of the reading to break the bond, or sprinkle salt over the cards to ground them, or burn some incense to clear the air. I don't really think any of this is necessary. Just pick up the cards and the bond is broken.

In teaching the cards over the years I also have found that most students find memorization of the cards is boring; trying to memorize the cards as you would flash cards is not only frustrating, but is also usually unrewarding. The way to remember what the cards mean is by doing them. So, in this book you're going to be learning the cards a little at a time, working only with those cards that you've learned, until you feel comfortable with them and are ready to move on.

So you can get used to working with them immediately in a layout, you will learn a mini-Celtic Cross spread at the end of this chapter. By working with a limited number of cards in a simple spread you will be learning the meanings of the cards at the same time you are learning to exercise the logic muscles in your brain. Eventually, this will lead to an unfoldment of your psychic abilities as well. We will be adding on more cards with each chapter, and will proceed to progressively more intricate versions of the Celtic Cross spread as we do. Move at your own pace, and don't move on to the next chapters until you feel you've mastered the material in the one you're working on.

I am going to be jumping around a bit in presenting the cards, but my method is not madness. In the second portion of this chapter you'll be learning the suits – not the individual cards, mind you, but the suits themselves. Each suit represents a different type of energy, and once you understand that energy, the placement of various suits in a reading gives a definite overtone and insight into a client's situation. Initially, you can separate the Major Arcana cards from the deck and lay them aside (remember, they're the ones with the roman numeral and a title on them). We'll only be working with the 'Minors' in this chapter. Remember to keep the cards with which you're working with you at all times, and to sleep with them under your pillow as well. It will help you learn them more quickly, and may even give you some additional information of your own along the way!

Once you have a good understanding of the suits, we'll take a long look at the Court cards. The Court cards are the people in your client's life. That's what we'll be covering in the next chapter: people. Many students seem to have trouble learning and integrating the people in their readings, so I like to introduce them early in your learning. Since we'll be working with them right from the beginning, by the time you've learned the rest of the deck their meanings should be second nature to you. You won't even have to think about them, you'll just know who they are.

Since we're progressing from hardest to easiest, the Major Arcana cards come next. They're not difficult to learn or to integrate, but they are very comprehensive and important. Chapters 4 and 5 will cover the meanings of the 'Majors.' While you're learning the meanings of the Major Arcana cards, you'll only be working with them, and the Court cards. The rest of the Minor Arcana will be set aside while you're learning these.

And finally, because they're the simplest and most straight forward, in Chapters 6 and 7 you'll be learning the meanings of the Minor Arcana.

Since I read the cards with both inverted and upright meanings myself, you will be learning them that way, too. Remember to scramble them before your first reading so that they face different ways. Some readers like to return their cards to order after each reading. I do not, believing that the way they were gathered up after the last client is exactly the way the next client needs them to be as he or she begins to shuffle. If this seems too complicated, remember that many readers only use upright meanings and seem to do perfectly good readings, intuiting the inverted meaning from the surrounding cards instead of the card's position.

The Four Suits of the Minor Arcana

As noted above, the Minor Arcana suits represent different types of energy. If you have a good understanding of the energy at work when you read a client, your reading will be much more insightful into the nature of the events and circumstances in his or her life. You're going to find as you become familiar with the various meanings of the overall suits that you can actually do an accurate mini-reading without actually knowing the meanings of the cards, just understanding the interaction of the energy at work by the suits appearing in the reading.

Wands

The first of the suits we'll look at is the suit of Wands, known in some decks as Staffs, or Rods, and in playing card decks as Clubs.

The suit of Wands has a fiery energy. The Wands in the deck correspond astrologically to the fire signs of Aries (March 22 – April 22), Leo (July 22 – August 22), and Sagittarius (November 22 – December 22). If you know anything about these signs, it will give you greater insight as to how the fire energy of the Wands works. All of these fire signs, and the fiery Wands themselves, are creative, generative, goal oriented, physically active, highly sexual, inspirational, and idealistic. Wands are male, or generative in nature.

Wands is the energy we find in Aries, the astrological sign that is on the horizon at the time of the spring equinox. Wands rule the spring, they rule youth and childhood, and they herald all new beginnings.

To get a true feeling for the wild, forceful, ungoverned energy of Wands, it helps to study nature at work in the spring. Imagine the snow caps on the tallest peaks melting with the spring thaw. Now visualize the trickling meltwater running downward to form streams, and then the streams combining into torrential rivers. Imagine those wildly surging rivers overflowing their banks, as they do every spring, washing away all before them in their rush to the sea.

Now take a mental journey to a wooded hilltop, and notice the two stags butting horns over a female watching from nearby. And down in a valley, watch the farm animals going through their mating rituals while the farmer is out in the fields clearing away the winter debris and getting the fields ready for spring planting.

Wands are an instinctive energy. We find them at the beginning of all cycles and they are always the change preceding the new beginning. They deal with physical changes, as the change from ice and snow into water.

When a predominance of Wands energy appears in a reading, you know that there are many physical changes, disruptions, and new beginnings happening in your client's life. It's important that you advise him or her to go with the flow because, like the torrential flow of a river, there is no holding Wands energy back. If you try, when the dam bursts the changes will only be swifter and more difficult to deal with. Yet if you flow with it, with awareness, the changes can be sculpted into the eventual form you want them to take.

On the positive side, a predominance of Wands energy can mean a lot of physical energy to do things, and a virtual well-spring of creativity that the client can draw on. On the negative, it's common to find Wands appearing in a reading where health issues are a major consideration. As you learn the actual meanings of individual cards, you'll see that many of these, when combined in a reading that contains Wands, can indicate specific health problems.

Wands always appear in a reading when there is sexual attraction or activity between the client and a partner. And of course they always appear when there is competition, battling or fighting of any sort. They can also indicate sports activities.

Since Wands energy is also idealistic, there is a traditional side to the energy that you might not expect. Although aggressive and impulsive in their nature, Wands will direct that intense energy toward traditional, or instinctive, goals. You often find Wands involved in issues concerning home and family, too.

When Wands are negative, we often see wasted energy and action, illness, fighting and brutality, power trips, gross immaturity, recklessness, and lack of any real direction.

For now, assume that any inverted cards in a reading are acting negatively, and any upright ones positively.

Cups

Cups correspond to the suit of hearts in the regular playing card deck.

The energy of Cups is feminine, or receptive. Cups are a watery energy corresponding to the Zodiacal water signs of Cancer (June 22 – July 22), Scorpio (September 22 – October 22), and Pisces (February 22 – March 22).

Cups are emotional, sensitive, intuitive, psychic, nurturing, and protective of the young and weak. If negative, they can be suspicious, paranoid, manipulative, given to intrigue, and potentially addictive.

If you imagine that all of the energy released by the Wands, running downhill as an uncontrolled river, must in some way be contained in order to be used in any positive way, then imagine the Cups as the natural container for that energy.

Cups, corresponding to the sign Cancer, which appears at the Summer Solstice, the longest day of the year, are the natural check-balance to the aggressive, surging energy of the Wands that preceded them. Cups rule the Summer, a time of abundance and carelessness; they rule early adulthood.

The Cups take the sexual prowess and urgency of Wands and develop it into love. The Cups receive the sperm released by Wands during the sex act and develop it into a fetus, a baby. They nurture that baby, or whatever was created through the interaction of Wands and Cups, causing it to grow and flourish.

The Cups are also instinctual, but their instinct is totally toward the creation of the security and stability necessary to grow a dream, a business, a family. If anything threatens this stability or security that they are creating, you will see the protective, ferocious side of Cups.

Consider the female mountain lion, safe in her den, nursing her young, maybe cuffing them now and again to teach them manners. Her world consists of her cave, her cubs, the food her mate will bring to her, and the safety and security of her family. She doesn't look beyond the walls of the cave unless something from outside threatens her well-being, or the well-being of those dependent upon her. But when threatened, there is no more dangerous predator in the wild! She herself is dependent upon the hunting skills of her mate, but she scarcely thinks about this, only expecting that the next meal will come. Again, if the mate fails her, she and her family are threatened, and she will act out accordingly.

In a reading, a predominance of Cups energy indicates that this is a very emotional time in the client's life, for good or bad. The issues that concern him or her will be love, home, family, friends, and security. They are probably not interested in anything beyond the confines of their own small world, unless the larger world is in some way affecting them. Cups are not interested in money and finance except as a means to security. They are not interested in competition except as a means to security. They are interested in sex for the sense of well-being, safety, security, and love the sexual encounter gives them, as well as their instinctive drive to reproduce. One night stands are definitely not for Cups.

But the suit of Cups is also, in its own way, driven. Its drive is to create greater and greater security. A bigger and bigger home and family. More and more love. More and more emotional issues. Since it is receptive, it is drawing upon the energy of those around it to produce this grandeur. In the extreme, this produces the alcoholic, the drug addict, the co-dependent personality.

Cups rules that time of life when we are entering into adulthood, establishing our own families and the foundation for our own life situation.

Cups and Wands are the two most creative and artistic of the suits – Wands in a physical sense, Cups in an intuitive, imaginative sense. When they occur together in a reading, there is always a burst of creative energy that results.

Pentacles

Before actually discussing the suit of Pentacles, perhaps I should diverge for a short time, to present a very real dilemma that exists among Tarot experts concerning whether Pentacles or Swords should actually follow Cups. There are, obviously, two different schools of thought on this.

According to one system, since Libra is the sign that appears at the fall equinox, and Libra is an air sign, and the element of air corresponds to Swords, Swords should follow Cups as we proceed around the Wheel of the Year. This same tradition validly points out that energy always passes from positive pole to negative pole to positive pole, and so on – so generative Wands should be followed by receptive Cups should be followed by generative Swords, placing receptive Pentacles last.

According to the other system, the Wheel of the year should be split with the male suits (generative) dominating from January 22 to June 22, and the female (receptive) from

June 22 to January 22. Interestingly, this system follows the Pagan philosophy. This system places Pentacles in the fall as the suit to follow Cups, and Swords in the winter, following Pentacles.

Confusing, isn't it? But this dilemma also accounts for much of the trade-off in meanings between Pentacles and Swords, which often seem to overlap.

I really don't care which system you ultimately decide to side with. What's important isn't which suit comes next, but what they mean. And wherever you place them, the meanings won't change.

The Pentacles correspond to the earth signs of Taurus (April 22 – May 22), Virgo (August 22 – September 22), and Capricorn (December 22 – January 22). They are receptive and oriented toward physical, material things. And yet, they are also the doorway to the spirit; you'll note that Christmas (a holiday celebrating the birth of spirit appearing under different names in almost every culture) occurs during Capricorn. Pentacles dominate our lives during our middle years. We have already birthed our material beginnings, established a foundation, and now we are building upon it and getting ready to bring in the harvest.

Pentacles are a patient suit, concerned with careful planning and work, with business, finance, and material success. They like physical work, to get involved, and to get their hands dirty.

I find that observing the natural environment during the fall of the year gives good insight into the Pentacles energy. Notice, as you observe the squirrels in your yard, that their fun and play has ended. They are going about the very serious business of organizing their store of nuts for the winter to come.

Now, notice the people in your community, as they repair their roofs, get their snow removal equipment in shape, and prepare in their own way for the winter.

And take a moment to visit a farm in your imagination. Watch the farmer harvesting the last of his crop, readying it for market. Now watch him counting his money as he gets a good return on the sale, and place it into his fund for that new barn – the one that's going to let him increase his harvest next year.

In Pentacles we see instinctual action, too, but it's the urge toward improving our lot in a material sense, and preparing for a future when we intuitively know we may not have the affluence we do now.

Earthy Pentacles can manipulate, scheme, and plan with the best, but will do so silently. And much of Pentacles planning is purely instinctive, not thought out at all. Just like the squirrel hoarding nuts for the winter.

Whenever Pentacles come up in a reading you know that your client is concerned about finances, a business, work, or perhaps something they are making with his or her hands. Less commonly, and only if certain cards turn up in the same spread with the Pentacles, spiritual growth could be indicated.

Swords

Swords are generative, but since they correspond to the element of air, what they generate is mostly ideas.

The Swords correspond to the Zodiacal signs Gemini (May 22 – June 22), Libra (September 22 – October 22), and Aquarius (January 22 – February 22).

Due to their correspondence to the element air, they are the most purely mental of the suits. When you group Swords with Wands, you are thinking about some action you want to take, or agonizing over a physical problem or conflict. When you group Swords with Cups, you are thinking about emotional issues. This is often a bad combination because the real emotional pain we feel concerning a situation that did not work out well for us is usually not directly related to our experience, but rather to our prolonged agonizing over it afterward. Grouping Swords with Pentacles works a little better – that usually involves our planning or scheming to earn more money, or buy something we want.

Swords, needless to say, have gotten a bad name in Tarot circles. It seems that most of the time when we over-think things, we only create more problems for ourselves. Swords are often indicators of strife in a reading.

But let's try to look at Swords in a somewhat positive light.

Swords deal with thinking, with education, with communication of all kinds, with socialization, with planning, and with short and long distance travel (after all, travel is a form of communication!).

And then again, headaches and difficulty sleeping could be a Swords reward.

Let's look at nature again to get a better handle on how Swords behave. I like to compare Swords to our activities during the winter months. Let's take a look at that farmer again. He's finished the work of gathering in the harvest, and now he's settled in for the winter. He might be working indoors on some projects he couldn't get to during the active summer months, but mostly he's organizing and planning his field layout for the coming spring. Being forced to stay indoors so much, he has plenty of time for reading, and for catching up with the neighbors. He may even indulge in a few social gatherings this season if the spirit moves him. He's also spending plenty of time alone, and he's working out a lot of things that bothered him this past year that he didn't have much time to think about until now.

In a reading, when you see a lot of Swords, you know that there is not a lot actually going on in your client's life, but there sure is a lot of thinking and communication happening. As I noted above, the other suits contained in the spread of cards will give you some insight into what the thinking or planning is all about.

Swords correspond to our golden years, when we should be looking back, assessing, understanding, and passing on the knowledge we have gained.

I said earlier that there are a lot of common denominators between Swords and Pentacles. We may see both of them going to school, but Swords goes to learn, Pentacles for the degree necessary to make money. Both may open businesses, but Swords does this for the mental stimulation, Pentacles for the money. They are both suits of work, but Swords works with the mind, Pentacles with the hands. Both can be involved in spiritual pursuits, but Swords pursues spirituality in books and learning, Pentacles through direct experience.

Now that you have a good overview of the Tarot Minor Arcana suits, here's a synopsis that you can use for quick reference:

Wands	Cups	Pentacles	Swords
(clubs)	(hearts)	(diamonds)	(spades)
Fire	Water	Earth	Air
*Physical	*Emotional	*Materialistic	*Mental
Spring	Summer	Fall	Winter
Youth	Early Adult	Middle Age	Old Age
Generative	Receptive	Receptive	Generative
Sexual	Nurturing	Sensual	Social
Initiates	Retains	Builds	Dreams
Explosive	Sensitive	Introspective	Emotionally Distant
Instinctive	Intuitive	Instinctive	Intuitive
Changing	Expanding	Stabilizing	Planning
Sports and Play	Family	Business, Money	Communication, Travel
Idealism	Psychism	Spirituality	Contemplation
Traditional	Family Values	Work oriented	Idea oriented

Table 1: Overview of the Minor Arcana Suits

*Qualities may be either a negative or a positive representation of the suit qualities, depending on individual card meanings and surrounding cards in the layout. Here are some particularly negative attributes:

Wands	Cups	Pentacles	Swords
Brutality	Escapism	Callousness	Emotionless
Obtuseness	Addiction	Dull	Slandering
Fighting	Obsession	Careless	Manipulation
Illness	Manipulation	Theft or Loss	Strife

Table 2: Negative Attributes of the Minor Arcana Suits

I think you have the idea! Now, here's a very simple variation of the famous Celtic Cross spread:

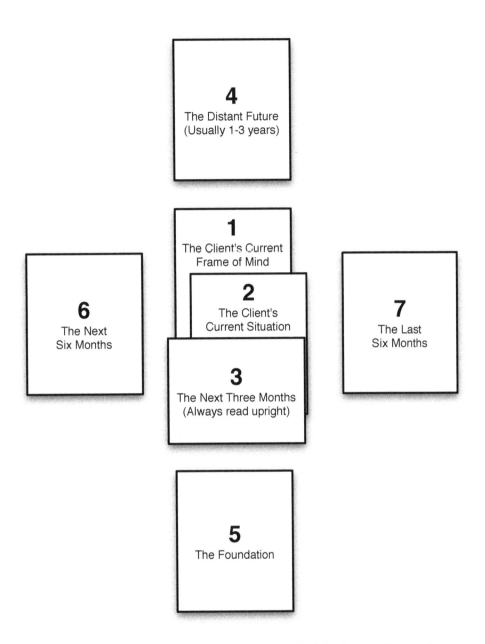

Figure 1: A Simple Variation of the Celtic Cross Spread

And here's a more lengthy description of each position:

1. This is the first card down, and will describe your client, as well as his (or her) state of mind, that is, what he is thinking about. Many Tarot readers actually select a card from the deck to represent the client, but I prefer to leave this to the cards. (Keep in mind that if you select a Queen or King from the deck to represent your client, you are removing that card from the deck so that it cannot

come up to represent another person in your client's life!) The suit will tell you a great deal about who the client is, as well as what type of issues are on his mind. For example, a Pentacle appearing here would mean that the client is earthy, perhaps materialistic, probably good at handling money, and is probably concerned about some material issue at the time of the reading. If a Court card turns up here, it may indicate that the client is preoccupied with that person. If this card is inverted, the client may be upset, or having trouble dealing with the matters indicated by this card!

2. This position represents the client's actual situation. Note that even though the card in position 1 might show his concern over a problem, say, concerning the suit of Pentacles, an upright Pentacle in this position would show no actual problem, just perhaps important business dealings. Conversely, an upright Pentacle in position 1 shows that business and money are on the client's mind, not necessarily in a negative way, but an inverted Pentacle in position 2 says he had better watch out anyway because some problems are developing. So, position 2 usually gives insight into the first, and develops it. It's important to remember that this position talks about the present.

3. This position gives you your first insight into the future for your client. It literally tells you what the major issues coming up during the next three months in his life will involve. Occasionally, if I am reading a client that I see fairly often, time will speed up, and this position will extend only to three weeks, or even three days. The important concept is '3,' and that it is his next major issue. If, for example, a Cup appears here, you know the client will be dealing with emotional issues over the next three months! By the way, this position is traditionally read right side up. Any negative interpretation would have to come from surrounding cards.

*The first three cards together show the client and his current direction. These three cards are at the center of the simple cross; they are therefore the most important cards in the spread.

When laying the cards out, I like to lay them down one at a time and thoroughly discuss each one before I move on to the next. Getting a firm grasp on these first three cards especially, and their interrelationship with one another, is necessary if you are going to pull the rest of the reading together well.

4. Position 4 shows the distant future, usually about one year from the time of the reading, but sometimes as far as three, if your client is future oriented in his thinking. Often this card refers to generalities, and has little to do with actual events taking place in the person's life now, although it is most certainly affected by the way in which events are being handled now. If you see the Celtic Cross layout as a simple cross, this position lies at the top of the vertical line, which is the *line of spirit*. The card, which appears here, shows what the result of the

choices the person is presently making will be. And now, of course, you can understand why the first three cards are so important. Our actions in the present determine the direction of our future, and these first three cards sit at the juncture of our spiritual direction and the material plane, which is the horizontal line, formed by cards 6 and 7 (the next six months and the past six months.). We are continually forced to travel the maze between spirit and matter as long as we are on this earth plane, trying to resolve our goals and ultimate desires with our material conditions and limitations.

5. Position 5, *the foundation*, represents the sum total of what has brought the client to his present point in life. This position becomes a jumping off point for the rest of the reading. Sometimes the foundation shows family or financial conditions; sometimes it shows a failed romance, or a succession of them. Sometimes it shows a decision made, a hope, or a desire. But whatever it shows, it is past, and it is the action or internal state that has brought the person to the point where he began his current life situation.

6. Position 6 is the left side of the Celtic Cross. I read it as the immediate future, but many other Tarot readers use this position as the immediate past. I have conducted several interesting experiments in which I have read the spread my own way (with position 6 being the future and 7 the past), and then had another person who reads them the opposite way look at them – we came up with similar interpretations. When you remember that on the physical plane we repeat our patterns over and over again, the idea that on this horizontal crossbar of the Celtic Cross, past could be read as future and future as past is not so strange. I've experimented with reading positions 6 and 7 first as both being past, and then after I've exhausted the resulting insights, I've reversed and read them as both being future and delivered a successful reading as well. My point is that if you are already reading the cards and have learned that position 7 is future, don't try to change – it works, just be consistent in your method.

   Since this position for me is future, here's how I read it: This will represent the next six months or so of the client's life, and will show the type of events, circumstances, and people he or she will be dealing with during that time. Obviously there is an overlap with position 3, and so by reading these cards together you can glean even more information. Since this position lies along the horizontal crossbar, it deals with actual events and material situations.

7. This position is our last in the simplified Celtic Cross, and shows (according to the way I read) the immediate past (about six months) in the client's life. Again, being a part of the horizontal crossbar of the Celtic Cross, it shows actual events and circumstances, perhaps even decisions or actions relative to them.

Let's do a sample reading with the simplified Celtic Cross, using only the meanings of the suits as I've described them earlier in this chapter.

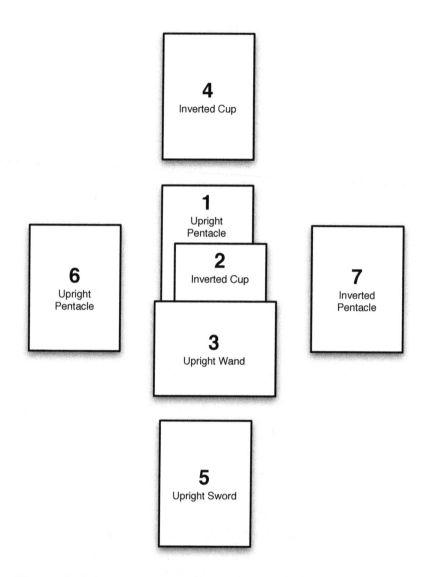

Figure 2: A Sample Reading with the Simplified Celtic Cross

Exercise #1

The following questions will help to guide you through your first interpretation. Using these questions as a guide will help to teach your mind the necessary logic required for a good Tarot interpretation. After you've completed your own interpretation, read on and compare it to mine and to the client's actual situation as recorded at the end of the chapter. Remember: every reader is an individual and your reading need not be exactly like mine to be a good one. But the comparison should give you some good feedback.

It is important when you do a reading to know for whom you are reading. The age of the person, for instance, as well as his or her sex will often determine the proper slant of the reading. Once you have this information for a general reading, the person need not be present. We are, in this case, reading for a 45-year-old woman.

1. Start with the client's frame of mind, card 1, which is an upright Pentacle:

    a. What qualities does the card say she possesses?

    b. What might be her primary interest at this time?

2. Continue with card 2, your client's present situation, shown by an inverted Cup:

    a. What does the card tell you about her present situation?

    b. Referring back to card 1, and combining their meanings, what might her emotional concern be about?

3. What does this card (a Wand read upright) tell you about what's coming into her life in the next three months?

4. This position, representing the distant future, shows an inverted Cup. What does this tell you about how she will be feeling about this situation approximately a year from now?

5. This position is the foundation and here we find an upright Sword.

    a. What does this tell you about her general past?

    b. Is this foundation card good or bad and what do you think it gave rise to?

    c. How do you think this card will affect the upright Wand in position 3 (the next three months)?

    d. How do you think this card will affect or help generate the inverted Cup in position 4 (the distant future)?

6. We see an upright Pentacle in the immediate future.

    a. What does this say will be occurring in the next six months?

    b. This position overlaps with position 3 (the next three months). How would you interpret these two cards together?

7. This position shows an inverted Pentacle. What does this say about her position during the last six months?

8. Look at the horizontal line of the material plane and see if you can pull together the cards representing the Self (positions 1, 2, and 3) and the last six months and

the next six months (positions 7 and 6). Where is the client's physical and material reality going?

9. Look at the vertical line of spirit and again pull together the cards representing the Self (positions 1, 2, and 3), the foundation card (position 5), and the distant future card (position 4). In what circumstances is the Spirit going to show itself?

Now, let's look at my own interpretation of the cards with the added benefit of the actual situation. As I said before, it's important when you do a reading to know for whom you are reading. This will determine the proper slant of the reading. In this case, we are reading for a 45-year-old woman.

1. Let's begin by taking a look at card 1, which describes her frame of mind when she visits us. The upright Pentacle describes her as a person, perhaps a businesswoman, who at this moment is primarily interested in material matters, her finances, her job, or perhaps an investment or other financial involvement. Personally she will be an earthy person; solid, stable, secure, and generally good relative to handling material matters.

2. But our second card, an inverted Cup, turning up relative to her current situation shows that she is emotionally disturbed about something. Since card 1 (frame of mind) is a Pentacle, she is probably concerned and overwrought about something involving material or money matters. Since it is the Cup that is inverted, these matters involve not only her emotions, but also her family and her sense of security.

3. Looking on to card 3, what she'll be dealing with over the next three months, we find a Wand. Any card in this position is read upright, remember. So we know that a change is coming, in fact a physical change, which will benefit her!

4. Card 4 is our distant future, and when we see an inverted Cup here, we know that a year or so from now she's still not going to be very happy about the situation, even though it will have changed for the better.

5. Card 5 is the foundation, and the upright Sword appearing here shows the good idea that is giving rise to the current situation. The change coming over the next three months (position 3), and the general unhappiness relative to this situation will still linger a year from now (position 4). This upright Sword also infers good social connections, good communication abilities, and good planning.

6. Card 6 is the immediate future, and shows the events and circumstances that will prevail during this time. The upright Pentacle shows material well-being, perhaps even increase. If we read it overlapping with 3 (next three months) the combination of Wand and Pentacle shows financial changes being put into action, which will be beneficial.

7. Card 7 shows that in the immediate past (about the past six months) the financial situation has not been good (inverted Pentacle).

8. Now, if we go back and read across our horizontal material world situation, we start with 7 (last six months), then look at positions 1, 2, and 3 (frame of mind, situation and next three months), and finally see what's to be done in 6 (next six months):

   The unpleasant financial situation shown by position 7 (last six months) is being dealt with by an effective means (positions 1 and 3 / frame of mind and next three months) that are not emotionally happy (position 2 / situation). The situation will be successfully dealt with as in position 6 (next six months).

9. Looking at the vertical line of spirit, goals, and long distance focus by following first position 5 (foundation), then positions 1, 2, and 3 (frame of mind, situation and next three months), and finally position 4 (distant future), we see:

   The idea of how to resolve the financial issue is good, the contacts necessary are there, the proper advice has been given and is being used (5 / foundation). The client is optimistic about positive results (1 / frame of mind) but is not happy about what she has to do to obtain them (2 / situation). But she will take the necessary action anyway (Wands, 3 / next three months) even though it will result in an emotional sacrifice still apparent in 4 (distant future).

*This woman is an actual client of mine; she is a well-educated businesswoman, as indicated by the Sword in position 5 (foundation), and the Pentacle in position 1 (frame of mind). Her business has not been doing well (see 7 / last six months) and the best advice she's been given is either to close it, which she does not want to do, or to sell her vacation home to finance it, which she also does not want to do. This is why we see Cups inverted in position 2 (situation). We know from the reading that the advice she's been given is sound since the Sword in position 5 (foundation) is upright, and that she will take one of these two actions in the next three months, since a Wand is in position 3. We know this will resolve her problem since the Pentacle in position 6 (next six months) is upright, but that she will not be happy about it in the future since the Cup in position 4 (distant future) is inverted.

Simple, isn't it?

When my students first realize that they can do a reading this accurately knowing only what the suits mean using the simple Celtic Cross, they are amazed. You will be, too..

When you do your own practice readings, at least one a day, you can read for yourself if you promise not to take it seriously, or you can read for a friend, or... you can think of a friend. Shuffle the cards yourself and do a reading for them without them being present;

then call them to get confirmation. That's right, it's possible to read for someone that you're just thinking about! Hold them in your mind while you shuffle the cards, and then proceed as for any other reading. Just remember that although this is great for practice, don't use it for spying – that's bad manners in psychic circles! Another way to practice the cards if you don't have anyone near to read is to take a newspaper or magazine article that has a photograph with it and concentrate on the photograph while you shuffle the cards. Then lay your cards out, read them, and when you're done, read the article for confirmation. Still another way to practice is to turn on your favorite T.V. show, without the sound. Shuffle the cards while you watch the first few scenes, and then lay them out, read them, then turn up the sound and get confirmation of your reading.

If you don't like the way a reading ends, as in my above sample reading, lay out another card or two or three in a row until you come up with a positive ending. Remember that in life there are no lasting ups and downs and it's a good idea to get into the habit of leaving your clients on an 'up,' knowing that no matter how bad things may be, they'll get better... because they always do!

Chapter 3

The Court Cards

The Court cards in a Tarot spread represent the people that your client is dealing with in his (or her) day to day life; the men, women and children he is involved with, or concerned about.

The Court cards may also represent the client himself, since we are all composed of all four elements, so that even though you may identify yourself more with one suit than another, you may find yourself acting like a different suit at various times and in various situations in your life.

For example, you may actually be a Queen of Cups (soft and emotional), but find that when work issues come up in your cards you always appear like a Queen of Swords (intellectual and unemotional).

When you read a Tarot spread that contains Court cards you must remember that each one that is the same sex as the client will represent a different facet of his (or her) character that is being demonstrated in the particular situation indicated, while at the same time it may represent a completely different person in his life. Thus, you may correctly infer that a single card may be read over and over, having a different meaning each time.

For example, I may read the same spread twice. The first time through I am reading all of the Queens that appear as being my client (a woman) moving through different situations in her life. When I read the cards this way, I am seeing her life totally from her own perspective, and I get a very internalized view of it. This perspective is excellent for counseling clients.

The second time through, I read the cards with all of the Queens representing different people she deals with in her life. Now I get an externalized view (though still from her own viewpoint) of people she is dealing with in these varying situations.

For instance, the first time through the spread I may see the Queen of Wands relative to her work as indicating that she approaches her work with energy and vitality. The second time through I may see this same Queen of Wands as an energetic woman that she deals with at work.

Eventually, with practice, you will automatically be looking at the Court cards in the spread from these two points of view.

You'll note that several times above I mentioned that you were seeing the Court cards from the client's perspective. That is also very important to remember. The fact that you and I may know the same person does not mean that we see him or her the same way. Remember, as a reader you must remain totally objective to your client's situation in order to do a good reading, and that means realizing that the people you see in a client's reading are from his or her point of view, not yours.

Here's a fun anecdote that confirms this. During a short period I read for a number of young women that belonged to the same social group, but did not know one another well. In one woman's reading I saw a young man she had just met that I described as brooding, quiet, artistic, and spiritual. She agreed that described him well. That is how she saw him. In another woman's reading I described her boyfriend as active and energetic, someone who had to constantly be doing something. Again, this girl said I had pinpointed her boyfriend exactly. This is how she saw him. In still a third girl's reading I saw her young man as being lazy, selfish, manipulative, and controlling. Again, this girl agreed because at the time of the reading this was exactly how she saw him. Imagine my surprise when I met the young man that all three girls were describing! Apparently, he was dating all three of them at the same time, unbeknownst to the others – and each one saw him differently depending upon how they interacted with him! Needless to say, I looked at him in quite a different light than his three girlfriends did.

The fact that we all see a person from our own point of view is the reason that it is not a good idea to do a reading for someone when his or her significant other or friend is present. If the client insists, go ahead and do it, but make sure they know that the other person being present will definitely affect their reading. You will unconsciously be picking up the slant of the other person when reading the Court cards, as well as the situation. The client will get a reading slanted from his or her friend's point of view, not just their own.

As I mentioned earlier, the Court cards represent the people in the reading. The Court cards are divided into Kings, Queens, Knights, and Pages. The Kings and Queens are the same as a playing card deck, and the Knights correspond to Jacks in the playing card deck. The Pages have no playing card equivalent. Each suit, of course, has one of each.

The Kings in the deck represent mature, responsible men. Let's linger on that word: *responsible*. Technically, a male Page (Pages can be either girls or boys) becomes a Knight sometime around when puberty begins, and the Knight becomes a King when he marries and assumes the responsibility of a family, which traditionally occurs sometime during his twenties. However, we know that this is not always the case. I have met some 16 and 17 year olds who are certainly Kings, since they are supporting a mother and several brothers and sisters and obviously learned responsibility earlier than most. Then again, I have also had occasion to read for some 75 year olds who were still definitely

Knights, never having developed a taste for responsibility, relying upon their family to take care of them instead of the other way around. I also know some Kings who are unmarried at 70, though very responsible, mature individuals – marriage is not necessarily a criteria to maturity either.

So even though we can make the generalized rule that Kings are mature men, Knights are teens, and Pages are children, remember that this rule is made to be broken. It is also a rule that follows the perspective of the client.

If I see my husband as younger than me (actually or emotionally), he will appear as a Knight. My son, on the other hand, could appear as a King if I see him as accomplished and successful, even though he may still be in his teens. Conversely, if I am a 60-year-old woman with a 40-year-old son whom I see as a failure, I may see him as a Knight, instead of the King he should be. Or I may even see him as a Page if I think he has been acting particularly childish. His wife, on the other hand, may be perfectly happy with him and see him as a King. All you have to remember, is that however he turns up is how your client sees him. And if you describe him well enough, they will have no trouble identifying who he is in his or her life.

The female cards in the deck are the Queens and the Pages (remember, the Pages can be either male or female). I have always found it interesting that the Tarot cards give no "in between" child and adult equivalent to Knights for women. It's as if they see that women, who actually go about the business of bearing children, have no choice but to accept responsibility and become Queens once puberty has passed. And then again, with changing values in our changing times, I could see where it may soon become necessary to invent a female equivalent to the Knights for those women who don't want to grow up. Until then, a man or woman who is seeing his or her grown daughter as acting in an immature manner, would have to see her as either a Page, or perhaps inverted.

When a Court card appears inverted in your spread it will mean that you have not met the person yet (the card must fall in a future position for this meaning to hold true); the person is ill or has problems; the person is acting in an immature, negative manner relative to your client.

Remember that both upright and inverted meanings are latent in every Court card, no matter which position you might find it in.

Knights in a spread are usually seen as young men, but they are also beginnings and endings of situations depending on whether they fall upright (a new beginning) or inverted (an ending) in the spread. The particular thing that is beginning or ending will be indicated by the suit of the Knight, as well as by surrounding cards in the spread. For example, if I see an inverted Knight of Cups, it is an ending of an emotional situation. If the inverted Knight is surrounded by Pentacles, the emotional situation has to do with material concerns, perhaps a job. Of course, after I have read the ending of this situation, I will go back and read the Knight as a young man, and integrate this into the rest of my reading.

One particular Knight in the deck, the Knight of Swords, also acts as a somewhat negative adjective to other male cards in the deck. When this Knight falls upright near another male card in the deck, it means the person indicated by that card is moving too fast. When the Knight of Swords falls inverted near another male card in the deck, it means the hasty actions of the man indicated will lead to disaster for himself and those involved with him. The male card the Knight of Swords is defining need not himself be inverted for these negative meanings to still work. Good people can make mistakes, too!

The Pages, who normally represent pre-pubescent children, both boys and girls (sorry, only your intuition will tell the difference here), also have a general meaning applicable in your readings. The Pages can represent news, offers, and messages. If the Page is upright, the message is good, and if it's inverted, it's bad. If the Page appears relative to an offer and it's inverted, the offer will either not be made, or will be turned down; upright, and the offer is a good one, that will probably be taken. Again, the suit of the Page will indicate what the news, offer, or message concerns, as will surrounding cards. Once you've read your Page as a message, news, or an offer, remember to go back and look at it as a child (you might first ask your client if they have children, or if there are any important children in his or her life.), then integrate it with the rest of your reading.

Two of the Pages also serve as special adjective cards. The Page of Wands upright near any Court card tells you the person represented by that card can be trusted, but inverted it means that they can't be. The Page of Pentacles in a reading is often a special message from your guides or your Higher Self – upright you are listening and getting the message, but inverted, it means that you are not paying attention.

The Kings

The Kings in the Tarot deck are mature, responsible men. But each of the four Tarot Kings displays a very different personality.

The King of Wands

Coloring – Light hair, eyes, and skin.

Mode – Cardinal (self-starting).

Element – Fire.

Corresponding Astrological Signs – Primarily Aries, Leo, Sagittarius, and occasionally Cancer or Virgo.

Simplified Meanings:

Upright – An idealistic, physically active, energetic man.

Inverted – A short-tempered, possibly abusive and dishonest man.

Famous Kings of Wands: Kirk Douglas, Bill Clinton, William Shatner (Captain Kirk from the original Star Trek).

In-Depth Discussion:

The King of Wands is an idealistic, honest, very physical personality. For him, thought transfers immediately into action. He is vibrant and sexual, though his honesty and integrity will usually work to keep him faithful in his romantic relationships, unless his family traditions preserve the old-world double standard in which a mistress is acceptable. He is a traditionalist, holding dear the values and traditions of his family, and according them the highest of honors. If this gentleman does maintain a mistress, she will be so well hidden from the family that her presence can in no way jeopardize the family's security or respectability. His family and children are very important to him; he sees them as part of his accomplishment in the world, and yet also seeks their love and approval in everything he does. He is eager to please and seeks recognition and attention wherever he goes – and usually he gets it! He is an innate romantic, and seeks to be the 'knight in shining armor' in every aspect of his life. If he has one major failing, it is his obtuseness — that is, his tendency not to notice how you're feeling or what your real needs might be. With this man you must be direct, and when he knows what you want he will do his best to please, but hints he will never notice. In business he can be a dynamo, having unlimited energy and ambition, but when things get slow or he is faced with roadblocks, he may lose patience and move on to more fruitful and immediately satisfying endeavors. He loves a challenge, but can't tolerate his own failure, especially if it's public.

When the King of Wands is inverted in the reading, the negative side of all of these characteristics may be enhanced. Instead of venting his frustrations and excess energy in the gym, he may vent them through physical abuse, or reckless driving. Instead of being proud of himself and following the ethics of honesty and integrity, which should be his, he feels he is a failure and therefore lies, cheats, and acts selfishly to get his own way. When inverted, he may be the cheating husband, or he may be the neighborhood thug. This King can make an unpleasant enemy in the extreme.

Being a Star-Trek fan, I like to see the King of Wands as the 'Captain Kirk' character from the original Star Trek series — a series that was so successful largely because of the perfect balance of elements of its four leading actors. If you are somewhat familiar with Captain Kirk in his ongoing Star Trek role, you will have a fair depiction of the King of Wands both upright and inverted. The other three elements were represented by Dr. McCoy as the King of Cups, by Scotty as the King of Pentacles, and by Spock as the King of Swords. The salamander at the base of the Rider-Waite version of the card is meant to represent the element fire. But if your family has a pet lizard or iguana this might well be its card.

Now, think of examples of the King of Wands in both his upright and inverted character type from your own life. Your insight into the real-life character of your King of Wands will give added dimension to your readings. Record your own examples here:

Personal Notes

_____

_____

_____

_____

_____

KING of CUPS

Coloring – Medium to dark hair, light skin and eyes.

Mode – Cardinal (self-starting).

Element – Water.

Corresponding Astrological Signs – Primarily Cancer, Scorpio, Pisces, and occasionally Sagittarius or Aquarius.

Simplified Meanings:

Upright – A warm, emotional, intuitive and sensitive man.

Inverted – A self-centered, manipulative and self-indulgent man.

Famous Kings of Cups: Richard Burton, Prince Charles, Deforest Kelly (Dr. McCoy from the original Star Trek).

In-Depth Meanings:

The King of Cups is an emotional, caring, very sensitive and intuitive personality. Sometimes he is shy and retiring, but just as often he can be friendly and outgoing, reaching out to anyone he sees in need. Because of this, we often find him in a healing or service profession. His family and friends mean the world to him, and he will spare no effort to see any wrong to them set right. He makes a wonderful father, sometimes being more of a mother to his children than his wife. He makes a good small-businessman, and loves being able to provide the security in which his family or his employees can thrive. He is so good at knowing what you need when you need it that you could almost swear he is psychic! He loves the good things in life too, like good, rich food, social gatherings with family and friends, and enough time off to enjoy life. He, too, is a romantic, though his idea of romance is more likely to involve a home-cooked meal followed by lots of cuddling by the fire. I have found that in many women's readings when a new romantic partner shows up, regardless of his real character he may appear in their reading as the King of Cups. This is because they are initially seeing him as soft, gentle and nurturing. Later on, if he truly is a different character, he will start to show up as his 'real' suit. If the King of Cups has a fault, it is that in his concern for those people and issues that are close to him he often fails to see the larger picture. As with Star Trek's Dr. McCoy, he may be more concerned with saving the life of the individual beneath his nose than the lives of the million sick people he's supposed to deliver a miracle medicine to. Due to his love of the good things in life, he may be prone to overeating, or to overdoing other potentially addictive substances.

When the King of Cups is inverted, he displays the negative traits of the character. He may be obsessive, manipulative, and compulsive. He is overly emotional, and overly sensitive to the point that he sees wrongs in the most minute actions of others. In a relationship, he seeks to keep his partner's attention all to himself by creating never ending emotional crises that keep the partner on a perpetual roller coaster of emotion. In the extreme situation, he may even subtly feed off of the emotional energy he is forcing his partner to release. He may cheat on his wife or lover – but be assured, if he does, he will be sure he gets caught, because it's really his partner's attention he wants. He is an addictive, co-dependent personality.

Now, think about the famous people that are Kings of Cups, and when you think you have a good grasp on what this King is all about, think of some upright and inverted Kings of Cups that you know personally. These people will serve you as a template or reference whenever you turn up a King of Cups in your readings. You may record them here:

Personal Notes

_____

_____

_____

_____

_____

_____

_____

_____

The King of Pentacles

Coloring – Dark hair, skin, and eyes.

Mode – Cardinal (self-starting).

Element – Earth.

Corresponding Astrological Signs – Primarily Taurus, Virgo, Capricorn, and occasionally Scorpio or Pisces.

Simplified Meanings:

Upright – A stable, solid, materially oriented man, good with money and mechanical things.

Inverted – A selfish, materialistic con-man not to be trusted.

Famous Kings of Pentacles: Richard Nixon, Howard Hughes, James Doohan (Scotty, from the original Star Trek).

In-Depth Meanings:

The King of Pentacles is a solid, stable, down-to-earth and practical personality. He is generally most comfortable working behind the scenes to further the interests of his family or business. As a family man, he is primarily concerned with supplying the material needs of the family, assuming that his wife will take care of everything else. In fact, he's usually extremely talented in handling finances and investments. Often he stays so far in the background relative to family matters that you may forget he exists until the paycheck comes in. He is very good mechanically, especially with his hands, so no matter what his profession, it's not unusual to find him quietly building a treehouse for the kids or laying a tile floor in his spare time. It is generally away from home in his business or profession that we see the more dynamic side of this King. For in his most positive representation, he is the corporate dynamo, the individual whose far-seeing insight results in schemes and actions that achieve great results. There seems to be nothing that he cannot do when he sets his mind to it, though those around him may have no idea of what he's planning until he decides they now need to know. For this reason, most of us see him as closed-mouthed and secretive, though he surely would not see himself that way. As far as he's concerned, if you want to know something, just ask, and he really will tell you, too – that is, if he is aware yet of what he's planning. Much of this Kings action results directly from intuition, and a great deal of his planning goes on at the unconscious level. Often times women become disillusioned with him, because when they first know him romantically he may really play the dating game with the best of them, yet after he's made his conquest he becomes the practical, earthy person that he really is. If what you want is security, responsibility, and a wonderful business partner, this is your man. His greatest fault may be an inability to sit back and enjoy life, because at heart he's a workaholic and in love with his work. All of the green and growing things shown around him in the Rider-Waite card represent affluence and the nurturing ability to make things grow and multiply.

When the King of Pentacles is inverted we see an entirely different personality emerge. This is the man who schemes and manipulates others into doing his work for him; the man who looks for the softest job with the best pay; the man who skims off the top, the bottom, and the sides, of whatever barrel he falls into. He is lazy, but knows how to look busy. He turns his business and financial abilities into looking for ways to beat the system. Or, he may seek to marry a woman who will take care of his considerable financial needs. He is prone to jealousy, and needs to control everyone and everything in his life, fearful that what he seeks so hard to control, will instead control him. He is the King who is most likely to keep his wife and family living in poverty, even though they might afford more. He is the King most likely to try to control you through your attachment to things. And remember, no matter how much he has, it is never enough. I personally feel that of the four Kings, the two who are capable of causing the most damage when they are negative are the King of Wands and the King of Pentacles.

Consider the famous Kings of Pentacles that you know. Now, think of both upright and inverted Kings of Pentacles that people your own life. Perhaps one came to mind when you were reading the foregoing section? Record them here:

Personal Notes

_____

_____

_____

_____

_____

_____

The King of Swords

Coloring – Medium skin, hair, eyes.

Mode – Cardinal (self-starting).

Element – Air.

Corresponding Astrological Signs – Primarily Gemini, Libra, Aquarius, and occasionally Aries, Virgo or Scorpio.

Simplified Meanings:

Upright – A quick witted, very intelligent man.

Inverted – A scheming, arrogant, and manipulative man.

Famous Kings of Swords: John F. Kennedy, Jimmy Carter, and Leonard Nimoy (Spock, from the original Star Trek).

In-Depth Meanings:

The King of Swords is the most mental of the Kings. He is so mental, in fact, that he actually processes his emotions intellectually. Because of that, he very often doesn't know what he's really feeling – he's already decided what he's feeling! Truth to tell, the King of Swords is not really comfortable dealing with emotions at all. Like the famous character Spock, from Star Trek, it is actually unhealthy for him to let his emotions get away from him. If you know a King of Swords personally, you will have witnessed the totally out of character (and generally rather destructive) behavior that results when his emotions occasionally override his mind. But if you can accept this King's generally emotionless demeanor you will find an ability for friendship and intellectual companionship that no other King is capable of. The King of Swords has a keen wit and a wonderful sense of humor. His quick mind can work its way through just about any problem in moments. He is a great communicator, although you have to catch him in the right mood because he also needs a lot of quiet time, which he usually chooses to spend alone. He's very social and he loves people, but again, only when he's in the mood for them. Families are not necessarily his forte. When he's in the mood, there's no place he'd rather be, but when he's not, he could disappear for several months. If he has children, he probably won't accept that they're alive until they can carry on a conversation with him. This King makes a much better father to teens than he does to infants. Like the King of Pentacles, we generally see the King of Swords in his best light in his career. Also like the King of Pentacles, he may be a workaholic, although this King usually works with his mind and his communication skills. We'll find him in any field that is intellectually stimulating and challenging. Women often find the King of Swords mysterious and magnetic, mistaking his intellectually reserved demeanor for romantic intrigue. Remember, that although he may have the gift for communication, it cuts both ways – he not only knows when to talk, but also when not to talk.

When I read this card I often find myself focusing on the two birds on the upper-right side of the Rider-Waite version. When this happens, I read this as 'distance,' perhaps between this King and his family or a loved one. In fact, this card usually shows up when a romantic relationship is being conducted from across a distance. The shaky ground beneath his feet tells you that this King does not necessarily operate from a solid foundation and may constantly change his life situation.

When the King of Swords is reversed, his mental nature is magnified into underhanded scheming. He is the King who plans, plots, and schemes his way into the bosses confidence to ultimately usurp his position. He is a chess player who is years ahead of his competition. He is verbally abusive. He lies. He is so far out of touch with his own emotions that he doesn't even know that his negative actions are stimulated by greed, fear, jealousy or envy.

Again, as you read the preceding section you probably thought of some upright and inverted Kings of Swords that you know personally. If not, take the time to think of one for the inverted position, and one for the upright. Record them here:

Personal Notes

_____

_____

_____

_____

_____

_____

The Queens

The Queens of the Tarot deck represent mature women past the age of puberty. Each Queen demonstrates a very different character, which reflects her suit.

The Queen of Wands

Coloring – Medium to light hair, eyes, and skin.

Mode – Fixed (stabilizing).

Element – Fire.

Corresponding Astrological Signs – Primarily Aries, Leo, Sagittarius, and occasionally Cancer or Virgo.

Simplified Meanings:

Upright – A strong, intuitive, physically active and impetuous woman.

Inverted – A short-tempered, physical woman, false to her ideals.

Famous Queens of Wands: Elizabeth, Queen of England; Barbara Stanwyck, Sigourney Weaver.

In-Depth Meanings:

The Queen of Wands is idealistic, direct, and extremely honest. She is not someone who notices things, so if you want her help or attention you have to make your needs clear. Once you do, she will expend enormous amounts of her time and effort to give you what you need. She is a doer and an actor, not a talker or a listener. If you do enlist her aid, be sure to let her know exactly what you want because she has a habit of assuming that she knows your needs already and is prone to go off in her own impetuous direction before you have a chance to tell her. In all of her relationships, with both friends and family, she is intensely loyal. She will defend someone she believes in first, and ask them questions later. She is an all or nothing lady. If you don't have her affection and good will, you may very well have her animosity. As a mother she is exacting, expecting a great deal from her children, and yet she will defend and support them like a lioness taking care of her cubs. At work she is a dynamo, the ideal employee who can be trusted totally, a team player, good at what she does, tremendously creative, and will always be there when you need her. But be wary that you do not abuse her or fail to give her recognition when she deserves it – because she can make an implacable enemy! She thoroughly enjoys men, both being with them and competing with them. Because of this, it is not unusual to find her at the gym, or working in a man's job, or making her very best friend a man.

When the Queen of Wands is inverted in the reading, we see a woman who is above all things false to herself. Instead of honesty, we see deceit. Instead of directness, we see subterfuge and stealth. This is the Queen who is most likely to cheat on her husband, or to lie, cheat, or steal. She is the Queen most likely to abuse her children physically, or to get into a fist fight with her husband. But remember, she took this turn into negative behavior when she first became false to her own values. This usually happens when she fails at something that is very important to her, or is refused the recognition she craves. All of this Queen's negative behavior arises from a poor self-image. She can be jealous and envious of her peers or family members and seek to undermine them. She may even resent all other women, seeing them only as competitors. But remember, the upright and inverted meanings of the cards are always present no matter which direction the card faces – it's only that the inverted position brings out the negative as opposed to the positive. That means that somewhere within her she still has the positive traits if she could only find out how to release them. This is true of all of the Court cards. This card may sometimes be used to represent the family cat. (Note the cat on the card.)

Think of examples of the Queen of Wands in her upright and inverted positions. Choose your examples from people you know, and record them here:

Personal Notes

_____

_____

_____

_____

_____

The Queen of Cups

Coloring – Light hair, eyes, and skin.

Mode – Fixed (stabilizing).

Element – Water.

Corresponding Astrological Signs – Primarily Cancer, Scorpio, Pisces, and occasionally Gemini or Sagittarius.

Simplified Meanings:

Upright – An emotional, sensitive, intuitive, nurturing woman.

Inverted – A selfish, over-emotional and manipulative woman.

Famous Queens of Cups: Princess Diana, Elizabeth Taylor, Ali Sheedy.

In-Depth Meanings:

The Queen of Cups is warm, caring, and sees everything in life from her own very emotional and intuitive point of view. She can make a good professional psychic if she learns to separate her emotions from her intuitions. Of all the Queens, she is the one who embodies the feminine qualities to the fullest. She is totally receptive and is motherly, womanly, and childlike all at the same time. Since she is ruled by emotion, she has a constantly changing and vacillating nature. Her emotions pass through her quickly, much like clouds passing across the sun. She is home loving and family oriented, although we may not actually find her at home all that much, since she is inclined to be involved with so many people outside of the home. She is always ready to listen to your problems and to offer her opinion, her empathy, and a shoulder to cry on. But don't expect too much in the way of tangible or physical help from her, that's more the province of the Queen of Pentacles or the Queen of Wands. In a romantic relationship with her, you'll never be quite sure whether you're dealing with your mother, your daughter, or a seductress. Her children will find themselves alternately mothering her, or being nurtured by her. In her nurturing mode there is no other Queen in the deck who can generate the quiet and sure emotional support that this Queen can. She has the ability to generate self-confidence and strength in everyone she nurtures.

When the Queen of Cups is inverted we see the selfish, insecure side of her. In this mode she is not a nurturer, rather she works to undermine you, to make you insecure. She is afraid you will leave her. Her moods fluctuate violently, and she does whatever she can to keep you in a state of emotional distress, tying into you emotionally so that you go on the same emotional roller-coaster ride she is on. When inverted, she may be chronically low on energy and be very draining to her family and friends. She may be prone to alcoholism or co-dependency, or demonstrate other addictive traits. In the extreme, and especially if an inverted Temperance, Moon, or Star appears in the reading with her, she may be experiencing mental health problems such as chronic depression, manic-depression, or schizophrenia.

Think of some Queens of Cups from your own life, and record them here as your own real-life examples:

Personal Notes

_____

_____

_____

_____

_____

_____

_____

_____

_____

_____

The Queen of Pentacles

Coloring – Dark hair, eyes, and skin.

Mode – Fixed (stabilizing).

Element – Earth.

Corresponding Astrological Signs – Primarily Taurus, Virgo, Capricorn, and occasionally Scorpio or Pisces.

Simplified Meanings:

Upright – A practical woman, good with money and things.

Inverted – An impractical, lazy woman. She is manipulative and obsessive.

Famous Queens of Pentacles: Hillary Clinton, Eleanor Roosevelt, and Helena Rubenstein.

In-Depth Meanings:

The Queen of Pentacles is a strong, stubborn, and practical woman who knows how to get things done. She is a top-notch organizer who uses her skills to find the shortest route to the greatest accomplishment. She is single-minded and thorough in all that she does. Her nature is secretive and if you want to know about something she's doing, you'll probably have to ask. She's good at making and handling money, has no trouble both working and caring for a family, and would probably do well in her own business. She and the Queen of Wands are beyond a doubt the strongest women in the Tarot deck. As a friend, she will always be there, yet will not be interfering. As a wife, she is loyal and supportive of her mate, being as much a partner as a wife. As a mother she is practical and attentive, and generally knows exactly what her kids are up to, though they may well think she doesn't! Her greatest fault is that she often expects too much of others, thinking that they have the same special organizational skills and abilities that she does. And remember, that although she will never interfere with your life unless she's invited, once you invite her help she may prove to be a real takeover artist, having little patience for what she may see as your incapability in dealing with the problem.

When she is inverted she can be an extremely negative influence in the reading. She may be the woman who cannot handle money, who squanders her own resources and then moves on to yours. She can be untrustworthy and manipulative, making a good thief. She may be weak and co-dependent, expecting everyone else to take care of her needs, even manipulating them through guilt, giving form to the term, 'tyranny of the weak.' She may try to manipulate her family and friends with her money, or with vague promises of what she will give you or do for you if you live up to her expectations. She always takes more than she gives. This is definitely a Queen to stay away from when she's inverted.

Note that the Rider-Waite version shows a rabbit in the foreground. Read this card as the family rabbit if you have one.

Think of examples of the Queen of Pentacles in her upright and inverted positions. Again, choose your examples from people that you know, and record them here:

Personal Notes

_____

_____

_____

_____

_____

_____

_____

_____

_____

_____

Coloring – Medium hair, eyes, and skin.

Mode – Fixed (stabilizing).

Element – Air.

Corresponding Astrological Signs – Primarily Gemini, Libra, Aquarius, and occasionally Aries, Virgo or Sagittarius.

Simplified Meanings:

Upright – A serious, very intelligent woman who does not display emotion easily.

Inverted – A malicious gossip. A cruel woman who lacks emotion.

Famous Queens of Swords: Margaret Thatcher, Joan Crawford, and Oprah Winfrey.

In-Depth Meanings:

The Queen of Swords is a serious-minded, very intelligent woman who usually has excellent communication and social skills. She makes a wonderful radio or television broadcaster, but we may find her equally successful in any career situation where she can make the best use of her talents in these areas, from psychologist to social director, and everything in between. Because of her fine mind, we often find her in pursuit of a scientific, medical or legal career as well. Of all of the Queens, the Queen of Swords is most likely to be well educated.

Often in her earlier life, the Queen of Swords experienced some major disillusionment or hardship – as a result, she finds it difficult to trust others, or to just let go and have a good time. She takes everything she experiences with the utmost seriousness, even though she may appear to be joking with you. Remember that, because with this Queen, what you see is not necessarily what you get. All the while she is joking, her mind is hard at work planning the next move in a complex chess game. Because she has difficulty showing her emotions, she will not be the most nurturing of mothers, but when her children grow to the age where they need the help and advice of a parent, no parent will do a better job. When this Queen looks for a marriage partner, she looks for a friend first. She will offer her wonderful ability to listen to her mate and good friends, and will share her invaluable insights into their lives as her offering of love and support. Like her counterpart, the Queen of Pentacles, she makes a good business woman, but the challenge to her intellect and social skills will be her motivator, as opposed to the money – motivation of the Queen of Pentacles. These two make good business partners. I often see the single bird over her head as the birth of an idea in the Rider-Waite version.

When the Queen of Swords is inverted, we see a most negative side of her character. She becomes a malicious, even vicious gossip. She uses her strong mental nature to obsess over supposed slights, and manufactures intricate plots to destroy the object(s) of her anger. She shows no compassion for anyone, and in fact displays a cruelty toward all whom she sees as weaker than herself. When inverted, this woman will use her strong intellect and communication skills to steal from, to undermine, and to browbeat all those around her. Essentially, she feels for no one and no thing except herself.

Think of some people from your own life who could be represented by the Queen of Swords in both her inverted and upright positions. Record their names here for your own future reference:

Personal Notes

_____

_____

_____

_____

_____

_____

_____

_____

The Knights

The Knights in the Tarot deck represent young men, past the age of puberty, but not old enough to have become responsible, in an adult sense. In your Tarot readings, the Knight is seen from your client's point of view. So if you are reading for a child or an adolescent, the Knight might very well be a young man older than your client. If you are reading for someone in his teens or early twenties, the Knight could be the client, or someone around that age. If you are reading for an older person, the Knight will be a man that the client sees as younger than he is, either physically or emotionally. That means he could actually be any age, even older than the client, but seen as immature.

Remember, Knights also can represent beginnings (if upright) or endings (if inverted) of situations relative to their suit. Additionally, if your client owns a horse or is fond of horse-back riding, any Knight could represent his pet or hobby.

The Knight of Wands

KNIGHT of WANDS.

Coloring – Medium to light hair, eyes, and skin.

Mode – Mutable (changing).

Element – Fire.

Corresponding Astrological Signs – Primarily Aries, Leo, Sagittarius, and occasionally Cancer or Virgo.

<u>Simplified Meanings</u>:

Upright – An idealistic, physically active and ambitious young man. A new beginning in romance or home life. A physical change.

Inverted – A selfish, destructive, and vengeful young man. An ending of a romance, home situation, or a negative physical change.

Famous Knights of Wands: The young Tom Cruise; Mel Gibson; Mark Hamill (Luke).

<u>In-Depth Meanings</u>:

The Knight of Wands is idealistic and impulsive. His thoughts turn almost immediately into action, so you will generally know exactly what he is thinking, wanting or needing – if not by his revealing actions, than certainly by his extremely expressive face. Sometimes he is like a bull in a china shop, appearing awkward and ungainly in situations requiring grace and charm. He may even be painfully shy. In sports or physical activities of any kind he is wonderfully graceful. Competition seems to bring out the best in him. He seeks to shine in all that he does, and usually succeeds. He has latent leadership abilities, but generally speaking, he is so concerned with maintaining the good will of friends and loved ones that he willingly takes a back seat to their leadership. It's usually only when an emergency arises that we see any of that leadership ability leak out. Often he is a dreamer living in a rather unrealistic rendition of his own reality, wanting only to see the best in those he cares for. When romantically involved, he truly seeks to be the 'knight in shining armor' to someone's 'damsel in distress.' We often see him brokenhearted after he's discovered his damsel has no further need of him. And in truth, he is so in love with *love* that he may never have known who she really was! His eagerness, loyalty, strong values, and desire to please make him a delight to know. But don't step on his values or otherwise hurt him, because then he'll turn over – and inverted, this Knight is not a pleasure at all.

When the Knight of Wands is inverted he may be physically over-aggressive to the point of brutality. He is selfish, and paranoid. He sees only his own desires. As far as he is concerned, any means to an end is acceptable as long as it gets him there. He has no values. He is extremely sexual and may seek to use sex for domination. He is untrustworthy and may lie, cheat, or steal to achieve his own ends. He may use a persona of rebel or present an I-don't-care attitude to the world. He probably has a major insecurity problem that he covers with macho and bravado. If his negative action is a reaction to having been hurt, and he really does know better, he may be prone to periods of deep depression as well, during which he will either withdraw from others, or lash out at them.

I generally like to think of how I would react to any of the Knights dating my daughter (if I had one). If the Knight of Wands was upright, I'd probably like the young man and encourage the courtship, though I'd keep an eye on him. Knowing that he'd do the 'right thing' and marry her after he made her pregnant would not impress me. If he were inverted I would certainly not let her anywhere near the brute!

Take a moment to record the names of some upright and inverted Knights of Wands from your own life:

Personal Notes

_____

_____

_____

_____

_____

_____

_____

The Knight of Cups

KNIGHT of CUPS

Coloring – Medium to dark hair, light skin and eyes.

Mode – Mutable (changing).

Element – Water.

Corresponding Astrological Signs – Primarily Cancer, Scorpio, Pisces, and occasionally Gemini, Aquarius or Sagittarius.

Simplified Meanings:

Upright – A generous, warm and gentle young man. The beginning of an emotional, creative, or intuitive situation.

Inverted – A selfish, emotionally unbalanced young man. The ending of an emotional, creative or intuitive issue.

Famous Knights of Cups: Robin Williams, Paul McCartney, and Paul Simon.

In-Depth Meanings:

The Knight of Cups is very emotional, sensitive, and intuitive. He is generally a caring and supportive companion, who both gives and receives nurturing freely. He is very artistic and creative, and flourishes in a warm and happy family environment. In fact, the well-being of his family and close circle of friends will be very important to him. His emotions pass swiftly, from joy to sadness and back again in only moments. Whatever he feels, he feels with all of his heart and soul. He is trustworthy and capable, if a bit given to dreaming. If you have a Knight of Cups son or lover, treat him gently, for he wounds easily. Nurtured in the right environment he can grow to be a man fully in touch with his own feelings, with his feminine side, if you will; a true rarity in our society.

When he is inverted, the Knight of Cups is an insecure and unhappy person. Perhaps he was not raised in the pre-requisite nurturing environment, or perhaps he was misused or abused early on. Whatever the cause, the result is a deeply moody young man who knows how to use his own emotions to affect yours adversely. Just being around him can be a draining or irritating experience. He knows how to keep all of your hair constantly on end, how to keep your nerves in a continuous state of fray. His moodiness is not the swift passing of clouds across the sun as in the upright position, it is the deep well of depression or anger, and it is usually used deliberately to control those around him.

Needless to say, if I had a daughter who wanted to date the inverted Knight of Cups, I'd do everything in my power to spare her the broken heart he'd be sure to leave her with. If he were upright, however, I couldn't want a better suitor for my daughter's first love!

When looking at this card as a new beginning, I often find myself focusing on the layout of the Rider-Waite version. The Knight, being the client, is standing in a desert representing his present life situation emotionally. But he has an opportunity to move forward if he can find the strength to cross the river of his own fears and insecurities. Of course the mountain on the other side represents the fact that the journey is not without pitfalls and is a long upward climb.

Now take a moment to record here any Knights of Cups, inverted and upright, that you know:

Personal Notes

_____

_____

_____

_____

_____

_____

_____

_____

_____

The Knight of Pentacles

Coloring – Dark hair, eyes and skin.

Mode – Mutable (changing).

Element – Earth.

Corresponding Astrological Signs – Primarily Taurus, Virgo, Capricorn, and occasionally Scorpio or Pisces.

Simplified Meanings:

Upright – A quiet, thoughtful and practical young man. The beginning of a financial or spiritual matter.

Inverted – A slow, plodding, lazy, and selfish young man. The ending of a financial or spiritual matter.

Famous Knights of Pentacles: The young Marlon Brando, Pierce Brosnan, and Henry Fonda.

In-Depth Meanings:

The Knight of Pentacles is a gentle person, quiet and laid back. He seems to see everything, taking it all in and weighing it. He doesn't talk much, but when he does, it's worth listening to. It may take him a relatively long time to reach conclusions, but those he reaches are carefully thought out and will certainly hold water. He's not good at sharing his thoughts and ideas with others, so unless you are comfortable with long silences he may not be the guy for you. But he is deeply caring and emotional, though he does not show those emotions readily. He generally shows his concern best by looking after the needs and comforts of those he cares for, and doing it so well and quietly that you may not even notice him until he is not there. He is wonderfully creative with his hands, especially at making things. He may be mechanically inclined as well. He is the slowest moving and probably the most mature of the Knights, since he is the only Knight who generally remembers to use his head. He spends a great deal of time thinking about and preparing for his future, though, and by the time he is ready to marry and have a family he probably already has the necessary finances saved to accomplish his dream.

When he is inverted, the Knight of Pentacles isn't thoughtful, he's thoughtless. If he spends any time thinking and planning at all, it's time spent trying to figure out how to get out of some work or responsibility, or how to get something for free. This is the Knight who is the free-loader or the boomerang kid. He usually doesn't have any money of his own, but he'll gladly borrow yours. He's a real escapist, and may be addicted to all kinds of physical and sensual experiences. He is the Knight least likely to change or grow up.

If I had a daughter she probably would not be interested in dating this Knight whether he was upright or inverted. I might approve of him in his upright position, even encourage the relationship, seeing his steadiness as a great benefit – but my daughter would probably find him boring unless security was her top priority. When inverted, he's definitely not the fellow for her – she'd be waiting for him to get a job forever, or be engaged to him for 10 years while she was waiting for him to set a date to end his bachelorhood!

Take a moment to record the names of some upright and inverted Knights of Pentacles from your own life:

Personal Notes

_____

_____

_____

_____

_____

_____

_____

_____

The Knight of Swords

KNIGHT of SWORDS

Coloring – Light to medium hair and skin, light to medium eyes.

Mode – Mutable (changing).

Element – Air.

Corresponding Astrological Signs – Primarily Gemini, Libra, Aquarius, and occasionally Aries, Virgo or Sagittarius.

Simplified Meanings:

Upright – A fast-talking, thinking, and acting young man. The beginning of a business, educational, or communication related matter. Swiftly moving times and events.

Inverted – A young man constantly in trouble because of his mouth or actions. The end of a business, educational, or communication related matter.

As an Adjective:

*This card falling near any other male card in the reading indicates that the person representing the companion card is about to bring trouble to himself and others. Whether the companion card is upright or inverted makes no difference other than defining the person's personality; i.e. – good people can make mistakes, too! But if the Knight of Swords is upright, the trouble usually comes from acting too quickly, without enough forethought; the timing of the resultant action is poor. If the Knight of Swords is inverted, it is the action itself that is the problem.

Famous Knights of Swords: James Dean, Peter Fonda, John Lennon.

In-Depth Meanings:

The Knight of Swords is the only Knight whose youthful personality is radically different than his adult personality. Possibly the reason that the King of Swords is a mental planner and schemer is because he learned the hard way. Because the Knight of Swords doesn't much give to thinking things out, faced with any new situation, he sizes it up in about 30 seconds or so, thinks through his best course of action for perhaps another heartbeat, and then opens his mouth and acts at about the same time. The Knight of Swords is indeed the fast kid on the block – fast acting, fast talking, fast cars and fast girls. He has a sharp mind, but he generally uses it to get himself in and out of life situations that can change as quickly as you or I might change our clothes. His mental agility and quick-wittedness are endearing, though frustrating qualities. His creativity is all mental. He can think up some of the most wonderful excuses. He loves Dungeons and Dragons, and fantasy and science fiction books, movies, and T.V. shows. He loves debate and can argue a point so creatively that just when you think you've won, you find him on the other side and wonder how he got there. His is an exciting personality that draws others to him, but emotionally he forms few bonds, needing constant new people in his life to stimulate his questing mind.

When inverted, the Knight of Swords is an almost frightening card. He is the Knight who is drawn to chance and living on the edge. He is the Knight who must push everything and everyone in his life to their furthest limits, himself and his own abilities included. He doesn't just have the fast car, he must see how fast it can go... again and again. He must test it, and himself, in every possible situation and condition, always pushing just a bit further until disaster results. And he will do this in every way, with every thing and person in his life, be it his lover, his wife, his family, his friends, his job, or his own physical body. You might say he is in love with death because in one way or another he constantly flaunts it. You can't talk sense into him, he is unreachable. He merely registers your concern as the necessary attention to fuel his next test. The only thing that will turn this Knight around is to barely survive one of his disasters, and to have to return to life through struggle, patience, and hardship. I hope you don't have any representatives of this Knight in your life!

If I had a daughter she probably would be very interested in dating this Knight, in either his upright or inverted position. He is quite magnetic. But I would certainly discourage her since I would not like to see her hurt, and this Knight is famous for the broken hearts he leaves behind.

Record here some examples of the Knight of Swords that you do have in your life, or that you have known:

Personal Notes

_____

_____

_____

The Pages

The Pages in the Tarot deck represent children, up to the age of puberty. The Tarot deck does not differentiate between the sexes, so it is not possible to tell boys from girls unless you get a strong intuition as to which sex the child is. Some readers assume that the Pages of Wands and Swords are male because those suits are generative, and the Pages of Cups and Pentacles are female because those suits are receptive, but I find this assumption limiting. After all, some boys can be soft, sensitive, and receptive, and some girls are certainly aggressive, tough, and generative. However, if I find a Page surrounded by those receptive Cups and Pentacles in a reading, then I am more likely to feel the Page is a girl, whereas surrounded by the generative Wands and Swords it is more likely to be a boy. The best indicator, though, is your own intuition. And if you really don't feel anything one way or the other, there's nothing wrong with asking your client if they have a child, and then asking whether it's a boy or a girl. Once you know this, go on to describe the child's personality according to the descriptions below. In some readings you may turn up an older person as a Page, but only if the client you are reading for actually sees that person as a child.

Remember, Pages also often represent news, messages, or offers. If upright, the news or thing being offered is good for the client, and if reversed, it is bad.

The Page of Wands

PAGE of WANDS.

Coloring – Medium to light hair, eyes, and skin.

Element – Fire.

Corresponding Astrological Signs – Primarily Aries, Leo, Sagittarius, and occasionally Cancer or Virgo.

Simplified Meanings:

Upright – An innocent, trusting, sweet, and gentle child who is creative and imaginative.

Inverted – A mean-tempered and world-wise child, possibly abused or abusive.

As an Adjective:

*This card falling near any other Court card in the deck tells whether the person can be trusted by your client. If the Page of Wands falls upright, the Court card nearest to it is trustworthy; if he is inverted, the Court card nearest to it is untrustworthy. This will hold true whether the Court card being considered is itself upright or inverted. It makes no difference.

Famous Pages of Wands: Tom Sawyer; Judy Garland (The Wizard of Oz); Noah Hathaway (The Never ending Story).

In-Depth Meanings:

The Page of Wands is a quiet, gentle and imaginative youngster. He (or she) is loyal and idealistic and both trusting and trustworthy. The Pages of Wands may also be very gifted physically and have tremendous reservoirs of energy. They are also probably the most artistically inclined of all of the Pages. More than anything in the world this Page wants to be liked by friends and acquaintances, and loved by his family. This is a child with a truly generous spirit. Generally he will try with all of his heart to please those around them. This unswerving loyalty and desire to please generally leads the Pages of Wands into difficulty since they are not good judges of character. These Pages are easily and often hurt. Their very innocence makes them a target for other, more world-wise children to take advantage of. But the Page of Wands has wonderful bounce-back capability and generally holds onto this naivete long after anyone else would have been clobbered with reality. Even he has his limits, though. If this Page comes down to reality too hard and fast, the card reverses and we see the opposite side of the character.

Inverted, the Page of Wands is very angry. This anger is taken out on the surrounding world in a physical way, by breaking things, and getting into fist fights. The inverted Page of Wands won't look you in the eye when you talk to him, and as you reprimand him you can tell he's not listening, just waiting to get away and get on with his selfish pursuits. He's always in trouble of one sort or another, and he's often the class bully as well. I have found in practice that the best way to reach this Page is through physical activity and competition. Putting him on the boxing team, for example, helps him to work through his anger in a more or less constructive fashion. This Page suffers from rejection and a resultant ego problem that the parents are usually unable to help with since they are intrinsic to the root of the problem. The best help comes from school sports or activity counselors.

Record the names of several upright and inverted Pages of Wands that you are familiar with here:

Personal Notes

_____

_____

_____

_____

_____

_____

_____

_____

_____

The Page of Cups

PACE of CUPS.

Coloring – Medium to dark hair, light to medium skin and eyes.

Element – Water.

Corresponding Astrological Signs – Primarily Cancer, Scorpio, Pisces, and occasionally Gemini, Aquarius or Sagittarius.

Simplified Meanings:

Upright – An emotional, intuitive, artistic and creative child.

Inverted – A selfish and spoiled cry-baby.

Famous Pages of Cups: Pip (Great Expectations by Charles Dickens); Elizabeth Taylor (National Velvet); the young Michael Jackson.

In-Depth Meanings:

The Page of Cups is everyone's ideal of the perfect child. He (or she) is sensitive and emotional. This child's feelings are always close to the surface and he is as quick to empathize with your pain or hurt as he is to cry over his own. He experiences emotions with the quickness of a summer storm, but seldom hold onto any negative feelings for any length of time. He loves physical closeness and will always look for hugs and kisses and soft laps to sit on. Both boys and girls of this suit love stuffed toys and dolls, and can play imaginatively with them for hours upon hours. This child might be a little shy upon being introduced to new people, but once he feels comfortable and accepted into a new situation, he interacts openly and emotionally with his new friends. We frequently find this child excelling in the arts, including music, drawing, painting, and acting. Family support and interaction is very important to him.

When inverted, the natural emotionalism of this child is perverted into a tendency toward extreme selfishness and oversensitivity. He is moody, depressive, jealous, and sometimes vicious with other children. This is the child who throws the temper tantrum in the grocery store because Mom has finally decided she's not giving in to him. It is the child who acts silly in a desperate bid for attention from anyone he can get it from. This inverted Page of Cups will do anything he can to get an emotional reaction from surrounding family and friends, and can be a real drain to be around.

This card can also be used to represent the family aquarium or favorite fish. Note here several upright and inverted Pages of Cups from your own life experience:

Personal Notes

_____

_____

_____

_____

_____

_____

_____

_____

_____

_____

_____

_____

_____

The Page of Pentacles

Coloring – Dark hair, eyes, and skin.

Element – Earth.

Corresponding Astrological Signs – Primarily Taurus, Virgo, Capricorn, and occasionally Scorpio or Pisces.

Simplified Meanings:

Upright – A quiet, imaginative yet practical child who is emotionally withdrawn. Good news about a financial, material, or spiritual issue. A promising business offer. Long range plans.

Inverted – A child who is severely introverted and unreachable. Bad news about a financial, material, or spiritual issue. A business offer that lacks substance, or is denied.

As an Adjective:

*This Page is also the Page that may indicate that information and messages are being given to your client by his (or her) Higher Self. If the Page is upright, he is listening and getting the message; if it's inverted, he is not. Use this meaning only if other cards with spiritual interpretations are present in the spread.

Famous Pages of Pentacles: Mozart, the child prodigy; Wesley Crusher (Wil Wheaton), from Star Trek, the New Generation; Alec Ramsey, main character in Walter Farley's Black Stallion series for young readers.

In-Depth Meanings:

The Page of Pentacles is a quiet and unobtrusive child who is easy to overlook. While all of the other children are making their wild bids for attention from Mom or Dad, he or she is focusing on important matters like completing an art project, working out an important new invention, or planning how to set up a babysitting or lawn mowing business. This Page does not welcome Mom or Dad's interference or attention until such time as he actually needs help – and that is rarely. In fact, this child can be so totally self-sufficient that Mom and Dad feel left out! Pages of Pentacles are used to solving their own problems. Usually the only indication that they have one is that they're unusually quiet (even for them), or that you haven't seen them for a while. But of course, that could also mean that they are working on some new project and are so absorbed by it that they've forgotten the rest of the world. Pages of Pentacles often have difficulty relating to other children. It's not uncommon for them to select their friends very carefully, and only on a one-to-one basis. They often find friends in older children, or even adults that may share a common interest with them. All too often, because of their dependability and practicality, these children are expected to take care of the other children in the family, or do jobs that no one else can be made to do. The Page of Pentacles sees no point in wasting time arguing over it – his or her approach is to just get it done and then get on with life. He or she makes an extremely loyal friend and are often gifted in some special area.

If inverted, the Page of Pentacles turns his attention inward to the point that he becomes unreachable. This usually happens only if the child has experienced some deep disappointment or has been in some way used or abused. In the extreme this could be autism. More often it is merely the child who spends his or her time sulking in corners, doing whatever possible to avoid attention and your bid to get him or her to "do something." These children appear lazy and unproductive, and indeed they avoid work of any kind – yet you might find them wistfully watching a group of other youngsters at work or play, until they see you and pretend again to indifference. These Pages are often left alone without the help they need because since they always do just enough to skate by, both they and they're problems tend to go unnoticed. As with the Page of Wands, the help this Page needs usually has to come from outside the family, from a teacher or a friend, perhaps, because the family is usually responsible for the initial turning-off of the child. The best way to reach these children is through pets, or activities that involve working with the hands. If they are going to act out, it usually is in a behind-the-scenes way that is so subtle that it's hard to catch them. Or they may even set you up so that although you know that they did something wrong, you are helpless to do anything about it! Yes, they are sneaks!

Take a moment to note here the names of several upright and inverted Pages of Pentacles that you know:

Personal Notes

_____

_____

_____

_____

The Page of Swords

Coloring – Light to medium hair, skin, and eyes.

Element – Air.

Corresponding Astrological Signs – Primarily Gemini, Libra, Aquarius, and occasionally Aries, Virgo or Sagittarius.

Simplified Meanings:

Upright – A bright, energetic, active and talkative child. Good news, a long-distance phone call, or meaningless gossip.

Inverted – A malicious, hyperactive child who is a troublemaker. Bad news, a phone call not coming or malicious slander.

Famous Pages of Swords: Dennis the Menace; Huckleberry Finn; Shirley Temple.

In-Depth Meanings:

The Page of Swords is a physically and mentally active child that is both a delight and a trial for any parent lucky enough to have one. These children are into everything. No stone is left unturned. Their curiosity knows no limits. The Page of Swords undoubtedly knows the contents of the house better than either parent does. Somehow he (or she) manages to be involved in every conversation or excursion of any import. Nothing is sacred! Here it is, the week before Christmas, and you've been carrying the child's presents in the trunk of your car for the past month just waiting for a moment when he's not around, to bring them in and hide them. Two o'clock in the morning, everyone's asleep, and you sneak out to bring them in. As you walk in the door a piping little voice says, "Oh, Mom, what's that?" – and you want to kill! This child makes a delightful companion because he is bright and fun to be around. But just try to get away! In school these children usually do well, and have lots of friends. Teachers love them. They're involved in every club and sports activity that they can find. When the Page of Swords is inverted, his basic character is the same as the upright Page, but the child tends toward jealously and manipulation. Not only will these children eavesdrop and overhear every conversation in the house, but they will selectively repeat what they hear for the greatest affect. They are natural born gossips, and they usually use their gossiping to cause trouble for their siblings, friends, and family. This Page may also steal, especially if he can blame it on someone else. This is the child who seeks to be the best, not through achievement, but by undermining and cutting down the competition from behind. Usually this child is cunning and good with words, but don't trust what he says even though it sounds plausible until you've heard everyone else's story first. The Page of Swords may very well be a chronic liar, a difficult problem to cure, if he is not immediately caught and exposed. As with the Pages of Wands and Pentacles, help for the child must usually come from outside the family since the basic reason for the behavior is to get negative attention from the parents. Usually the child only reverses the behavior pattern when he develops friends and feels as a part of a group outside of the home.

Record here any upright and inverted Pages of Swords that you know, that you can refer back to as a character reference when doing your own readings:

Personal Notes

_____

_____

_____

_____

_____

_____

_____

_____

_____

_____

Now, let's look at a sample reading and interpretation using the Minor Arcana suits as we did following Chapter 2. This time, however, we are going to fully interpret the Court cards in the reading.

The following reading is for a 65 year old gentleman that is a regular client of mine.

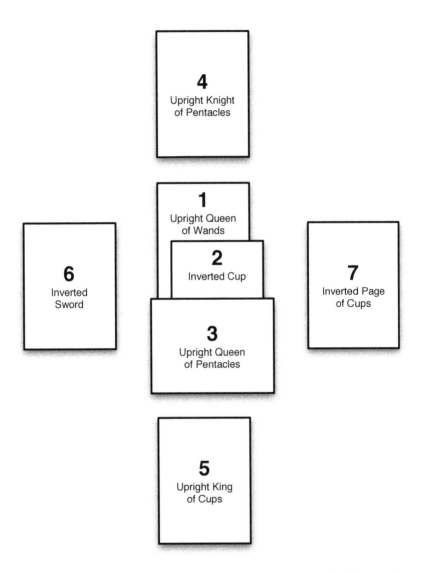

Figure 3: A Sample Reading from a Client Using the Simple Celtic Cross Spread

End of Chapter Exercise

1. What is this gentleman's current frame of mind? Whom or what might he be thinking about with the upright Queen of Wands in position 1?

2. Describe his current situation as shown by the inverted Cup in position 2. How does this relate to the Queen of Wands in position 1 and the King of Cups in the foundation in position 5?

3. What's coming up in the next three months as shown by the upright Queen of Pentacles in position 3? How does this card relate to the Queen of Wands in position 1 and the inverted Cup in position 2?

4. What can you predict that he will be dealing with in a year or so from now as shown by the Knight of Pentacles in the distant future or position 4? How will this relate to what's coming up in the next three months as shown by the Queen of Pentacles in position 3? Since we are reading for a man, any 'male' card in the reading can be represented as a part of our client. How would this card relate to him and what will he be doing in the future?

5. What does the King of Cups in the foundation in position 5 tell you about this client? Whom else might this King represent in this reading relative to both the client and the Queen of Pentacles in position 3?

6. What does the inverted Sword in the immediate future in position 6 tell you about what's coming over the next six months? When you look at this card together with the inverted Cup of the current situation in position 2, what do you expect the emotional climate to be? How do you relate this inverted Sword in the immediate future in position 6 to the upright Knight of Pentacles in the distant future in position 4?

7. The Page of Cups is inverted in the immediate past in position 7. What does this tell you about what may have happened over the last six months? Now read across and tie this card into the Queen of Pentacles in position 3 (the next three months) and the inverted Sword in position 6 (the next six months). Who might that Page actually be relative to the client and how has he or she been acting? Tie this meaning of the Page into positions 3 and 6 again and project into the future. Does the Knight of Pentacles in the distant future in position 4 give you any more insight?

Now, here's what I had to say about this spread:

Position 1 is our client's frame of mind, and tells us what, or who, he's thinking about as well. This elderly gentleman we are reading is certainly not a Queen of Wands. Or is he? As a matter of fact, the Wands suit itself will describe his frame of mind at the time of the reading. He comes to us interested in action. His ideals (Wands) are a focus for him. He's concerned about home and family. As you can see, the first step in interpretation is to read the suit. Next, let's take a look at the card itself. The Queen of Wands relative to him could indicate that the gentle, feminine side of his nature is being brought out by circumstances at this time.

It can also indicate that he is thinking about a Queen of Wands. The woman in question is a "strong, intuitive, physically active and impetuous person." In fact, there could be several women in his life who meet this criteria. This could be his wife, his good friend, his sister, or even his daughter. As a reader who knows nothing about him, you have no idea exactly who this could be. Just describe the person. As you describe her, he will begin to focus on a particular person that comes to his mind as you speak. As soon as he focuses, you will begin to feel a stronger connection, and will be more confident of your description. You will begin to unconsciously tune-in to him and describe his Queen of Wands much better than you know! In this case, let's assume he's focusing on his wife (who actually is a Queen of Wands, by the way). Since she is upright, you know that he has a positive attitude and involvement with her, that she is healthy, and that she is probably feeling pretty good about herself now.

Position 2 is the current situation. In this position we find an inverted Cup. Negative emotion (Cups, inverted) is evidently running high at the present time, both for him, because it's his reading, and for her, because the Queen of Wands leads directly into this card. Now, they might very well be upset about two different issues, but since they are married it is fairly safe to assume, for now, that it is the same issue. Cups deals with nurturance and family values, and the preceding card, a Wand, deals with tradition and therefore, also family values, so it's probably accurate to say that there is some sort of family crisis happening that is producing emotional tension. Since the preceding card, the Queen of Wands (his wife), is upright, and since the King at the Foundation of the reading (position 5) is also upright and can be assumed to represent him, it is probably not one of them that is going through the crisis, although they are certainly upset about it.

Position 3 is what's coming up in the next three months, and here we find a Queen of Pentacles. Remembering that the card in this position is always read upright, we read her as "a practical woman, good with money and things." Now, this could be his wife again, turning up during the next three months to offer her practicality in dealing with the situation, or it could be a totally different woman. Perhaps it's the woman with the problem? Or perhaps it's another woman who's going to have a positive affect on the whole situation. Maybe it's all three!

Position 4, the distant future, shows an upright Knight of Pentacles. We always read the Knights, first, as beginnings (if upright), or second, as endings (if inverted). This Knight's meaning is "a new beginning in financial or spiritual matters." It's beginning to look like all of the versions of the Queen of Pentacles in position 3 are making some new beginning. The wife, in her Queen of Pentacles mode, may be making a new beginning at handling the situation, the Queen of Pentacles with the problem is making a new beginning perhaps spiritually and materially in how she handles the problem, and the Queen who may be helping everyone is certainly aiding all of these fresh starts. Meanwhile, the Knight is also a person, isn't he? The Knight of Pentacles upright is "a quiet, thoughtful and practical young man." Since he's upright in the reading we can assume that he will be helpful and a positive influence in the life of our client. Maybe this is his son or son-in-law? Or perhaps just a man that he sees as younger than himself? Since he turns up in the reading so far in the future, it is unlikely that he is involved with the present unhappy situation but he may be involved with its outcome. Since he is upright, it is fair to assume that his interaction with each person in the reading will be positive. In fact, he could very well represent several different young men of similar character, each relative to one of the various Queens of Pentacles that we've looked at. Also, since any man in the reading can be read as a different aspect of the client, we might also infer from the positioning of this card that our client is going to begin some new financial endeavor in the future, which will take careful planning.

Position 5 is the foundation of the reading, and here we find the King of Cups. Reading this first as the client, we say that he is "a warm, emotional, intuitive, and sensitive man." In fact, he is a Cancer, one of the signs we associate with Cups. Since we find him in the foundation position, and upright, we can see that he sees himself as a cornerstone of his home and family, the support. He is upright, so he is both happy with the foundation he has created for himself and his place in it. Now going back, and re-reading this card as someone other than him, we can tell him that he had a "warm, emotional, intuitive, and sensitive man" around him that was a positive influence in his life. This gentleman is, in some way, involved with the current situation, though not directly. But he has somehow helped to set the stage for what is transpiring in this reading. The King of Cups may also be read as a separate person entirely, being the person who is the foundation for each interpretation of the Queen of Pentacles.

Position 6 is the immediate future, and here we see an inverted Sword. Swords deal with mental things, and communication, so we can assume that over the next six months there will be a lot of unpleasant communications and mental tension relative to the situation. When combined with the inverted Cup in position 2, this makes for a major emotional crisis (i.e., the negative emotion experienced in the current situation is not being let go – it's going to be re-hashed over and over again). On the other hand, it's probably because of this that the new beginning we see in position 4 (Knight of Pentacles) is taking place.

Position 7 is the immediate past. Somewhere over the last six months a message of negative emotional import was received. We know this because that's the first way to read the Page of Cups inverted. An offer of an emotional nature may also have been turned down, or never received. Reading across positions 3 and 6, you can see that it is probably this negative message that is producing the current emotional anxiety and will produce the future mental anxiety. Of course, next we can read the Page as a child. Since the gentleman we are reading is 65 years old, we can assume he doesn't have any children this age, but we might also ask. Even if he has no young children, this Page could be a grandchild. If so, the grandchild is a selfish and spoiled cry-baby. Or perhaps the child is just not feeling well or is upset about something. Since the position of this card is past, the inversion of the card could not mean that the child's not in his life yet, as it could if the card was in the future. If we do read this card as a grandchild, we can see by looking at the cards in positions 3 and 6 that the problems with the child will continue over the next six months until finally some practical action (position 4, the Knight of Pentacles), or possibly a young man (the Knight), deals with it!

Of course there is far more that could be said about this spread of cards, but I want to keep it simple for now. Let's look at this gentleman's actual situation:

As usual, we didn't know exactly what we were talking about; we were just reading the cards. But our client sure knew!

To begin with, the Queen of Wands is indeed his wife, as I said earlier. She recently received news that her sister is chronically ill (Page of Cups inverted, position 7). She is understandably very unhappy about this (position 3, inverted Cup), and it looks like she will continue to be unhappy over the next six months, relative to this problem (position 7, inverted Sword). She does, however, have another sister (our mysterious helping woman, the Queen of Pentacles, position 3) who is going to step in and offer help to the sister who is ill (yes, the Queen of Pentacles again). It appears from the reading that the ill sister has been refusing help from the healthy sister (position 7 again, Page of Cups inverted), but the upright Knight of Pentacles in position 4 makes it look right now like she'll finally accept it. The King in position 5 is indeed our client, who supports all of these gals in their close association with one another emotionally. But this King can also be read as the ill sister's husband. Following the cards straight up the center, he's obviously giving her positive support, where she appears in position 3, although he is unhappy about the situation as we see from position 2 (inverted Cup), and will gladly accept the help of the other sisters (positions 1 and 3). We see him doing something financial that will benefit the situation and perhaps help to alter the direction of her illness in position 5, the Knight of Pentacles.

If you have had a little trouble following all of this, don't be concerned. With practice you'll get it. The important thing to remember is to go slowly – initially lay each card out and interpret it first, then go back and tie it into the others. Don't try to pull all of the cards together until you have them all laid out and have understood, as best you can, each card individually. And remember to take the time to consider each of the meanings of each card before you move on to the next. The way to memorize the cards is by doing them, not by trying to memorize them. If it's too confusing to read each card now as several different people, then just read them as one person and let your client place them. I just wanted you to see that a card can be read over and over again, each time representing a different person and having a slightly different meaning. Understanding this from the beginning will prevent you from getting too narrow minded in your readings.

Chapter 4

The Major Arcana

The Major Arcana cards of the Tarot deck are undeniably the most important cards in the deck. These 22 cards alone can be used as a mini Tarot deck, so some readers choose to read only with these, or with just the Court cards added. In the Rider-Waite deck you will recognize them as the cards having a roman numeral at the top and a title on the bottom. Many scholars have noted that the 22 cards of the Major Arcana correspond perfectly to the 22 Paths contained in the *Tree of Life* represented by the Kabbala. The connection to the Kabbala is further strengthened when the Minor Arcana, 1 through 10 of each suit, is compared to the 10 types of consciousness represented on the Tree of Life as the 10 *Sephiroh*. The 22 Major Arcana plus the 10 cards of the suits gives a total of 32, which again are known to Kabbalists as the *32 Paths of Wisdom*. Now, if you look at the 32 Paths coming down into creation, and add to them the 32 Paths moving back up out of creation, you get the number 64. And 64 is the number of hexagrams in the *I Ching*, the ancient divination system used by the Chinese. It's a small world, isn't it? It seems obvious that all of these various disciplines derive from the same root! And they all attempt to show the evolutionary process, the purpose behind existence!

The Major Arcana in the Tarot deck is so important because it deals with evolution. These cards show the evolution of a life, of a person, of a job or business, or of a nation. They show the individual emerging at birth and passing through every conceivable growth phase. There was a wonderful book written by Richard Gardner, called *Evolution Through the Tarot*, that described this journey most beautifully. Unfortunately, it is currently out of print. If you should happen to come across a copy in a used book store, scarf it up immediately! Meanwhile, just keep in mind that each and every Major Arcana card has great importance when you are doing a spread of cards using the whole deck, relative to life lessons the client is learning, and major, sweeping changes may be entering his life. If you are only using the Majors in your reading, or just the Majors and the Court cards, you would not give them this extra weight in your reading.

This weighting of the Major Arcana cards when doing a spread involving all the different types of cards in the deck is so important that when I do a reading and a majority of Majors turns up, I know that my client is feeling as if he or she is tossed about by the winds of fate. Now, we all know that nothing just happens in your life – one way or another, through your action or inaction, you have drawn to you every event that occurs in your life. But when a majority of Major Arcana cards turns up in your card spread, you feel like the hand of fate has just swooped down, picked you up, turned you upside down, and given you a good shake! I often find that when I turn up a lot of Majors in someone's reading, it helps if I point out his or her own responsibility in the situation – it sort of helps the client to regain focus and feel a little more in control of a life that at the time of the reading feels totally beyond the client. It is especially important in these readings to end the reading on an up note.

Some readers connect the Major Arcana cards to particular astrological signs. Although I see an affinity between certain cards and certain signs, and will draw attention to them where I see fit, in general I feel that the Tarot Major Arcana each apply to some aspects of all of the signs, comprising as they do, the journey of the soul.

0 – The Fool

THE FOOL.

Simplified Meanings:

Upright – A new beginning. A decision to step forward. A special soul ready to be born. A special child. Your inner child.

Inverted – An ending. An opportunity passed up. A decision not to move on. A soul waiting to be born. A special child in trouble. Denying your inner child.

Number – 0 is the number that is before the beginning and after the end. Just as a circle completes itself, the 0 completes the Tarot deck as a never ending cycle.

In-Depth Meanings:

Key 0 in the Major Arcana is the Fool. Interestingly, some decks number the Fool Key XXII. This is confusing to some students until they realize that just as a circle has no beginning and no end but endlessly repeats, so do the Major Arcana cards. The Fool is both the beginning and the ending in the endless cycle represented by the cards. He is the soul coming into life for the first time, the spirit of the individual beginning any new pattern or taking any new action as life progresses, and he is the soul taking its last step out of life and into spirit at the end of life.

The Fool turns up in a reading any time your client is about to take a major step forward into the unknown. Of course, anything that we haven't already been involved in before can be defined as the unknown. The step forward indicated by this card could be a step into marriage, into a business, a new job, an educational pursuit, or even a change of residence. Surrounding cards will tell you what area of life in which this major step forward will occur. If the Fool is upright in the reading, the client is probably going to take the step forward. The decision of whether to do it has been made, at least inwardly, since he (or she) is following the inner voice which says, "Do it." If the Fool is inverted, the client is hearing the voice that says, "Do it," and wants to, but is likely to choose not to because other issues in his life are taking precedence right now. The client may feel he can come back and take the opportunity at a later date. As a reader, you should advise the client that if the Fool is inverted, to re-think the decision, since the opportunity presented in this easy-to-do manner will come but once. Since the Fool is Key 0, and the 0 is a circle, and circles are protective in nature, there is a suggestion here that as your client steps forward into this unknown venture (whatever it is), he will be protected! Mind you, the protection extended only involves the actual time of transition. Once the change is made, the action taken, the spiritual protection offered by this card is ended. If your client chooses to pass up the opportunity now, he is passing up the protection the Fool offers during that transition time. In the future, the client may very well be able to do his venture, but not nearly as easily or smoothly as if he did it when the Fool appeared.

In some readings the upright Fool may represent a young child (similar in nature to the Page of Wands) or a special soul getting ready to be born. You'll know if it's a baby about to be born because surrounding it in the reading you'll see cards that mean pregnancy. You'll know when to read it as a special child in whom the soul quality is very close to the surface because the situation the child is involved in will appear in the surrounding cards. However, whatever meaning you are using, this card always carries with it the feeling of innocence and purity of heart. If the Fool is inverted, the soul waiting to be born may not yet be in the womb of the mother, or if the Fool represents a child, it may indicate that the child's inner light has been quenched by unfortunate circumstances. I always feel particular sorrow when this meaning applies because it means that a serious wrong has been done to a very special soul that had a mission in incarnating that it may now be unable to complete.

On a somewhat happier note, the dog in the foreground may even represent the family dog in some of your readings.

*Special Note: In a reading when this card falls near the Empress, the Sun, or the Ace of Cups, Ace of Wands, or Ace of Swords, it will represent the birth of a special child who has a special mission.

Personal Notes

_____

_____

_____

_____

_____

I – The Magician

THE MAGICIAN.

Simplified Meanings:

Upright – Creativity. Strength of will. Sexuality. A magician or powerful leader. Administrative ability. A virile young man. The power to manifest your desires. Energy. Power.

Inverted – Blocked creativity. Impotency. An undermining influence around you. Physical incapacity. Lack of will power. Helplessness. Blocked energy.

Number – 1 is the number of beginnings, creativity, independence, and individuality. The I Ching regards it as "The Creative" or the natural active power of heaven.

In-Depth Meanings:

The Magician is the most energy-packed card in the deck. He is reminiscent of the sign Aries, the first sign of the zodiac, and like Aries, he is fiery, aggressive, competitive, ambitious, creative, and highly sexual. He achieves his desires. I describe the Magician as male because these characteristics are generative, or male, in nature. But the magician can represent a man or a woman in a reading – it's just the male nature in both that he brings out.

If he turns up in position 1 in your Celtic Cross spread he may indicate that the person you are reading is strong, virile, willful, has both creative and administrative capabilities, and has the power to manifest his (or her) desires. If your client is a man, this card may describe him, in which case you know that he sees himself as young, sexy, strong and invincible. And yet it may also describe someone else that he is thinking about, in which case this other person would also likely be male, and would be someone in whom he admired these qualities. If your client is a woman, the Magician here would describe her as possessing these qualities herself, but would also indicate that she has a young man on her mind whom she perceives as very sexual and capable. In your readings, the Magician will either describe your client, whether male or female, or any other young and aggressive male. A woman would not see another woman as this card unless she were gay, since the Magician may also be read to represent the sexual partner, especially if there is a very magnetic attraction.

As a matter of fact, the person indicated by the upright Magician has considerable sexual prowess and may even use his (or her) intense sexual magnetism to his advantage. In extreme cases, where the Magician falls next to cards meaning control or dominance, sex can be used to manipulate or control another person. Generally speaking though, as long as you find the Magician upright in a reading, he speaks well of the sexual relationship your client may be in.

When you occasionally read the Magician as an actual person, he will be a man who is young (perhaps late teens or early twenties) or who has managed to preserve that quality of combined innocence, egocentricity, fearlessness, carefree abandon, sexual aggressiveness, and ambition, into adulthood. It's as if he's at the threshold of life, full of prowess and eagerness, and not yet having experienced failure, or even entertained its possibility. As long as you find him upright, he will be dynamic and fun, and probably very successful. But upside down, he may be the person who is totally out of control because of his refusal to release those same youthful characteristics or because there is some undermining influence involved. Remember, even though it may be inverted, the Magician would not be in the spread at all unless the potential for its upright meaning was also present.

Inverted, the Magician is a block to sexual activity; as a matter of fact, since the Magician represents energy itself, inverted, it's safe to say that the person indicated by him in the reading is low on energy, and probably is blocked in every way. If the person is your client, one of your jobs as a reader should be to look at the surrounding cards to try to determine what is causing the energy block, whether physical, circumstantial, or psychological, and to try to advise your client in how to overcome it. Usually, in this case, the client has handed his personal power over to another person, or has given it up due to circumstance, and needs to take it back.

Interestingly, when the inverted Magician signifies sexual impotency, it is not possible to tell if it is male impotency or female frigidity that is the cause. All the inverted Magician tells us about the sexual interaction of the two partners is that sex is not occurring. But by looking at the way in which the surrounding cards fall, especially the Court cards, you may be able to tell which partner has the problem and what is causing it – and thereby help them to overcome it.

The very best thing that can be said about the Magician is that he represents our God-given capability to manifest our desires. All of the plants and bounty in the picture on the card suggests the procreative and creative capability inherent in the energy represented by this card. The reason all four elements are represented in the card by the Cup, the Sword, the Pentagram, and the Wand, is that the magician knows that to magically form any idea into manifested reality requires all four elements fused into one through application of the magical *Will*. By unifying our Will with that of the God force, we can accomplish anything – even the impossible. The infinity sign above his head is the symbol of energy, eternity, and karma – meaning that anything we begin we must complete, but we are free to complete it after our own fashion.

__Special Note__: When the Magician falls upright near the Devil, also upright, sex is being used for control. To find out who is being controlled, look for the inverted Court card. The person doing the controlling will be upright. If there are also a lot of Wands present and perhaps an inverted Ten of Cups, there may also be sexual abuse involved. When the Magician falls inverted next to an inverted Ace of Wands, it may indicate sexual impotency.

Personal Notes

_____

_____

_____

_____

_____

_____

_____

_____

_____

_____

_____

II – The High Priestess

Simplified Meanings:

Upright – Secret information. Spiritual knowledge and insight. Balance and detachment. The Virgin. The Nun. The teacher of mystic truths. A 'High Priestess.' The perfect woman. A woman, secretive, knowledgeable and helpful, but unobtrusive.

Inverted – Lies. Slander. Secrets used against you. A devious woman who appears to be a friend but will use her knowledge against you. The 'other' woman whom you suspect but of which you are never sure!

Number – 2 is the number of duality, black and white, male and female, yes and no, Yin and Yang, balance and imbalance. The I Ching regards it as "The Receptive" or what is considered the uncarved block representing all possibilities.

In-Depth Meanings:

The High Priestess is one of the most profound cards in the Tarot Deck. She is also one of the cards with the most obvious Kabbalistic symbolism.

One of the most basic tenets of the Kabbala is that life can be seen as two opposing poles of force, masculine and feminine (or if you prefer, active and reactive), that we are constantly trying to balance. And of course, more often than not we fail in our balance entirely, swinging from one pole to the other, from action to reaction and back again. The Kabbala talks about a mysterious *Middle Pillar* that mystics throughout the ages have sought to travel upon in their journey through life, thereby balancing the processes of action and reaction, taking complete control of the self, and increasing the rate of evolution. In her deepest sense, the High Priestess symbolizes this process and the secret knowledge necessary to achieve this state. In this Tarot card, the High Priestess is situated between two opposing poles. The Rider-Waite deck labels these B (which stands for Binah, found at the top of the left pillar on the Kabbalistic Tree of Life) and J (which stands for Jokmah or Chokmah, found at the top of the right pillar on the Kabbalistic Tree of Life). She herself becomes the Middle Pillar. In essence, she is the 'Way' or the 'Gateway.' The reason her knowledge is considered secret is that it involves the use of intuition and can only be accessed through a leap beyond logic into pure feeling, pure knowingness. Just as the Magician represents the male side of our nature, the High Priestess represents the female side.

In your actual readings you may indeed come across someone, male or female, who has attained this state, or is following the path of the Middle Pillar, but more often than not, you're going to be reading the cards for the average individual who is interested in the mundane matters of his or her life. In the average reading the High Priestess is going to represent a woman.

Sometimes she refers to a girl, an actual virgin, but more often, she refers to a woman who is worldly and wise, has deep insight and understanding into life's many little idiosyncrasies, and is more than willing to give help and advice, but only when asked to do so. She likes her privacy, so it is unlikely that you will know a great deal about her (here she preserves her virginal nature), although she conceals herself so well that you may not even realize how much more she knows about you than you do about her. It doesn't really matter that she has so many of your secrets, for as long as she is upright in the reading, you can be sure she would die before telling them. But if she's inverted, watch out, because she may turn on you in a moment and use those secrets of yours to her own benefit and your detriment.

Sometimes the woman the High Priestess represents is hypothetical. She is then the ideal woman. If you see her in position 1 in your Celtic Cross spread in a man's reading, for instance, he may either be searching for his ideal of the perfect woman, or he may think that he has found her. This may sound wonderful, but it isn't, really. You see, the perfect woman simply does not exist on this plane we live on, so the man in this reading is setting himself up for some real disillusionment at a later date if he doesn't come down to earth. As a reader you can help him here, by reminding him of reality. If the High Priestess is inverted in his reading, he may have already become disillusioned. It is the secrecy and the perfect woman connotation of the High Priestess that often causes her to appear in a spread of cards as the other woman in a man's life. If you're doing his cards she'll be upright, but if you're doing his wife's she'll be inverted.

Then again, the High Priestess may turn up in a woman's spread indicating that she is trying to be the perfect woman. This is also not exciting to see, especially since it's usually someone else's idea of perfection she's living up to (Mom's, Dad's, husband's, etc.). Usually a woman in this position is not really happy with herself because she can't possibly succeed – although she could pretend for a long time before she wakes up! Usually the wake-up call is accompanied by the High Priestess reversing her position, and by your client clearly announcing that she never intends to be anything other than who she is for anybody again.

The High Priestess, when she is real, has a way of detaching herself, setting herself apart. You find yourself looking up to her, perhaps even admiring her, but you don't really feel close to her. She often represents the psychic advisor, the female psychologist, the woman minister or Nun, or your coven's High Priestess. She might even be your Tarot teacher, because the information she imparts is always the "secret" truths, the information that is far from mainstream. In practice she is often a Gemini, Scorpio or Virgo woman because the planet which rules all forms of communication, from telepathy to channeling to talking, is Mercury – and Mercury rules Gemini and Virgo on the Physical level, and Scorpio on the Spiritual level. Virgo is also the sign of the virgin.

Remember, too, that the High Priestess is not always read as a person at all. She can represent secret information, or the need to become detached and balanced. Or, she could be your higher guidance reaching out to help you move through opposing forces during a difficult juncture in your life!

__Special Note__: Which meaning(s) to use for the High Priestess will be determined by the cards surrounding her in the layout. If she falls near the Hermit or the three of Pentacles, she may refer to a learning experience; if she falls near a King or Knight she may be the other woman; standing alone in your reading she is a woman, secretive and strong, but she always tells you that something secretive or hidden is afoot!

Personal Notes

_____

_____

_____

_____

_____

_____

_____

_____

III – The Empress

Simplified Meanings:

Upright – A Mother or Mother figure; emotional and material plenty; possible pregnancy.

Inverted – A Mother or Mother figure who is physically or emotionally ill, or whom the client is not getting along with. Barrenness. Emotional and Material lack.

Number – 3 is the number of expression. The I Ching regards it as "Difficult Beginnings" as with the needs of a small child who initially needs total support.

In-Depth Meanings:

The Empress in the Tarot Major Arcana is the archetypal Earth Mother. She is generous and bountiful, and supplies all that one needs to grow and to flourish. She is fiercely protective of her young, and of those she considers a part of her family. She is emotional, intuitive, and wise. She sometimes appears all-knowing and seeing. In a sense, she is the High Priestess after she has mated with the Magician to produce children. She always represents a Mother figure when she's representing a person.

If you're reading the cards of a woman, and she comes up as the indicator card, she could mean that the client sees herself in the role of Mother, especially in regards to the issue the cards are dealing with. Then again, she might have her own mother, grandmother, or a matronly friend on her mind. In a man's cards, this same position for the Empress might indicate that he is thinking of someone he thinks of in a maternal role. That could be his actual mother, grandmother, or any older woman that he relates to as a mother figure. I have even occasionally seen the Empress come up indicating the man's wife, if he relates to her strongly in her role of mother, either to his children, or even to himself. You might, in this position alone, even see the Empress as the feminine, nurturing side of the male client.

When the Empress represents a person, upright she is warm, generous, and comfortably well off. She is happy, and more than willing to share her happiness and material assets with you. But inverted, she is emotionally unbalanced, and probably is in pretty poor shape financially, too. She certainly is not capable of fulfilling any of her maternal responsibilities. If this card falls inverted near the Moon, the Chariot, or the Star, also inverted, it can mean emotional illness. If it falls inverted in a spread surrounded by Pentacles, you will know it pertains to financial problems. If it falls inverted surrounded by Wands and any cards that could represent illness, this mother figure could be physically ill. If it falls inverted in a future position in the reading, any of these issues may be coming up, or it is possible the client does not know this mother figure yet.

I've even seen the Empress come up in some men's cards representing the ex-wife, since he's now seeing her in the role of mother to his children. And often when I am reading the cards of a woman who is dating a married man, his wife will turn up as the Empress. Note that in this case your advice to your client should be to cut her losses and move on, since it's unlikely the gentleman she is dating will cut his apron strings to Mom and marry her.

The Empress also frequently turns up relative to pregnancy. However, I want to caution you against using this meaning too easily. First of all, if your client is not of childbearing age, and has no children or close friends of childbearing age, your assessment might be a little ridiculous. Secondly, in many cases an announcement of, "Gee, I think you're pregnant!" can produce an extremely panicked reaction. This is not generally something you want to suggest unless you're pretty sure. Here are some of the ways you can be as sure as possible:

First, follow your intuition. If you see the Empress turn up and you immediately have a strong feeling that someone is pregnant, follow your inclination, and continue to look for other indicators of pregnancy in the cards. Secondly, even if you have no intuitive feeling, if either the Ace of Wands, Ace of Cups, Ace of Swords, or Sun turns up near her, and especially if a Page or the Fool is present, SOMEBODY is pregnant. Now all you have to do is to figure out who the Empress represents to know who's pregnant.

The scenario of pregnancy is interesting. Some women want to be pregnant and have trouble getting that way, some women are and don't want to be, some women are and love it. Some of the don't-want-to-be's get abortions, and some of the want-to-be's have miscarriages. And the cards can show you all of these scenarios. Pull out of your own deck the cards I noted in the preceding paragraph, along with the Ten of Swords, and a couple of Wands. Lay them out so you can see for yourself as I show you how these scenarios might appear in a reading.

Usually when pregnancy is an issue you're going to see the Empress and at least one Ace (or the Sun). The inverted (no) and upright (yes) position of the Ace will tell if there is a pregnancy or not. The inverted or upright position of the Empress will tell you how your client (or the pregnant woman, if not the client) feels about the situation. So, for example, if the Empress and Ace are upright, she's pregnant and happy about it. If the

Empress is upright and the Ace inverted, she wants a baby and is trying, but the child has not been conceived yet. In this case, if you also see a Page or the Fool present (upright), it probably means she'll be pregnant soon. If the Page or Fool is inverted, the soul coming in is either not present yet, or is not ready to be born. Getting pregnant could take awhile. If the Empress and the Ace are both inverted, she could be unhappy about not being pregnant. Or perhaps she is not capable of having children. I'd expect to see lots of inverted Cups in this reading. But if instead, or in addition, I saw a lot of Wands, and maybe the Ten of Swords (upright or inverted), I may be seeing a miscarriage or abortion. Sometimes you cannot see the difference between the two, but usually when the Ten of Swords is present it's abortion. Lastly, if the Empress is inverted but the Ace is upright, you've got a baby going to be born, and a mom who is not happy about it.

So much for the varied scenarios of pregnancy. We've already looked at the Empress as a Mother, a Grandmother, a Wife, an ex-wife, a matronly friend or relative, your male client's nurturing side, and a possible pregnancy. What else could she possibly be? Plenty.

Not plenty more meanings, but simply plenty. When the Empress turns up in your reading you are usually entering a time of material abundance. Finances are either good, or will soon be looking up, and the pregnancy meaning of this card can be applied to the situation being 'pregnant' with opportunity. Possibly it is this one of her meanings that prompts me to associate her with the sign of Taurus.

Of course, when she's inverted, you can expect a reduction in finances and material assets, and financial opportunities may not measure up to your expectations.

__Special Note__: To see what type of abundance she's bringing, look at the cards surrounding the Empress. Remember, don't jump the gun and tell your client she's pregnant unless you see other cards to support this conclusion.

Personal Notes

_____

_____

_____

_____

_____

IV – The Emperor

Simplified Meanings:

Upright – Security, stability, strength. A Father or father-figure. A boss, a husband, a man in control.

Inverted – Insecurity, weakness, impotency; a Father or father figure who is physically or emotionally ill, or who is not meeting his obligations or has lost control.

Number – 4 is the number of foundations, work, stability, and being grounded. The I Ching regards it as "Inexperience" requiring work to establish a solid foundation.

In-Depth Meanings:

The Emperor is essentially the Magician after he has mated with the High Priestess, become a father and taken on all of the responsibilities a family entails. He maintains all of the magnetism, sensualism, and overt sexuality of the Magician, but that energy now has a polished veneer of responsibility, capability, security, and accomplishment. What in the Magician was largely promise, in the Emperor is fully realized. He generates an aura of confidence because he has been successful in life. The sign of Aries, the Ram, is a part of his chair, because the Magician, so reminiscent of Aries, is still a part of him, and much of his foundation is built upon this energy. Yet in him are balanced the male and female energies, as symbolized by the apple and the wand he holds balanced in his hands. The sign of the zodiac the Emperor most closely emulates is Cancer.

The Emperor is stable, solid, and secure. He is an administrator, a boss, the head of a family. His family will consist of whatever sphere he finds himself in – business, government, or wife and kids. He is a font of good advice, a rock in the wildest storm; his function is to guide and support, not control or manipulate. But when we occasionally see him in a reading near the upright Devil, he may be overreaching his responsibility, and controlling or attempting to control that which is none of his business(Inverted Emperor and upright Devil).

I have often seen this combination in the readings of women who are dealing with manipulative situations in their lives. This shows a tendency on the woman's part to attract controlling, manipulative men, and in fact, depending on where he falls, the Emperor might be her father, her husband, or her boss who is exerting a controlling influence on her. In extreme situations where the Magician or the Ace of Wands is also present, sex can be the control issue. If there are a lot of Wands in the spread, and both the upright Devil and the inverted Ten of Cups are present, there could be some form of physical abuse involved as well.

But, generally speaking, the Emperor is a solid, and loyal figure deserving of respect. Usually in a woman's reading he will represent her actual father, or grandfather, or a man she relates to like a father. He might be a boss, a teacher, or an advisor. She looks up to him. Sometimes, if the woman has married 'Daddy' (which most of us do at some time or other), he might be her husband. If this is the case, you will now have some deep insight into the nature of her relationship with her husband. If she sees him as the Emperor, she respects him, relies on him, and expects him to take care of her.

In a man's reading the Emperor might represent him owning his own power. It's especially common to see a man represent himself as the Emperor in his own reading when he's just become a father for the first time, or when he is the sole parent in the family and sees himself primarily in the role of father. But more often the Emperor represents his father or grandfather, his boss, or perhaps some professional colleague he has great respect for. Remember, as long as he is upright, the Emperor shows the positive qualities of loyalty, reliability, strength, maturity, and keen insight. He can be a wonderful asset to have on your side professionally.

But when he is inverted he has lost his power, lost his will. I have often seen older men appear as the Emperor inverted when they retire from their lifelong careers. It's as if their identity was so wrapped up in what they did that when they retired they literally lost themselves. Likewise, after a serious or near-fatal illness or accident, it's not unusual to see a man turn up as the inverted Emperor. Looking death in the eye can be a nerve-shattering experience! In a woman's reading, if she is finally successfully breaking free of the bonds of control in an abusive relationship, the inverted Emperor will often show up, indicating that this man no longer has control over her. This is particularly exciting to see because it is generally an indication of a karmic pattern being broken (i.e. – those of us who had controlling or abusive fathers usually find a mate who just takes over the job). When we finally break the control problem with the mate, we're generally ready to overcome the one involving Dad as well.

In a situation where the Emperor represents a father or husband in a reading, his inverted position could also mean that he is not being much of a father to his children. The inverted Emperor falling near the inverted Moon or the inverted Chariot in a reading could mean Alzheimer's, or some other emotional or hormonal disorder, especially if a lot of Wands are present.

In fact, if the Emperor represents a specific person in the reading, and appears inverted, it could mean that the person is emotionally or physically ill. Falling in a future position, it could mean that he will become ill, or will lose control in the future – or, it could mean that the client simply does not know him yet.

__Special Note__: The Emperor falling near Justice, the Hierophant, the Chariot, or the Three of Pentacles, Eight of Pentacles, or Ace of Pentacles, will be a professional man. Surrounded by Cups he's likely to be a romantic partner or a family member. As always, look to the surrounding cards to define the role he is playing in the client's life, and the client will know who he is.

Personal Notes

_____

_____

_____

_____

_____

_____

_____

_____

_____

_____

_____

V – The Hierophant

Simplified Meanings:

Upright – Convention. Organized Religion. Government. University learning. A Priest, Bishop or Pope. A conventional marriage. Big business.

Inverted – Unconventional. Bending the law. Outside normal Governmental channels. Leader of an unusual religious order or organization. An unconventional marriage.

Number – 5 is the number of change, adaptation and communication. In the I Ching it is regarded as "Calculated Waiting" or patience.

In-Depth Meanings:

The Hierophant is essentially a male version of the High Priestess. Like her, he forms the Middle Pillar on the Kabbalistic Tree of Life. And also like her, he holds the key to higher wisdom and knowledge. But unlike her, he deals with exoteric knowledge and wisdom, with form and tradition. In the middle ages many of the Tarot decks depicted this card as the Pope. And how fitting that was, seeing that at the time the Catholic Church, headed by the Pope, was the primary unifying and governing force throughout the Western world.

Whenever your reading includes governmental, big business, or legal issues, the Hierophant is likely to turn up, bringing his form and structure to the issue. As long as he is upright, the straightforward approach will be the best way to deal with the situation. But if he is inverted, then an unconventional approach is in order. The cards surrounding him will help you to define the issue itself.

As a person, the Hierophant can represent a person in the professional trappings of religion or government. He could just as easily represent a supreme court justice as a Bishop. As long as he is upright, he is the representative of officialdom, of one sort or another.

And of course, upright, he represents all of the deepest traditional structures of our society, like marriage. The Hierophant as a marriage card does not require that the two people love one another. All he requires is that they obey the outer trappings of the form. They get a license, they have a wedding, they adopt the male and female roles expected of them in the marriage.

However, if the Hierophant turns up inverted representing a marriage, we are looking at an entirely different situation. This is a marriage that is unconventional and not interested in the traditions of society. It may be a marriage where wife works and husband takes care of the kids, or a marriage between people of two different cultures or religions, or a marriage between people of the same sex. All you really know, seeing the inverted Hierophant in the reading as a marriage card, is that the marriage is not by any means traditional. I remember seeing this in one of my client's cards near the Eight of Wands (a travel card) and saying that the marriage would be unconventional and would involve a lot of travel. My client laughed. Her job kept her in Florida, while her husband's kept him in New York. They took turns visiting each other for long weekends and had a very happy marriage.

You would know to read the Hierophant as a marriage card if you saw other cards indicating marriage nearby, or if there were a lot of Cups in the spread with it.

When there are a lot of Pentacles in the spread with the Hierophant it usually deals with business or legal issues. If your clients work for the government, a lawyer, or a "big business" like banking, expect to see the Hierophant turn up pretty often for them.

Since the Hierophant shows the extremes of the conventional versus the unconventional, doing what's expected verses what you want, it deals with the Zodiacal axis of Leo – Aquarius. When it's acting traditionally, it's Leo; untraditionally, it's Aquarius.

__Special Note__: When the Hierophant falls upright next to the Chariot, watch out. This could be the judge presiding at the hearing for your traffic ticket. And as long as he's upright, he's fair and honest, but a stickler for the law.

Personal Notes

_____

_____

_____

_____

_____

Simplified Meanings:

Upright – Choice, decision. Higher Guidance; a need to follow the intuition.

Inverted – A choice made. A choice yet to be made, but that may be regretted. A need to reconsider and look within.

Number – 6 is the number of decisions, but also success through mastering crisis. In the I Ching it is regarded as "Conflict" resulting from a commitment.

In-Depth Meanings:

The Lovers is clearly a choice card, but its title, "The Lovers," confuses many readers. This card's meaning is not that your client is about to meet a lover, but rather that they have a choice to make between two people, things, or issues that they love. This is a very profound card, simple to understand, yet extremely difficult to work through.

Your client may have a mother who cannot get along with her husband, and she must choose between them. Or her ex-husband refuses to let her leave the state with her child, but she really wants to accept that wonderful job transfer. Can she leave her child behind for the job? Or perhaps she has been dating two people – one of them is her intellectual equal, the best friend she has ever had, but the other really turns her on. Now they're both pushing her to make a choice. Can she?

The choices vary. But when the Lovers is involved they are always choices that wrench the soul, and break the heart. These choices cannot be made with the mind, they must be made with the intuition, with whatever higher guidance is available. You must tell your client that if he (or she) tries to make the choice with the mind alone, inevitably his heart will trouble him later.

If your client is about to make a choice he will be troubled by in the future, the Lovers will turn up inverted in the present. But if he has already made the choice, it may also turn up inverted. To advise the client, you need to know if he has made a choice yet. If not, don't tell the client his choice is wrong. Remember, there are no wrong choices in life, just longer and shorter routes to the same destination. You should merely advise him that he might want to re-think this one, just because it's so very important, and follow his own gut-instinct in choosing, not the advice of family or friends. If the client doesn't thank you then, he will later.

It is through making these kinds of choices throughout life that our value systems are formed, and that we gradually come to know who we are. Learning about who we are through choice and the interaction with others is the realm of the planet Venus. Since Venus rules both Taurus and Libra, you could probably assign this card to one of them; or, like most readers, you could associate it with the 6th sign of the zodiac, Virgo. Virgo is a sign that sees what needs to be done and does it, and we certainly need that outlook to be able to handle the Lovers.

__Special Note__: The cards surrounding the Lovers will tell you the scenario involved, and what choice your client is faced with.

Personal Notes

_____

_____

_____

_____

_____

_____

_____

_____

_____

_____

Simplified Meanings:

Upright – Being in control. Travel over land. Travel between two places. Your car. A police officer, military man, or someone who drives or wears a uniform for their living.

Inverted – Being out of control. Emotional problems. A trip not taken, or already taken. Car problems. Problems with a uniformed man.

Number – 7 is the number of mastery of one's material and social conditions. In the I Ching it is regarded as "The Army" or gathering ability.

In-Depth Meanings:

The Chariot is a card of power and accomplishment. It shows the client as the Chariot driver, in total control of his (or her) current life situation emotionally, financially, physically, and mentally. This is the person who has spent time and effort to bring each aspect of his life into perfect balance and symmetry. There is little in his life that can throw him into a state of imbalance. The Rider-Waite version of the card focuses first on the Tree of Life symbology placing the Chariot driver on the Middle Pillar of Balance between the two outer pillars of Severity and Mercy (appearing as two cities in the card). It also uses the chakra symbology. The chakras, or psychic energy centers, shown in the card are the lower four: the Root Center, Sacral Center, Solar Plexus Center, and Heart Center with the Crown Center shown at the top of the card. This symbology is meant to show that the Charioteer has mastered the development and expansion of the four lower centers thereby attaining perfect balance and control over his corporeal life, and has opened the gateway to the higher consciousness. He has now set the stage for his spiritual development, or, he may merely continue to exercise his supreme command of his physical and material situation.

In essence, when the Chariot appears upright, you know that the person described by this card will be successful and accomplished in his current pursuit, whatever it is. He is in control.

However, when the Chariot turns up inverted, the individual or situation depicted by the card is out of control, probably both emotionally and physically. Your client feels that life is running him, not that he is running his life. Often if this card appears near the Moon, the inverted Empress, or inverted Temperance, the person may be in need of psychological counseling. If you can't help the client yourself, then send him to a professional counselor.

The Chariot has several more mundane meanings as well. It is, for example, your car – a modern day chariot. Upright, you probably love it, and it runs well. Inverted, either you just don't like it, or you're having problems with it. Surrounded by Pentacles, it could be costing you a lot to run, or have a lot of mechanical problems. Surrounded by Wands or near the Tower, a car accident could be indicated. If this is in the future, advise caution. Remember, nothing is cast in granite in a reading. The reason you should be doing the reading in the first place is to know what things you want to change. This is one of them.

The Chariot is also travel via a land vehicle. This could include anything from a train or bus to your own car or motorcycle. Upright, it could mean a trip, or that your client is doing a lot of driving. As long as it's upright the trip will be a good one or your client likes the driving. Inverted, either the trip is past, or will not happen, or it will not be enjoyable or successful. Usually if a trip is indicated, there will be other travel cards such as the World or the Eight of Wands present in the reading. With the World, the trip could be long distance. With the Eight of Wands, it could combine driving and flying. With the Ace of Wands, there could be a change of residence.

Because of the strong polarity indicated by this card with the charioteer being the balancing agent, I often find this card in the readings of people who travel between two different places. Upright, the arrangement works; inverted, it doesn't.

If upright the Chariot can also indicate a person who is in the military, the police, or drives or wears a uniform in whatever work he or she is in.

This card could be assigned to the 7th sign of the zodiac, Libra; or, since it places so much emphasis on travel, you might prefer to associate it with Sagittarius, the sign of travel.

__Special Note:__ When there is any legal issue involving the police, the Chariot will be sure to turn up representing the arresting officer, or the person giving you the traffic ticket. If the Hierophant is also present, you may very well get a day in court. If the Devil is present, the result of all this could be jail.

Personal Notes

Simplified Meanings:

Upright – Strength and fortitude; intuition and creativity. The ability to achieve whatever goals you set. A woman with Leo-like characteristics.

Inverted – Weakness, poor self-image. Abilities and creativity blocked. A Leo-type woman who is ill or in trouble.

Number – 8 is the number of power, sex, karma and material completion. In the I Ching it is regarded as "Unity" or all cycles.

In-Depth Meanings:

Strength appears in most decks as a beautiful young woman in various poses with a lion. The lion symbolizes the Leo attributes of this card, being the astrological symbol for Leo. In the Crowley deck she is called Fortitude rather than Strength, and in the Aquarian Tarot she is depicted as a 'he.' Needless to say, if you are reading with that deck, you would most likely see Strength as a man, not a woman.

In most of the modern decks, Strength is Key VIII in the Major Arcana, but in some of the older decks she is Key XI. In those decks she is switched with the Justice card, which we will discuss as Key XI. There has been an ongoing argument among Tarot experts as to which is the correct placement, and usually these arguments are based upon the meanings of the numbers 8 and 11. The number 8 is a number of power, of karma, of materialization, and of sex. The number 11 is a master number of balance and karma, but also of two individuals working together to achieve a single goal that is greater than either of them could achieve alone, maximizing both of their abilities. I personally feel that Strength better suits her position as Key VIII, but if you like her better as Key XI, so be it! Wherever you place her, her meaning will be the same.

Strength represents the 'female' strength within all of us. There is a certain stamina, endurance, stability, focus, and inner knowingness that combines to create a totally feminine kind of power. This power draws on the individual's creative and intuitive nature, as well as her (or his) faith in her own abilities or the abilities of those she has placed her trust in. When Strength appears upright in a reading, especially as an indicator card, it may mean that your client, whether male or female, is presently exhibiting this type of strength. If Strength falls next to a Court card in the reading, particularly a Queen, it may be read as an adjective to add these qualities to those the Queen already possesses. (Likewise, if you use the Aquarian Tarot deck, the male version of Strength falling next to a King would do the same for him.)

In the now out-of-print *Evolution Through The Tarot*, Richard Gardner presented Strength as being the female version of the Magician – and indeed she is. But her power is inwardly directed, whereas the Magician's was outwardly directed. Both cards demonstrate the individual's ability to manifest his or her desires. Both cards are also very sexual and sensual.

In my favorite version of the Strength card, the young woman in the card is not petting or otherwise restraining the lion with her physical hands – she is emitting an energy from her hands that causes the lion to be as tame as a house cat. Remember, her strength is the inner, magnetic strength that comes from the center of her being and radiates outward. This control of the lion is also symbolic of her own control of the animal within her own nature, allowing her humanity to shine forth.

As a person, Strength is usually a young or at least youthful woman (or man in the Aquarian deck), who is energetic, dynamic, honest, generous, and very competent. And yet, she also generates a certain amount of innocence, in a subtly childlike way. We often see her representing a Leo, an Aries, or a Sagittarian (these are the three fire signs of the zodiac). Sometimes she even depicts a person who is light or red-haired.

As long as she is upright this Leo-like individual will give her support; her generous and courageous spirit will not only enable her to succeed at whatever she tries, but will make her a dynamic asset to others as well. But when she is inverted she can be a liability to herself and others.

Inverted, Strength reverts to weakness. Somehow, the person this card represents in your reading has been undermined and has lost touch with the feminine strength within herself. The result is lack of confidence, blocked creativity and intuition, and very often self-destructive behavior that could cause trouble both for this person and those close to them. Individuality is replaced by dependency; generosity and gregariousness by selfishness and introverted behavior. There may be a need to get attention through self-destructive actions or a poor-me attitude.

But remember, that all cards inherently contain within them their opposing meaning. So when she appears inverted in a reading, if she represents your client, spend some time helping her to build confidence. Help her to turn herself around.

*_Special Note_: *Don't forget when you're reading Strength, that although she usually is an actual person in the reading, she could also be read as an adjective to describe the client or some other person in the reading.*

Personal Notes

_____

_____

_____

_____

_____

_____

_____

_____

_____

_____

_____

_____

Simplified Meanings:

Upright – A teacher. A hermit. A learning experience. Gaining insight. Higher guidance available.

Inverted – Refusing to learn from one's experience. An old pattern repeating. Leaving an educational opportunity behind. Refusing guidance.

Number – 9 is the number of Spiritual Completion and of the teacher. In the I Ching it is regarded as the "Taming Power of the Small" or the refining of the outer nature.

In-Depth Meanings:

The Hermit is a card of learning and education, but not necessarily in a traditional sense. In its broadest sense, this card represents the life lessons we learn on our journey through life. The Hermit sees life as a school that we are born into to learn our lessons through direct experience. Whenever you see the Hermit upright in a reading, be assured that one of these life-lessons is being experienced by your client; as long as the Hermit is upright, your client is doing well and is learning the lesson intended. But if the Hermit is inverted, he or she is not getting it. Like Peter Pan, the client is refusing to grow up because it is only through experiencing and assimilating life's many lessons that we attain spiritual adulthood.

While we are learning that lesson, the higher guidance of our many guides and the guiding light of our own Higher Self is available, as shown by the lantern the Hermit carries. We have only to listen to our inner voice, and to look for the road signs we have left for ourselves along the way, to find our way back home through the many life lessons the Hermit teaches us.

I often have clients come in for a session, hoping the Tarot reading they are about to get will enable them to accept as reality such promises from loved ones as, "I'll never see that other woman again," or, "I've given up drinking," or, "I'll never do it again!" If the Hermit turns up in that reading, his upright or inverted position will give you the answer; if he's upright, your client is hearing the truth, he (or she) can put faith in the promises being heard. If he's inverted, though, the individual making the promise will not keep it, even if the promise was made in good faith. Remember, the inverted Hermit means that the same old behavior pattern will prevail, the lesson was not learned.

Often the Hermit represents the client. In this case his upright or inverted position tells you a great deal about the client. If upright, the client has teaching ability, or may even be a teacher. He has the ability to impart knowledge, wisdom, and guidance to others, whether or not he has a teaching degree. Remember, the Hermit's primary education is in the 'school of hard knocks.' In fact, it's the assimilation of life's varied lessons that makes him such a good teacher. When the Hermit is inverted, though, it means that the client may have teaching skills, but is not applying them. In fact, it means that he is likely stuck in an unhealthy pattern that he is unwilling to change, or that he is about to repeat an old lesson not yet learned. For example, many, many times I've had someone ask me if she took her husband or boyfriend back again, "Would things be different?" In these instances, when the inverted Hermit appears the answer is a definite NO. In fact, the client has not learned whatever new behavior pattern is necessary in order to better cope with her partner. The client is probably still at the point where she believes a successful relationship depends on her partner's changing. In this case, the renewed relationship is doomed to failure for the same reasons it failed the first time.

The upright Hermit's presence in the reading may mean the client is just in the process of assimilating a life lesson, or may even be considering going to school for something. School is especially likely if the Hermit falls near the Ace of Pentacles or Swords, the three of Pentacles or the Hierophant. Another possible meaning is that the client has just gained some important insight or information relative to something central in his life at the time of the reading. The surrounding cards should tell you more about what that is.

When the Hermit is inverted the person you're reading has not learned an important lesson in his life, and indeed, he may be about to repeat a past error as the old pattern begins to repeat itself again, as in the above examples. It is your responsibility as a reader to let the client know this. Many times, in pointing this out to clients I've been able to alert them to mistakes they are about to make, which gives them the ability to step back and take a second look before they leap, so to speak. Again, the surrounding cards should tell you more about what the situation entails.

The Hermit inverted may also mean that an opportunity for an educational pursuit is available – but, it will not be followed up on, or that your client is waiting for some news or insight that is either delayed, or that will not be received.

The Hermit may have similar meanings when applied to other people. If he falls near one of the Court cards in the reading, he may be read as an adjective to that card and the above meanings may be freely applied. Falling central to a situation being described in the reading, these meanings may be applied to the situation and its circumstances directly.

The Hermit may also represent an actual person in the cards. As such, he will always be a person who is some kind of teacher. I have even seen him occasionally represent a client's spirit guide. In some instances he could represent an individual who dislikes people and lives his life on the fringes of society, just like a hermit. He might choose this private life because he is running away from society (if inverted), or because his assimilated life lessons have given him such deep knowledge and insight into people with whom he is no longer comfortable (upright). Most readers associate him with Virgo or Sagittarius; both signs are associated with teaching.

__Special Note__: The cards falling adjacent to the Hermit tell what lessons are in progress. For example, with the Ace of Pentacles he may indicate learning a new trade, with the Ace of Swords, going to college, surrounded by Pentacles his lessons have to do with money, by Cups, with love, and so on.

Personal Notes

_____

_____

_____

_____

_____

_____

_____

_____

X – The Wheel of Fortune

Simplified Meanings:

Upright – Change; a karmic cycle ending. Major events over which you have no control. A time for learning and growing.

Inverted – Exactly the same as the upright meaning, but slower.

Number – 10 reduces down to a 1 (1+0 = 1), but this 1 is a higher octave of the 1 we saw in the Magician. It still represents new beginnings, creativity, and individuality, but on a level that signifies a new cycle with greater responsibility. I Ching regards it as maintaining a responsible "Conduct."

In-Depth Meanings:

The Wheel of Fortune is one of the most karmic cards in the deck. Remember that karma is nothing more than the need for an action, once begun, to complete itself. The many cycles and patterns in our lives are the result of the actions, and reactions to those actions, that we have repeated over and over again until they have essentially become a habit. We no longer need to think about doing them, they have become automatic. They have become karmic.

All of our emotional and physical action patterns were originally created by us as a survival technique. For example, when you were a child and you first learned that there were some things that you enjoyed doing that your mother did not approve of, and might even punish you for, you either learned to lie to her about doing them, to simply hide from her that you did them, or you learned to curb your own desires out of respect for her wishes and/or fear of her punishment. No matter which reaction you had, once you began the action, you had to follow it to its completion. And the next time the same situation, or one similar came up, you probably reacted the same way because having done it once, it was easier to do it again the same way than to think about it and alter your action the second time. In fact, you were more likely to embellish the original action pattern the second time than you were to originate a new one. Eventually, with repetition, the action became a habit and the habit turned into a predictable pattern of behavior for you. Such patterns are repeated all through life, and the stronger ones may even be carried into the next life as what we might see as inborn character traits or emotional problems.

By the time we reach adulthood we have created or brought on with us from past lives many such patterns. In fact, most of us live our lives so much on automatic that when we one day wake up to the fact that one of our survival oriented behavior patterns is no longer functioning to help us survive, but rather is creating some of our major life crises, we are usually at a loss to know what to do about it.

Take, for example, the young boy who lies to Mom about playing in her garden. He establishes a precedent for lying. His lying becomes a pattern over the years as he discovers that these small lies help him to avoid confrontation. Let's suppose he dies with the pattern still intact.

In his next life, lying comes automatically the first time he is presented with an issue requiring confrontation. He develops his little survival technique into a comprehensive pattern of lying to get ahead. Suppose again, that he dies with his lying pattern, still rewarding him, in place.

Now, in the following life, there is no hesitancy in his jumping right into the same pattern of lying to achieve his goals. But one day he begins to realize that his family and friends never believe him and don't really respect him. He's hurt, but he doesn't know how to change their feelings. Following his old pattern, he still lies to them to gain their respect, but doesn't understand when it doesn't work.

Finally, in his present life he faces the fact that although lying may have helped him to escape some uncomfortable situations, and may have helped him to get ahead, it is now hurting more than helping him. He is presented with a crisis. The old pattern must change for him to grow.

It is at this point in his many lives that we would see the Wheel of Fortune coming up in his reading. He has now come full circle (note the circular pattern of the Wheel). He is at a point in his karmic cycle when he can, if he chooses, stand back and see the pattern for what it is. It is as if the Wheel has spun completely around once, and he has returned again to his initial position, where he again has the choice of action patterns. And he again has three choices. He can continue the behavior pattern exactly as it is, without change; he can continue the same behavior pattern, but maintain his awareness as he does so, allowing him to make subtle changes as the pattern progresses; he can choose to step off the Wheel relative to this pattern, taking steps to eliminate the pattern in himself completely.

Whenever the Wheel of Fortune turns up it signifies a turning point. Consciously or unconsciously, you are at the top of the Wheel of your own life deciding whether to continue or to modify a karmic pattern in it. Often people are not conscious of this. All they see are broad sweeping events that are happening in their lives that seem to be beyond their control. It is very hard for them to understand that the current events, whatever they may be, are the results of actions, attitudes, and choices that they have made long ago, that are only coming to fruition now.

With some clients you will be able to take the time to help them see these patterns in their entirety; with others you will only help them through the change in their lives, whatever it is.

The Wheel of Fortune in a reading can refer to the client, or to someone in the client's life, or to a situation, depending upon where it falls, but it will always tell of circumstances that he (or she) feels helpless to change or avoid. These circumstances are by no means always negative. The Wheel of Fortune can portent good as well as bad events, but they are always on a grand scale.

I have seen the Wheel of Fortune often during divorces, marriages, deaths, births, illnesses, career changes, home changes, etc. – in short, whenever life's sweeping events catch us up and say, "It's time for a change."

Astrologer's reading this text may be interested in knowing that the Wheel of Fortune is likely to turn up during a Saturn Return (for you non-astrologers, Saturn Return's occur around ages 28, 56, and 84. Astrologer's consider Saturn the planet of Karma). I've also seen it commonly in readings where the client is experiencing some other major planetary transit as well.

When the Wheel of Fortune is inverted its meaning is essentially the same – major changes, and the opportunity to alter a karmic pattern, only slower... much slower. When the Wheel of Fortune appears upright usually the client is in a lot of turmoil because things are changing NOW. But when the Wheel is inverted the same change is occurring, but may take several years. In fact, it's been my observation that when it's upright in the reading the client is likely to be somewhat frightened and concerned about whatever change is coming, but when it's inverted he (or she) has been working toward the change for so long he just wants to get it over with, regardless of if it is good or bad! Again, for you Astrologer's reading this text, I've noted that in the readings I do for fixed signed individuals (Taurus, Leo, Scorpio, and Aquarius), it usually turns up inverted – these people seem to need plenty of time to make life changes or to break their habits.

The Wheel of Fortune cannot really be assigned to any one sign. It might, however, represent the four fixed signs of Taurus, Leo, Scorpio, and Aquarius, which are represented in the corners of the Rider-Waite version. Some readers see these as the four 'Elemental Kings,' having the ability to combine forces to give form to the material world.

*<u>Special Note</u>: *The Wheel of Fortune alone will not signify a divorce, marriage, or any other particular issue; but once surrounding cards have helped you to clarify the issue, the Wheel tells you that what is going on is karmic, that your clients are being given opportunities to make sweeping and permanent changes in themselves and their lives. I always see change, approached with optimism and enthusiasm, as leading ultimately to a good ending.*

Personal Notes

_____

_____

_____

_____

_____

_____

_____

_____

_____

_____

_____

Simplified Meanings:

Upright – Justice will be served. A legal situation works out fairly. Balance is achieved. A wrong is righted.

Inverted – Injustice. Unfairness. Lack of balance in a situation. A legal situation is decided unfairly.

Number – 11 is a master number, but is still reduced to the 2 (1+1 = 2). The 2 represents duality. 11, as a master number, gives the '2' an opportunity to rise to a higher level by becoming greater than itself. I Ching regards it as "Peace."

In-Depth Meanings:

In our society where there are so many rules and regulations, Justice most commonly represents some situation the client is in that requires a bill or tax to be paid, a traffic ticket to be dealt with, a loan or some important legal document to be signed, or perhaps an actual court battle to be undertaken. When I first began as a reader, it amazed me that so many people had legal issues of one sort or another in their lives, until I began to look closer at the system we live in, where there is so much government regulation. Although this is certainly not the original meaning intended for this card, Justice usually will refer to one or more of these legal situations when you see it in a reading. Upright it usually means everything will proceed smoothly and have a positive outcome; inverted it means there is some difficulty that may either slow the whole process down or prevent a positive outcome altogether.

Justice, for instance, falling next to the Ace of Pentacles or the Ten of Pentacles, could represent an inheritance. Near the Chariot it's often a traffic ticket. Near the Eight of Pentacles it will be a work related legal issue. Near the Sun or Judgement it might pertain to a divorce settlement. Near the Devil it's particularly bad because it could mean someone's going to jail!

And then again, your client could merely be a member of the legal profession. I recall one client that always had some legal issue or other going on in every reading I did for her. I finally discovered she was an attorney. After I knew that, the legal issues I routinely saw in her readings disturbed me a lot less.

Justice may also merely mean that given the situation portrayed in the cards, justice will prevail. It does not always pertain to a legal situation. Remember, this does not represent an automatic win for your client. Rather, it means the situation will be brought into balance – that means your client may have to do a little bending, just as his (or her) opponent in the situation will. For example, you might see Justice turn up in a spread when you are reading for a client who just had a major misunderstanding with a friend. In this case returning the situation to balance may require both individuals to make apologies.

Often, in fact, Justice inverted may mean better news for your client (I've often noted that people are usually not interested in justice, but rather in coming out ahead). If Justice is inverted it means that the situation at hand will be resolved in an "unfair" manner where balance is not achieved. If, for example, your client is a woman going through a divorce and you see the Justice card inverted next to the King who is her husband (also inverted), you are seeing his unhappiness resulting from an unfair resolution – this means that your client comes out ahead in the division of his or her property. Now, in this same example, if the Queen representing the client is inverted while the King representing her husband is upright, the outcome is probably reversed and the resolution of the situation will be in his favor, not hers. So in your interpretation of this card it is particularly important to look at the surrounding Court cards. By their disposition they will tell you who is coming out the winner or the loser.

When Justice is upright the surrounding Court cards also give insight into who is happy or unhappy with the resolution, but you as the reader know that here any unhappiness is sour grapes because 'universal justice' has also been served and the situation has been returned to balance.

Justice is a karmic card. In our universe there is always a tendency for any individual or circumstance to swing back and forth between the poles of good and evil or, if you prefer, the generative versus the receptive poles of universal force. On a broad scale, this could mean that an individual lives through several lifetimes as a priest or nun who is and does only good, and then proceeds to live several lifetimes where he or she is involved in crime, in order to create an inner balance. On a smaller scale, it means that if you live out your life as Miss- or Mister-Goodie-Two-Shoes, you are going to attract into your life many evil or negative people as the universe seeks to balance the overly good nature you are demonstrating. In such a case, as you learn that you should be accepting the negative side of yourself, as well as the positive, and allow yourself the luxury of your humanity, you become more inwardly balanced, and you stop attracting negative people – you no longer have need of them. Justice is that force in the universe that eternally seeks to bring all people, all things, and all situations into a perfect balance within themselves. When that balance has been achieved, the karma incurred by the constant swinging from one pole to another is eliminated. Note, especially, the blindfold worn by the figure in this card. Justice is blind and can show no favoritism. Whatever needs to be done to rebalance the situation will be done, whether your client likes it or not (note the two-edged sword).

Justice may also represent an actual person in some readings. He may be the actual Judge in a court, or he may be an attorney representing your client. If he falls next to the Three of Pentacles, he may mean that the attorney is part of a team. Justice is usually seen as a Libra card.

__Special Note__: Remember that Justice may be read in four different ways. It may be read as a legal situation. It may be read as a moral situation. It may be read as a person. It may be read as a karmic rebalancing of an area your client has been too over or under developed in.

Personal Notes

THE HANGED MAN.

Simplified Meanings:

Upright – Trapped in a situation where you cannot act. Objectivity. Insight. Channelling Higher Mind or Spirit.

Inverted – Freedom to act on your ideals and principles. Practical application of higher intuitions. Lack of objectivity.

Number – 12 is actually a 3 (1+2 = 3), but again the concept of expansion is raised to a higher level, making this one of the most spiritual cards in the deck. The I Ching regards it as "Standstill."

In-Depth Meanings:

The Hanged Man represents an interesting dichotomy. He is depicted as a man actually hanging upside down, feet, (or foot, as in most decks one leg is crossed over the other in a very obvious effort to form a cross) in the world of spirit, illuminated head (or mind) in the world of matter. The conclusion is that the Hanged Man, when upright, represents the individual who has the ability to see clearly and objectively all aspects of the material world around him, and apply his spiritual insight to it. He blends into the situation around him, thereby easily earning the trust of others. Unfortunately, he is also tied or otherwise fastened to the cross, or tree, that he hangs on. A little thought on this shows that he may very well channel his insight, even share it when asked, but he is incapable of actual action, so long as he is in the upright position.

What comes to mind here is the Star Trek law of non-interference in the development of any culture the exploring ship's crew might come across. You see, once the person in the position of the Hanged Man has obtained all of the knowledge and the insight that would give him the ability to act intelligently in a situation, he also has gained the insight that any action upsets the necessary balance and development of other individuals in the situation, having far reaching and often uncontrollable affects, as those individuals react to the action he takes. Recognizing this, the Hanged Man usually takes no action, only gives advice if asked. (And rarely is he asked, since the players in whatever scenario he's observing seem to instinctively know his insight will upset the balance and force their hand.)

As soon as the Hanged Man enters the fray by taking action, he turns upside down. This places his head in the world of spirit, and his feet firmly on the ground. He therefore loses his objectivity and his extraordinary insight at the same time. Your advice to the client in this position should be to base any further actions on past insights that had a clarity that future ones will lack, now that objectivity is lost.

Let me recount for you a situation from one of my client's lives that depicts the meaning of this card beautifully. My client is a young woman, unmarried, and still living at home with her parents. At the time of her reading with me, her sister-in-law and two nieces were living downstairs in the same house. Her brother, estranged from his wife, was living down the block with another woman. Needless to say, this was a tense situation at best. The sister-in-law did not work and was therefore totally dependent upon her in-laws, who completely supported her and their two grandchildren. The brother refused to contribute to the financial care of his family since his parents, his estranged wife, and his children refused to talk to him. My client was the only individual in this situation who still conversed with every one of her family members. She very carefully remained uncommitted to any side, and so was able to see each person's point of view. She knew that the woman her brother lived with was actually a nice person. She knew that her brother had long tried to work things out with a wife that had shut him out of her life and her bed, over financial stresses, before taking a girlfriend. She knew that her nieces still loved their dad, but couldn't talk to him because their mom, her sister-in-law, forbade them to. She knew that her sister-in-law still loved her husband (my client's brother) but wanted him only if he changed his values relative to money. Finally, she knew that the whole situation was placing a severe emotional and financial strain on her parents, who were siding with their daughter-in-law only because they hoped that by doing so they would pull their son's family back together.

In her unique position of objectivity, my client had special insight into each individual's motives and actions. At any time she could easily predict what was coming next. If any one had asked her advice, she could have given real insight into all aspects of the situation. For a long time she maintained her upright Hanged Man position relative to her family situation, knowing that to take any action, to take the side of any one individual, would cost her not only her objectivity, but probably also a relationship as well. Ultimately, however, she was forced into action, as usually happens when we see the Hanged Man, because she could no longer stand coldly by while her parents depleted all of their savings supporting her sister-in-law and the children, and were emotionally hurt by their own actions that alienated their son. Using her insight gained when the Hanged Man was upright, she encouraged her parents to demand rent from their daughter-in-law, and to stop paying her bills as well. Her parents began to see that their daughter-in-law's spending habits were at the root of their son's marital problems. They agreed to provide child care, but insisted that if the daughter-in-law were to continue to live with them she must return to her career. They began talking to their son again. Pleased that his former wife had returned to work and was now footing her share of the bills, he began again to contribute to family support. My client's insight, gained while the Hanged Man was upright in her life, showed her exactly where to act in order to bring about the necessary changes to end this stalemate.

But as soon as she acted, she became the inverted Hanged Man. She was free to act, free to apply her beliefs and insights, but she lost the total objectivity, the insight, into why each family member acted as they did. She had sided with her parents, which was in her own best interests. The situation worked out well, but once she had started the ball rolling, everything else was beyond her control – her insight was based on the former situation, and could no longer help her.

We also see the Hanged Man in readings where the person the card pertains to is making a major personal sacrifice based upon her spiritual belief system. In these cases you can see the selfless side of the card, as the individual puts his or her needs second to the needs of the family, group, or cause. It's also in this meaning that the connection of the card to the sign Aquarius, which most readers give it, is apparent. When the Hanged Man reverses, the individual is done with his sacrifice.

If your client, or someone close to him (or her) is missing a leg, the Hanged Man may also indicate that individual. In your readings, he may refer to a situation, to your client's position relative to a situation, or to a particular individual in the reading.

__Special Note__: Often in readings the Hanged Man's appearance denotes a spiritual awakening of sorts that your client is experiencing. Look for other cards in the reading that are also spiritual and you will know for sure.

Personal Notes

_____

_____

_____

_____

_____

Now let's do another reading for an actual client using only the Court cards and the Major Arcana cards that we've covered in this chapter. For now, remove your Minor Arcana cards and the remaining Major Arcana cards from the deck and store them in a safe place. For the next few days, use only the Court cards and the Major Arcana cards we've covered here in your practice readings, until you have the meanings fairly well rooted in your mind. When you feel you've got a fair command of all of these cards, move on to the next chapter.

Our sample reading is for a 35-year-old woman, who was born under the sign of Libra. Here's what the spread looks like. Note that I've added a row of cards up the side of our simple Celtic Cross spread. This complex Celtic Cross gives us a little more information, as you will see. Use the questions below to help guide you through your own interpretation. Then go on to read my interpretation, and the woman's actual situation that follows.

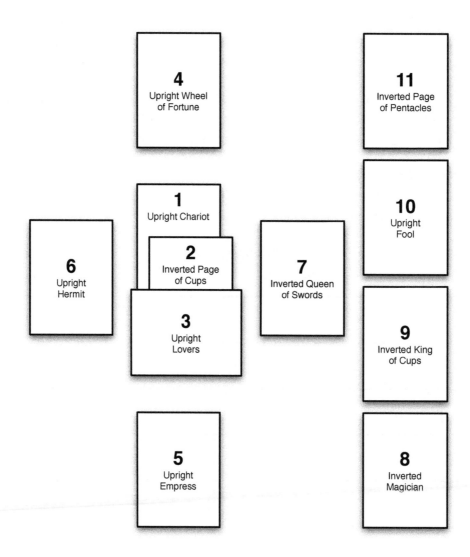

Figure 4: A Sample Reading from a Client Using the Complex Celtic Cross Spread

1. The Chariot appears upright in the indicator position. What does this tell you about her frame of mind at the time of the reading, about her personality, and about what she may be thinking?

2. The Page of Cups is inverted in the position representing the present situation. Who and what may this refer to?

3. The Lovers is read upright in this position, that tells us what she will be dealing with over the next period of '3' – usually months, but occasionally days or weeks. What's coming up for her in this time period?

4. The Wheel of Fortune appears in her distant future. Where does this tell you her life is going?

5. The Empress is in the foundation position. What does this tell you about where she has come from in her life, about the foundation that her life is built upon? When you tie this into the vertical line of spirit leading up through the Lovers, the inverted Page of Cups, the Chariot, and the Wheel of Fortune, what does this tell you about where her life is going in the long run?

6. The Hermit is in the position that represents the next six months. What will he bring into her life? When overlapped with the Lovers in the next three months position, what additional information can you intuit?

7. The inverted Queen of Swords is in the immediate past, usually looking back not more than six months. What's been going on in the last six months? Who could that Queen be? Now, if you tie the inverted Queen of Swords into the inverted Page of Cups and the Hermit, you'll be able to read the horizontal line of the cross that tells you what the physical issues in her life during this immediate time period concern.

8. The inverted Magician falling in the 'home' position gives insight into what is going on in and around her actual home at the present time. Usually this refers to the client's own home, but sometimes if she (or he) spends a great deal of time at work or owns her own business, this could also be seen as her home. What do you think is going on in her home right now? Often if we tie this position back into the foundation card, in this case the Empress, we get additional insight. Can you get any more information by doing this here?

9. The inverted King of Cups falls in the position defined as the next 10 days. This position literally tells you what the client will be dealing with in the next 10-day period. So, what's coming up for our client here? Again, by tying this card back to the home position, which is the inverted Magician here, we may get additional insight. Do this, and see if you get more information.

10. The Fool falls in the position I designate as 'concerns.' Most readers call this position the hopes and fears of the client. I prefer not to use this title because all

too often readers consequently always see this position as dealing with negative issues, which surely is not the case. This position is simply the concerns that the client has at this time in his or her life. Those concerns may be either good or bad, they may tie in with the rest of the reading, or reflect some totally different issue that's on the client's mind. So, what's on our client's mind here?

11. This last position in the complex Celtic Cross shows the outcome of the current major life situation as indicated in the reading. This outcome often affects the direction the client's life is going, as shown by the card in position 4, the distant future. The outcome of this reading is shown by the inverted Page of Pentacles. What do you think the outcome will be? How will this outcome affect the distant future?

Now that you've had a chance to work through this on your own, take a look at how I read this spread. Remember, if your interpretation differed, it does not necessarily mean it was wrong. You may have simply worked with different meanings for the same cards. When you're done with this, you may want to go back and read through the chapter once again, and don't forget to take a look at the lines of force diagrams I've included at the end of the chapter. These will help you to draw the cards together as you read them.

Here's my interpretation:

1. The Chariot in this position (1) tells me that she is a strong woman, very much in charge of her own life. Since this card has an affinity with the signs of Libra and Sagittarius, she might very well be one of these signs. In fact, she is a Libra! She may also be doing a lot of traveling, thinking about taking a trip, or be thinking about her car. I'm going to have to read further to tell which of these, if any, she is doing. But it's good to have the possibilities in mind right from the start. She also may have a person on her mind who drives, or wears a uniform, for a living. If so, he or she is probably a good person, since the Chariot is upright.

2. The inverted Page of Cups in this position (2) first tells me that she is waiting for some emotional news, or perhaps an emotional offer, that she isn't getting. She also may have just received an emotional message that bothered her. The Page of Cups, inverted, could also indicate a child, perhaps her own, since she's of the right age to have one, that either she is having trouble with, or that is going through some hard times of his or her own. If I relate this card back to the Chariot, perhaps the child is upset at her traveling or even about a trip she's taking. Perhaps the child wants to drive and she's not allowing this. Perhaps the bad news is even about that, or about a person represented by the Chariot.

3. In the next three months (position 3) she will be dealing with The Lovers, which tells me that she has a major decision to make between two people or things that she loves. Perhaps it's between the Page of Cups and the Charioteer? Or, perhaps it's between the child and the traveling. We'll have to wait and see.

4. In the distant future (position 4) the Wheel of Fortune comes up, which means that she is moving into a time of great change. A karmic pattern will come full circle and she will have the opportunity to end or change it. As we continue with the reading, we will see something of what this pattern is.

5. In the foundation we see the Empress (position 5). This could be her, in her role of Mother to the Page of Cups; if so, it appears she does a good job – the Empress is upright. It could be her mother, or a woman she sees as motherly. We can't tell yet which one. She may very well have a decision to make concerning her mothering, though, in the next three months. I know this, because as I look up the vertical line of force, I see a decision she will make (the Lovers) because an emotional offer or opportunity (inverted Page of Cups) is denied her. Making the decision, though, will empower her (the Chariot), which I see as I continue to follow the same line of force back over the cards I just laid down.

6. The Hermit appearing in the immediate future (position 6) tells of a lesson she is going to learn in the next six months. She may be going to school. If so, she will probably have to drive a long distance to get there (note that this card, too, ties back into the central grouping, which contains the Chariot). Or, the lesson may pertain to the offer or opportunity she is not getting, or even to the decision she will make. Indeed, it may be all three. Maybe she's going to learn something about the charioteer.

7. In the immediate past we see the inverted Queen of Swords (position 7). This may be my client again, in which case I see that she has not been feeling well, or has been upset, over the last six months or so. Perhaps, as I tie this back into the central grouping, it's because of the offer she's waiting for and not getting or she and her child are not getting along. If we look at the direction the Queen faces in the card, which in the Rider-Waite version of the Tarot is toward the right, or back toward the past, perhaps she is upset because she is dwelling on the past. Don't be afraid to let the picture on the card talk to you! Now, this inverted Queen could be someone else, as well. Perhaps it's a friend or close relative that she is either concerned with or has had a falling out with. Note that by tying this card into the center grouping it's also possible to say that she may be waiting for some message from this woman and either not getting it or getting bad news about her.

8. The home position (8) tells me what the situation in her home is right now. If she feels like work is home, you might occasionally see her work environment here, too. The inverted Magician indicates that at home she is feeling incompetent or ineffective. Relating this back to the upright Empress in her foundation, this may be relative to an older woman, or to her own mothering abilities. The Magician may also be a man she lives with or is very close to (a husband or boyfriend?). If he is an actual person, he is having problems or she is seeing him as ineffective in his life. He may find himself lacking in her eyes, or in the eyes of his mother

(by relating this back to the Empress again). Lastly, since the Magician represents sexual activity, there probably is none going on at home right now.

9. In the next 10 days (position 9) the King of Cups shows up inverted. This tells me she will have trouble with a King of Cups during this time. Relating this card back to the Magician in position 8, her problems with an ineffective male at home could be escalating, and/or, relating it across through the central grouping, she could be waiting to hear from a certain King of Cups (by tying him into the inverted Page of Cups) that she sees as the Charioteer, who is not contacting her.

10. Her concerns show up in the next position (10). The Fool here means she is deciding to move forward into a new situation, and is concerned about its affects on her life, and whether it will be beneficial.

11. The outcome (position 11), shown by the inverted Page of Pentacles, says that the emotional offer or opportunity she's presently waiting for will be unlikely to come anytime before a year from now. Reading the Page of Pentacles as a child, she could be having trouble with two children (remember the Page of Cups) or the same child could be turning up here a second time, in which case she'd still be having trouble with it a year from now. The inverted Page of Pentacles may also mean that a year form now she will have a new career or business offer. Since he's inverted, he just may not be in her life yet. Remember, too, that the inverted Page means she is not following her higher guidance.

Now, let's look at her actual situation, which mirrors the cards very well:

My Libra client is a divorcee, living alone with one son. She is indeed having trouble with the son, who up until now has been a model child, but has begun acting out as, after many years following her divorce, she began to date again. The Empress in the foundation is her, as she placed her mothering before everything else in her life until now. The first man she dated turned out to have both emotional and sexual potency problems that she discovered after he had practically moved in with her (note the inverted Magician in the home position). He borrowed money from her, which she is still trying to get back (note the inverted Pages in the current situation, and in the outcome position). It doesn't look like she will get it back. She has recently met a police officer (the Charioteer) who seems to be interested in her. She's waiting for him to call, but it seems that at least in the next 10 days she is unlikely to hear from him. Remember, the King of Cups may represent the romantic interest in your life, and he's inverted in hers, and the Page of Cups in the current situation is inverted as well. He apparently represents both of her love interests here and she's not happy with either one! Since the choice card, the Lovers, turns up in the next three months, it does look like she will have the opportunity to begin a new relationship with the policeman, but it also looks like her son will keep acting out. She will have to make a choice to go on with her life or not, chose between her two love interests and also, between her son and her lover. That choice will change her life. Note that it leads to both the Lovers and the Wheel of Fortune. She's learning an important lesson about herself (the Hermit).

Meanwhile, there's another story underlying this one that's also apparent in this spread of cards. This woman does a great deal of driving on her job (the Chariot). The driving and consequent time away from home have caused difficulty with her son, and many problems for her (inverted Page of Cups and inverted Queen of Swords). She has applied for a new position that would require additional training (the Hermit). Since the Page of Cups is inverted, we know that she has not yet received the offer, but the Lovers in the next three months position, and the Hermit in the next six months position do indicate the likelihood of her landing some position that will require more education and another choice on her part. Her son, by the way, wants a car (he's just learned to drive) and she's afraid to give it to him.

There was a great deal more apparent in the reading that I did not touch upon, so if you came up with different interpretations, don't consider them wrong – just different!

Now, let's look at these lines of force that I used in this reading and that will help you to tie the cards together before going on to complete the Major Arcana definitions in the next chapter.

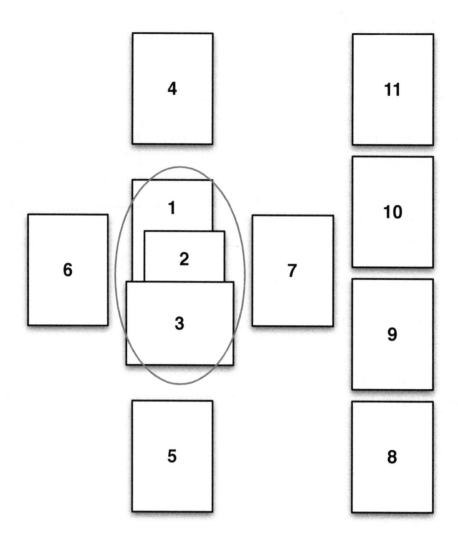

Figure 5A. The central self = positions 1, 2, and 3.
This pertains to the client and his or her immediate situation.

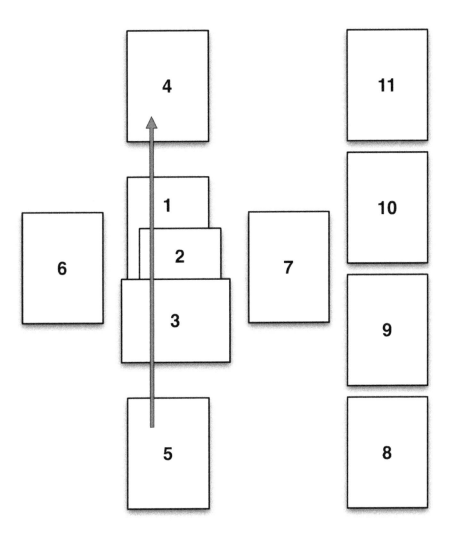

Figure 5B. Vertical line of spirit = positions 5, 3, 2, 1, and 4.
This is where life is supposed to be heading.

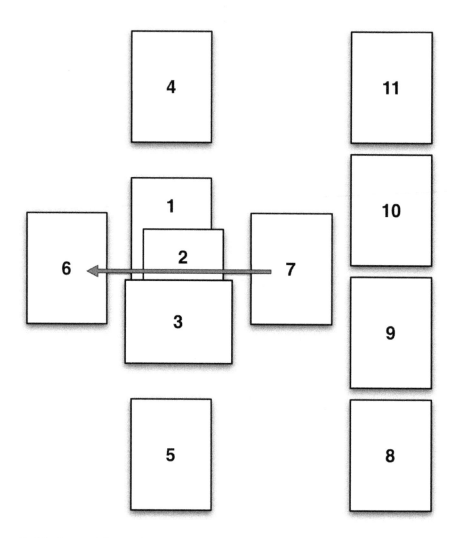

Figure C. Horizontal line of the material work situation = positions 7, 3, 2, 1, and 6. This is where we usually find our major obstacles and present existing conditions.

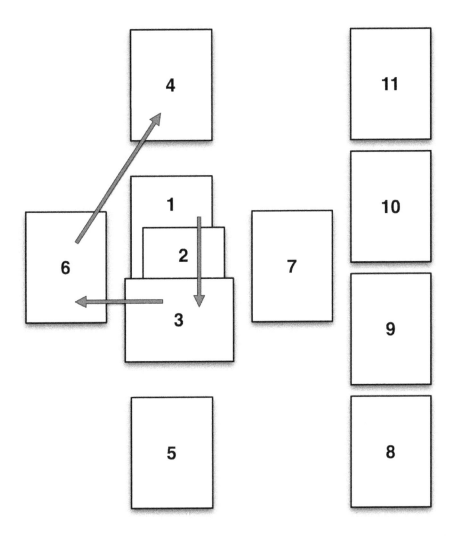

Figure 5D. Present situation's probable future = positions 1, 2, 3, 6, and 4.

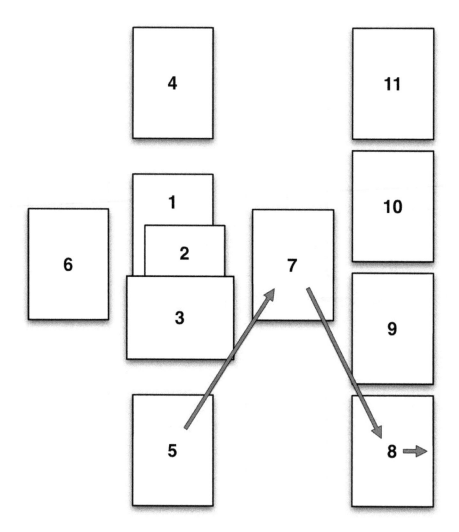

Figure 5E. How the past relates to our present home situation = positions 5, 7, and 8. Combining this with (D) shows how our past will lead to our future.

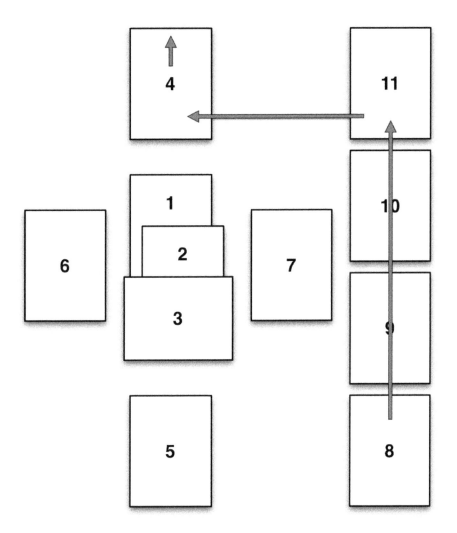

Figure 5F. Shows how what is going on at home will ultimately result in our outcome (11) and our distant future (4) = positions 8, 9, 10, 11 and 4. Combining (E) with (F) gives greater insight to our past experience.

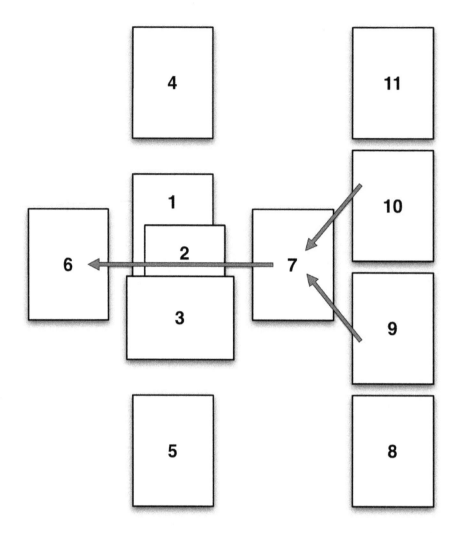

Figure 5G. How our next 10 days and our concerns will affect the present situation and its immediate future = positions 9, 10, 7, (1, 2, 3), and 6. This can be combined with (D) for insight into the final outcome.

Chapter 5

The Major Arcana Continued

XIII – Death

Simplified Meanings:

Upright – Change; transformation; the death of something physically or emotionally. Letting go.

Inverted – A slow change. Resistance to inevitable changes. The death of something or someone has occurred already.

Number – 13 is actually a number 4 (1+3 = 4). Remember that 4 is the number of the physical plane, foundation and work. But derived from the 3 and the 1, it gives a need for the spirit (1) to expand (3) beyond what binds it. In the I Ching it is regarded as "Brotherhood."

In-Depth Meanings:

All too often in my readings my clients will suddenly point to the Death card, shudder, and ask, "What does that mean? Is someone going to die?" I almost always answer, "No, that means that something in your life, perhaps an old attitude or belief that is holding you back, is getting ready to change. Let's look at the surrounding cards to see what it is you're changing!"

People do get frightened by the Death card because it represents an ultimate ending that most do not want to deal with. But when you explain that Death most often merely represents the transformation of old ideas or attitudes, which allows you to make much needed changes in your life, your clients will become eager to see what the changes are going to be because they already know their inner attitudes and values are changing – that's probably one of the reason's they have come for a reading! This card is reminiscent of the sign Scorpio, the sign of death and regeneration.

I often see the Death card in readings when clients are realizing they are in the wrong job or career and are getting ready to change it, or when they are just coming to the conclusion that their marriage is over, or when they realize that they no longer feel the same way about a friend, lover, or family member. An inner death of some kind always precedes a major life change. In fact, usually a change in attitude is necessary before one can take steps to initiate any new things in life. In essence, Death must precede Life. The two are intricately connected. Nothing new can be born until something old has died, be it an old attitude, job, relationship, residence, vehicle, or the like. This is not just a card of death, but of rebirth as well.

The Death card does sometimes signify the physical death of a person, but needless to say, I am very careful in mentioning death to a client, and will never do so if the Death card is the only indicator of a death in the reading, unless my intuition is screaming at me that that is what it means this time. As you can see, Death could pertain to so many other things, that usually, unless you see other cards in the reading that could also signify a physical death to back it up, you will be wrong. Other cards that often appear with Death to signify a physical death include the Ace of Swords or Ace of Pentacles, the Five of Cups, the Ten of Swords, or Judgement. Obviously, the more of them you see, the more likely a physical death may occur. You'll notice that I still used *may*. It's been my experience that people die when they are ready, not when a reader says they will. As an Astrologer as well as a Tarot reader, I have seen very clear deaths in readings that have never occurred. Usually in these cases the individuals who should have died had close calls, but survived. The Death card transformed their lives as they re-evaluated what was important to them. If a physical death is actually indicated, you should also see the cause of death in most cases. If you do predict any deaths in your readings make sure that you make it clear to your clients that your prediction is not carved in granite, but is dependent upon the will to live and the resultant action of the individual concerned.

Many of my students ask me why I would predict a death to begin with, when it is such a dreaded subject, and I might be wrong anyway and may just have stirred up some ungrounded worries. The answer is simple: The future is changeable. When we read our clients, our accurate predictions only remain accurate as long as they follow their previous, predictable patterns of behavior. When our clients change those patterns, those inner values and attitudes, they also change the future. If I see a death, I predict it so that the client may take steps to prevent it. The closer the client is to the person who is dying, the greater the likelihood that they can help to change the outcome. I have, in fact, been able to save several people's lives through my readings by both making the prediction and explaining that they could take steps to alter it.

Of course, when you're counseling a client you have to be exceedingly careful how you approach this subject. If your client is a woman waiting for a sick Uncle to die so she can claim her inheritance (yes, you will run across some of these), you can be totally blunt. But if you're talking about a husband, child, lover, parent, or the client themselves dying, please approach the subject delicately. In fact, you might even refer to it obliquely, as I did here:

My client was a young woman. In her reading, I saw her father dying of a heart attack. (We will learn later on how to determine various illnesses through the cards). I approached the subject delicately, asking first, did she know that her father had a bad heart? She answered that she did, that he was under doctor's care and that as long as he took his medicine he was alright. I then told her that his condition was probably much more serious than she knew, perhaps was even life threatening, and that it should be looked into more thoroughly. I didn't dwell on this aspect of her reading further, but went on to other issues. I had informed her of the need to look into this, but didn't want to unnecessarily upset her. I saw this same client several months later and she told me that after her reading she had taken my comments about her father's heart seriously and had insisted upon accompanying him on his next visit to the doctor. The doctor told her that her father needed a quadruple heart by-pass operation or he would not live long. He apparently had been telling her father this for the past year, but her father, fearful of surgery and in denial of his condition, was ignoring the advice and telling his family that as long as he took his medication he was alright. The family was insistent that the father have the surgery. He did, and today he is still alive and well. In subsequent readings I did for my young client I saw her father's surgery, recovery, and transformation as he realized he could no longer live in denial of his fears. In this instance, the meaning of the Death card itself was transformed, from an actual death, to a change in attitude.

When the Death card appears inverted in a reading it may mean that the transformation or death has already occurred or that it is in process, but moving forward very slowly due to the person's resistance to change. Its position in the spread should tell you which of these meanings to use.

A last comment – many times you will turn up the death that has already occurred. If the person or thing that has died was close to the client, it may be, unbeknownst to himself, that he has come for the reading to purge by talking about it, or that there are things about it that he needs to let go of now. One of your functions as a counselor, as well as a reader, should be to help the client to deal with that death, which wouldn't show in the spread at all if it wasn't an important issue still.

Special Note: Remember that Death usually means transformation, not physical death. If you're predicting an actual death, make sure there are other cards in the spread that back up your interpretation.

Personal Notes

XIV – Temperance

Simplified Meanings:

Upright – Balance, harmony, good health, the arts, medicine, an artist, a medical practitioner, an herbalist. The higher self reflected in the personality.

Inverted – Imbalance, possible poor health or addictions. Blockage of higher inspirations.

Number – The number 14 is actually a 5 (1+4 = 5) which is a number of evolution and change coming through the balance and foundation (4) of the spirit (1). In the I Ching it is regarded as "Sovereignty."

In-Depth Meanings:

Temperance is one of the most important cards in the deck because its representation of balance versus imbalance gives you great insight into the state of things in your client's life. If Temperance occurs upright in the reading, whatever it pertains to will be in a state of balance and harmony. If Temperance is inverted, whatever it refers to is out of balance and is causing the client problems as a result. The imbalance could be whatever the surrounding cards tell you it's in. In particular, when Temperance is inverted and surrounded by Wands, there could be physical illness indicated.

The surrounding Wands are what tells you that the imbalance is physical. But if you want to know what particular illness might be indicated, you have to look for particular cards. For example, the Three of Swords indicates problems with the heart, blood, circulation, or general chest area, but only when it falls near an inverted Temperance and one or more Wands. If Temperance were upright with the same surrounding cards, it would still mean there was illness, but that healing was occurring since physical balance is indicated. The same Three of Swords surrounded by Wands but lacking the Temperance card may not indicate illness at all. Temperance is our indicator of illness or health – but only when a Wand appears near it.

Here is a list of cards that can indicate specific illnesses, when they fall near both Temperance and one or more Wands (it will help you to see where these meanings come from if you take each card out and look at it as you read).

- The inverted Ace of Cups, Wands or Swords or the inverted Empress or Sun could mean termination of a pregnancy due to physical illness. If these cards are upright they could simply mean difficulties with the pregnancy.

- The Ace of Wands or Magician inverted near a male Court card indicates impotence caused by a physical illness.

- The Two of Swords indicates physical blindness or eye problems.

- The Five of Pentacles indicates a head injury or illness involving the head, or injury to a leg, limb or bones.

- The Hanged Man also indicates the loss of or injury to one leg.

- The Five of Wands aggravates any condition – if it's inverted, it means the person who is ill is fighting a losing battle.

- The Seven of Wands indicates the illness will be overcome, but if it's inverted it will not be.

- The Moon means female organ or hormonal problems are being dealt with.

- The Devil, upright, means the illness is chronic in nature – i.e., it will not go away (cancer, diabetes or asthma).

- The Eight of Swords indicates a debilitating condition preventing mobility, eye problems or even blindness.

- The Eight of Wands indicates a problem with communication – speech or hearing.

- The Nine of Swords gives insomnia or headaches.

- The Nine of Wands may indicate a past illness returning – if inverted, it may not be overcome this time.

- The Ten of Swords usually indicates some form of surgery.

- The Ten of Wands indicates a problem with the back or the bones.

- The Ten of Pentacles doesn't tell what the illness is, but lets you know that it is an elderly member of the family who is ill. In most cases the person who is ill will show up as an inverted Court card near those cards indicating the illness.

- If, in addition to these cards that indicate physical illness, you also see Death, Judgement, the Ace of Pentacles or Swords or the Five of Pentacles, the outcome of the illness could be death unless something changes.

- In addition, Temperance falling near the Three of Cups, the Nine of Cups or the Four of Pentacles, even with no Wands nearby, can indicate a tendency to overdue by pushing the digestive system past its capabilities. If Temperance is upright, the individual indicated is keeping this tendency in check, if inverted it's out of control.

- Usually with the Three of Cups or Nine of Cups the substance is alcohol or drugs, with the Four of Pentacles it's usually food (overeating or under eating, or just eating the wrong things).

- When the Devil also appears upright in the same spread, an addiction is often indicated. With a large number of Cups, the substance abuse is enhanced, with a large number of Wands, it's having debilitating affects on the body of the person indicated by the cards. If the Moon appears in the same spread, it could be either the cause of or the result of a hormonal imbalance – this is common in diabetes, where diet control is so important.

Temperance is also commonly present when emotional problems are being dealt with. In these cases we usually see either an inverted Empress, Chariot, Moon, Star, or even Five of Pentacles falling near the inverted Court card who is the person with the problem. It's not unusual to see emotional problems and addictive problems surrounding the same person.

Now you can see why an upright Temperance in a reading is so nice to see. It tells of good health, emotionally and physically, and that any potential addictions are under control and balanced. No matter how bad the client's situation may be at the time of the reading, if Temperance falls upright in any future position, the outcome will be positive, as his or her life returns to wholeness.

Because this card has so much to do with physical balance and centeredness, it follows that it also is one of the most artistic cards in the deck. It shows the inner harmony necessary for the artist to be inspired. It's particularly good for arts like interior decorating, which require a good grasp of balance. It also shows the inner harmony necessary for us to know where we stand relative to our life's direction. It's as if when Temperance turns up, the client is taking a momentary time out from life to center and regroup. Very often that harmony and balance that can be achieved at this time is helpful to other people in his or her life as well. That is the reason why this card is also the card of the healer. It never fails to amaze me that the same quality in a person that can open him to higher inspiration artistically and spiritually also enables him to be a healer! Small wonder that this is the card of all those involved in the healing professions, as well as the arts. This card is most often associated with the sign Libra.

__Special Note__: Temperance is one of the most spiritual cards in the deck; in the Rider-Waite version of the card, the dotted circle on the angel's forehead is not a stethoscope (although this serves as a good reminder that this is the medical indicator card in the deck) but is actually the symbol for the Sun. Placed here, it symbolizes the inspiration of the Higher Self. The triangle in the square on the angel's breast shows the spirit contained within matter. The pose of the angel, with one foot on dry land and one in the water, shows the perfect balance and communication between the intuitive and the rational mind, as well as the Higher and lower Selves.

Personal Notes

_____

_____

_____

_____

_____

_____

_____

_____

_____

_____

_____

_____

_____

_____

_____

Simplified Meanings:

Upright – Bondage. Addiction. A contract or obligation. Government or big business. Controlling or being controlled. Jail. Attachment. Obsession. Enslavement to the world of the senses. Black magic.

Inverted – Freedom from bondage, addiction, contracts or obligations.

Number – The number 15 is actually a 6 (1+5 = 6), so here success (6) is arrived by the spirit (1), undergoing change and evolution (5), to achieve freedom. In the I Ching it is regarded as "Moderation."

In-Depth Meanings:

The Devil is a very easy card to understand and to remember, but it is also very hard to deal with when it actually appears in your life. This is one card where the upright meaning is usually far worse than the inverted one.

When the Devil appears upright it usually indicates that there is something or someone in the client's life that is controlling him (or her), either in thoughts or actions. For example, if the Devil falls next to the upright Emperor, your female client may be controlled by her husband, father or boss, but when the Devil falls near Pentacles the controlling factor might be finances. When he falls near Temperance and Wands the controlling issue is probably a chronic illness, but if instead of Wands you see Cups, especially the Three or Nine of Cups, it's an addiction. Near the Ace of Wands, the Magician, or the Emperor sex could be used for control. Near the Chariot or the Hierophant someone could be going to jail. These days it's not uncommon to see the Devil near the Chariot, Temperance and either the Three or Nine of Cups – when someone is about to get stopped for DUI.

In all of these instances, the situation in which control is exerted is shown by the surrounding cards. The upright Devil only tells you that the client, or whomever the cards are indicating, is in a situation wherein he is being controlled and is not free to exercise personal freedom.

Or at least that's the way the client sees it. I'd like you to take just a moment to look at the Rider-Waite version of the card. Note that the chains by which the Devil holds the humans in the card are loosely fastened around their necks. This gives a whole new look at the old adage, 'putting your own neck in the noose,' because that's exactly what the people in this card have done. You can see that the chains are so loose that to be free they have only to lift them off. So why don't they?

The Devil teaches us a lesson. We can only be in bondage to that which we allow ourselves to be. We can be controlled by our addiction, by our greed, by our perceived needs, by our possessiveness, our guilts, even by our love. And if your clients are in situations where the Devil appears upright in their cards, you can be sure that their own need is what is keeping them in bondage, not another person or situation. This is important to know and understand because usually the only way for your clients to break out of their bondage is for them to make some internal changes that allows them to no longer need whatever is causing them to be controlled.

Take for example, the following configuration: Next to an inverted Queen of Cups, you see the upright Devil, the upright Emperor, inverted Temperance, the Nine of Cups, as well as several Wands – including the Five of Wands. The inverted Queen of Cups is your emotional female client who is upset about her husband, who is an alcoholic and tends to become violent when under the influence (lay out these cards next to one another and the scenario will be clear). Your client is understandably fearful in this situation, and is dealing with the Devil's bondage in two ways. Firstly, she sees her husband's bondage in his addiction. But secondly, she is herself in bondage because her fear prevents her from taking action to stop his drinking and his abuse, while her love for him prevents her from leaving him. She can do nothing about his bondage to his addiction. But she can do something about her bondage to it, and that first requires her to change. She must either change her fear or change her love. Once she does either one, she is free from the bondage of the situation, and can begin to formulate a plan of action.

When the Devil turns up in a reading you are doing for a client, you should take the time to explore what it is that is binding him. Find out how your client feels about it. Unfortunately, there are many people who actually derive a sense of identity from the bondage they have placed themselves in, and though they may loudly complain about it, they are not yet ready to change it. But if they are truly ready to break out of their confines, you, as a reader, can be a great help. You need to make clear to them that they have to let go of whatever it is within themselves that keeps them in the situation.

If they're in bondage to their three jobs because they bought a house they cannot afford, they need to sell the house, or find a way to share the payments with a spouse or roommate. If they're controlled by their jealousy over a lover who's indiscriminate, they need to find a new lover who's loyal. If they're addicted to something, they need to get help and deal with the addiction. If someone they love is addicted and they feel they're controlled through that addiction, they need to give an ultimatum to their loved one – "get help, or lose me." And they need to mean it. The Devil has a habit of turning up in almost every co-dependent relationship. If they're controlled by Mom because they want her stuff, they've got to let go of the stuff, and make it on their own. If they're controlled by someone whose love they want, but never can get, they have to stop wanting it. The possible positions we all put ourselves in where we can so readily become controlled by things outside of ourselves is unlimited.

Once your client has made the inner change necessary to take the outer action, the Devil will appear in his cards inverted because inverted he means 'freedom from bondage.' And you should give your client a pat on the back because he deserves it. Breaking the bondage of the Devil may feel like cutting off your right arm, perhaps more so because it's your own attitudes, values, and actions that allowed the bondage to take place to begin with.

In a more positive sense, the Devil may also indicate contracts (remember, a contract is binding, even though it may be good for both parties). If upright, the contract will go through; inverted, it will not. He may represent your own conscience, the need to discharge an honest obligation. When inverted it would mean that obligation has been filled. The Devil may also indicate big business and government, especially in the sense of monetary control and legal action. Upright, the business is in charge and in control; inverted, it is not. This is also the card that represents Capricorn.

Lastly, the Devil is sometimes associated with the devil and black magic. I don't expect you to come across this meaning often, but if your clients involve themselves with people or groups that are involved in real magic, and the Devil turns up, it could indicate that some very nasty magic is taking place – the kind that binds people and forces them to do the magician's bidding. Look for the Magician or the High Priestess, and perhaps the Nine of Swords to be nearby in the reading before you ask your clients if they have friends involved in magic. Then, if they do, tell them the worst, and encourage them to break their ties to these people. All magic is not bad or wrong – but black magic, the upright Devil's only kind, is always wrong. If you feel your clients are the target of this black magic, don't tell them to fight back but, rather, just to protect themselves. Magical wars go on for lifetimes and are not worth being involved in. Protecting oneself always works because eventually the opposition has to tire and look elsewhere. There are plenty of books available on how to protect yourself psychically. Recommend one to your client. Don't become involved yourself!

__Special Note__: The Devil is a natural precursor to change. Until you have overdosed on chocolate, for example, you are unlikely to give it up. This is the single most materialistic and possessive card in the deck – and in many ways it characterizes our society better than any other card. We are at the most materialistic period in our Earth's long history, *and until we 'OD' on all of these material things in our world, we will not change our addiction to them and allow ourselves to be free!*

Personal Notes

_____

_____

_____

_____

_____

_____

_____

_____

_____

_____

_____

_____

Simplified Meanings:

Upright – Sudden, shocking change. Overthrow of the existing order. Ineffectual values and behavior patterns are discarded. Loss.

Inverted – Freedom, but at great cost, emotionally and materially. Major life change completed.

Number – The number 16 is actually a number 7 (1+6 = 7). This means that self mastery (7) is attained by successfully overcoming one's own enslavement to the senses (6) under the guidance of spirit (1). In the I Ching it is regarded as "Harmonize."

In-Depth Meanings:

The Tower is one of the most difficult cards to experience. When it turns up in your clients' readings, spend a bit more time with them, helping them to understand the scope and meaning of the changes they are going through. The Tower always brings change – major, sweeping changes that erase all that has gone before.

The Tower does not follow the Devil by accident. In the Devil we saw our addiction to pleasures, our obsessive attachment to people and things, as blocking our growth and evolution until we have gone so deeply into them that we are nearly suffocated by them, and of our own accord, seek freedom from them. It's at this point that the Tower enters the story, showing us that it is the very foundations of the life that we have built for ourselves that must be shattered to set us free.

The Tower is a shattering experience. When it comes up in the reading of a client, that client is going through massive upheavals in his (or her) life. Often, with the Tower showing, these upheavals are occurring in several areas of life at once. It is the Tower's function to overturn the foundations of the life, to upset the client's reality base to the point that none of his previous attitudes, values, or habit patterns can work in the situation in which he finds himself. The only viable solution is to pioneer new attitudes, values, and patterns. In a positive sense, the Tower is one of the major agents promoting personal evolution in the Tarot deck. Most of us dislike its methods, but eventually come to appreciate the results.

In counseling your clients who are experiencing the Tower in their lives, I advise against telling them how much they are going to grow by losing everything important to them. If you're lucky, they won't throw something at you, they'll just begin to cry. If you see the Tower in the past, or if it's inverted in the present (which means its influence is recently passed), go ahead and tell them about their growth – they're already beginning to see some of it and are probably ready for the pep talk. Often during the period following a major life upheaval your clients are existing in a state of shock; they're not moving on with their lives because they have not yet fully accepted the changes they have gone through. Hence the value of a pep talk at this point. Tremendous energy is always released following the Tower's action, but until the individual has accepted the change and moved on, he cannot take advantage of it. If the Tower is upright in the present, on the other hand, what he needs is a hand to hold, and perhaps some good, earthy advice on how to make it through this time of change with his sanity intact and with the least amount of loss.

You can be sure that the Tower will bring loss. But what is supposed to be lost are those things you don't really need anymore, those things that are holding you back (even though you may not see it that way just yet). The problem is, once the Tower gets going, it builds up momentum and, like a landslide, may wipe away everything before it, including some things not really meant to be lost at this time. So when you see the Tower upright in the present situation for clients, endeavor to slow them down. Get them to think about their actions. Help them to bring awareness and control to the inevitable change they are going through.

When the Tower falls near the Ace of Pentacles, Ace of Swords, Three of Pentacles, or Eight of Pentacles, the change involves a job; the client might be getting laid off, he might be quitting, or getting transferred – the surrounding cards will tell the rest of the story. With the Sun or the Four of Wands (upright), the change could be a marriage – with the Tower present, you know adjustment to marriage won't be easy! With the Sun or Four of Wands (inverted), Judgement, or an upright Five of Cups, it may bring a divorce. With the Five of Wands, and Temperance, a major illness that will transform the life of the person it aspects in the reading. With the Five of Wands and the Chariot, it's a car accident. With Death, and either the Ace of Pentacles or Five of Cups, it may be a physical death of someone that will radically affect the client's life. These are just a few of the things that the Tower may transform in your life. Remember – any card it falls near will be transformed according to its nature.

For those of you who are astrologers, you might compare the Tower to the interaction of the energies of Mars (pure energy and force) and Uranus (revolution and change). The Tower cannot be resisted. In fact, the longer a change has been resisted, the more sweeping and violent the action of the Tower will be. Of the signs of the zodiac, the one that I think most accurately mirrors the Tower's energy through its ability to totally transform itself is Scorpio.

Remember, that when the Tower is inverted, its meaning is the same, except that the change has already occurred – your client is either just dealing with the tail end of it, or internally accepting its ramifications.

__Special Note__: If you see the inverted Tower in a future position in a client's reading, you may infer that the Tower is really upright in the present, and that your client is presently going through some sudden, major upheaval in his or her life. Surrounding cards will define the areas in his or her life where this upheaval is occurring.

Personal Notes

XVII – The Star

Simplified Meanings:

Upright – Material wealth and happiness. Balance between one's inner and outer world. Love is given and received. Joy. Heightened intuition.

Inverted – Depression and imbalance. Material depression and loss. Dwelling in the past.

Number – The number 17 is actually a number 8 (1+7 = 8). Here, the 7 of mastery of the material (and freedom from attachment to it) combines with the 1 of spirit to give 8, the number that completes physical and material karma, and that gives mundane power and material wealth. In the I Ching it is regarded as "Following."

In-Depth Meanings:

In my eyes, the Star is the most wonderful card in the deck. Remember, it follows upon the heels of the Tower, which through its action has induced a loss, created a 'vacuum' in the life of the client. The client now has no expectations. He (or she) is no longer hanging on to old, outmoded values, belief systems, or habit patterns. In short, there is now room in his life for a new, growth oriented and spiritually expansive experience. Enter, the Star!

The Star has tremendous power and energy. It's enormously creative. It encourages a flow of energy that allows no holding on, just a constant pulling in of new experience, combined with a total giving back to the universe of experience gained. It's as if the more that is shared, the more one receives.

As long as the conduit through which this energy flows remains open, the individuals experiencing the Star are in perfect balance and health, both physically and emotionally. All of the riches the universe has to offer, emotionally, physically, and materially, flow through them, enriching them and all those they are in contact with. In fact, the more open and receptive they become, the more of these universal goodies will become available to them. Under this card, it is possible to receive and generate incredibly high spiritual energies as well, attaining new heights of awareness, even becoming a conduit for one's higher self and one's guides to work through. But remember, the conduit must remain open; the receivers of this bounty must be willing to keep passing on what they receive. If they begin to hold on they become blocked, and the powerful energies passing through them will back up, producing both physical and mental illness, and resulting in material and emotional loss. In these cases the Star appears inverted.

In mundane readings when the Star appears upright it will tell you that your client is now, or will soon be (depending on where the Star falls in your spread) experiencing great happiness, joy, and love shared with another, or with many. Material concerns have vanished, balance between the material and the spiritual has been attained. Your client is naked to the world, has been exposed to his innermost self, has accepted that self, and can give the same quality of love to himself that he can give to others. This card always indicates a period of joy and harmony that your client wishes would go on forever. And it can – as long as he does not try to hold on to what is being received.

But of course we humans hate to let go of anything good (in fact, we have a difficult time letting go of the bad things in our lives, too). When your client tries to hold onto the wonderful things he is experiencing, or when your client cannot let go of the past and is still holding on to those things he has already lost as he experienced the Tower, the Star reverses itself in the reading.

Inverted, the Star is one of the most difficult and sad cards in the deck. Sadly, because the upright wonders this card has to offer are there, but just out of reach of the client; the inability to let go and go with the flow prevents the client from recognizing even the barest glimmer of Star light energy.

When the Star appears inverted in a reading your client is depressed – sometimes to a point bordering on emotional or mental illness. Financial and material matters are perhaps at the lowest ebb he has ever reached. It's as if your client has experienced the Tower, lost everything important – and stayed there!

Everything in the client's life is out of balance. When inverted, the water (emotional and psychic energy) is on the top of the card, showing that emotions are out of control and the client is drifting in negative emotional and psychic currents. He feels to have indeed been exposed for all the world to see, but that exposure has weakened and embarrassed him. The client cannot accept himself, the situation, or even those around who try to help. He yearns only for what was thought to be in his possession, and in that yearning, blocks himself from the healing energies of the Star that lie just out of sight.

If you can, when you read a client and the Star comes up inverted, try to gently encourage him to let go of whatever issues you see in the reading that he is holding onto so tightly. The client will resist you, so go gently. Letting go of the past, or of expectations, is the only solution to the problem.

*<u>Special Note</u>: *The Star is both the best (upright) and the worst (inverted) card in the deck. When it's upright, share in your client's joy, encourage him to go on with whatever he is involved with. When it's inverted, help your client to let go, and to heal, knowing that the upright Star is still available if he can only let go of fear and reach for it! The Star is closely associated with the sign Aquarius.*

Personal Notes

_____

_____

_____

_____

_____

_____

_____

_____

_____

_____

_____

_____

XVIII – The Moon

Simplified Meanings:

Upright – Beginning a new path; unfolding of psychic abilities; a psychic link to someone close to you; Strong emotions; the female organs; the path to initiation.

Inverted – Negative emotions; depression; an unhealthy psychic/emotional link; problems with the female organs; emotional illness; low energy; a woman who either has emotional problems or causes them.

Number – The number 18 is actually a 9 (1+8 = 9). Nine is the number of spiritual completion. It is the last number in our numerical system, and as such contains a bit of all the others, completing their cycle and raising them to a higher vibration for the next cycle to begin. This '9' derives from the 8 and the 1, so what is being completed and raised is everything pertinent to the number 8 – material achievement, finance, karma, sex, power, business and so on. In the I Ching it is regarded as "Repair."

In-Depth Meanings:

Let me begin this discussion by saying that many other authors and I do not agree on the meanings of the Moon in a reading. I have read such varied meanings as danger, mental illness, viciousness, and disaster in the works of various authors that I will leave unnamed. In fact, it often seems difficult to find any positive meanings for the Moon at all. Perhaps this is an indication of the demoted position of the Goddess energy in today's world. For the Moon surely encompasses that energy, and in fact, all that is feminine.

When the Goddess energy, or otherwise stated, the energy of the unconscious, subconscious, and unseen worlds, around us is understood, it is not at all fearful. It is wondrous and just as necessary to us as the God or Sun energy that is outer directed. As mankind continues to evolve and to become more in touch with the inner planes within himself, the Moon will take on progressively more positive meanings.

Take a moment to look at the card. The crayfish, or lobster-like creature is just crawling out of the water in the foreground of the card. (Incidentally, paleontologists have recently discovered that a lobster-like creature really was the first animal to crawl from the primordial oceans of our newly formed earth. Perhaps the original symbolism remains intact in this card.) Now, we usually see the element of water in the cards as representing the psyche, the unconscious, or the emotions. You will see as I continue that the moon may mean all three. In this case, look at the water as the great pool of unawareness in which most of mankind swims. The crayfish has just set foot (or claw, if you will) on a long and winding path. This is indicative of the individual who is just waking up to the possibility of a greater reality opening to him, if he is willing to commit to the journey. As he moves forward he will have to pass between a wolf and a dog, representing the wild and domesticated versions of the animal. The symbolism of the dog is rich. We initially saw him in the Fool, where he represented unconscious guidance and help that we brought into life with us. In this card, we see two sides of the animal, the wild and the tame – representing the two sides of ourselves – the man and the animal, that must be balanced before we can follow the path. The path continues to lead between two towers reminiscent of the two opposing pillars on the Tree of Life that show the forces within and without that must be continually balanced to move forward. Finally, at the end of the path, we see a symbol of the Moon united with the Sun – in the East, this is always a symbol of initiation; the union of Higher Self and Lower Self and the erasure of all boundaries between conscious and unconscious, so that awareness is complete and initiation is achieved.

Clearly, the Moon is a card depicting the beginning of the path to attainment. Ideally, of course, the attainment the card suggests working toward is that of the spirit. But we often see the Moon in readings where it merely shows that your client is embarking upon a new course in life that will be a long haul yet will help him (or her) to grow and learn as he moves toward the achievement of the goal. In these readings, the Moon does not guarantee that the goal will be achieved; it merely illuminates the fact that the journey has begun. And remember, too, that learning and developing a talent or ability, or even some mundane achievement like finding a job in a new field, can lead you on your own path toward enlightenment.

For most people, the beginning of spiritual awareness is marked by looking inward. For some, it means getting in touch again with their early religious beginnings, for others, becoming involved in psychology, astrology, or another field that teaches self-awareness. Still others find that their inward search results in an unfolding of psychic abilities such as developing empathic and telepathic abilities, and the ability to astral travel and receive precognitive dreams and visions.

Often, too, when the Moon appears in a reading it merely refers to a strong emotional and psychic (the two work together in this case) bond that your client has to another person. The person, of course, should appear in the cards as one of the Court cards. So long as the Moon is upright, the bond is a healthy one and benefits the two people involved, but if the Moon is inverted, the person represented by the Court card nearest it may very well have mental or emotional problems that create difficulty for your client because of the "link" between them. I remember, for example, reading a woman who had such a strong emotional-psychic bond to her sister that when her sister (who lived far away and was seldom in touch with her) divorced her husband, my client had such severe problems in her own marriage that she came close to divorce as well. It was only after the sister announced her divorce that she realized where the pressure on her had been coming from.

The Moon rules all things feminine. In our physical world it rules the night, the oceans and tides, and a woman's cycle. All magic must follow the lunar cycles as well, since the Moon rules the inner planes on which all magic is worked. When the Moon is upright, whether you're male or female, you're in touch with your feminine side; reversed, and you're out of touch with it. Upright, you're emotionally healthy and well-balanced; inverted, you are having some major emotional problems. Upright, you are in touch with your intuitions and are using them wisely; inverted, your intuitions are galloping away with you, your psychic receptivity is making you so open to other people's feelings that you feel out of control, not knowing what is real and what is not real, what is your own feeling, and what is someone else's. Upright, you are learning to be receptive to the emanations of your own higher nature; inverted, you have blocked yourself off from those emanations, wallowing in your own emotional depression. Remember, that whenever the Moon appears in a reading, the opportunity to use it positively is there, but if it's inverted, the client is choosing to block its more positive side, and refusing to awaken to the higher purpose he feels inside.

Often when the Moon appears in a reading, the subject the reading discusses will reach fulfillment within a month, since the physical moon's cycle is 28 days. Sometimes the Moon will represent a person, male or female, who is born under the sign of Cancer, which the moon rules astrologically.

If the Moon falls near Temperance (our health indicator card) in a spread, it can indicate illness, especially if inverted. If no Wands are present, the illness may not be physical, but rather emotional or mental. This is especially true if the Three of Swords, the inverted Empress, or the inverted Star is also nearby. When Wands are also present the illness is physical, and will focus in the female or reproductive organs. In a man's reading it is probably not him who is ill, but rather a woman close to him. The only exception to this would be if the inverted Moon fell immediately adjacent to a King or Knight, and in that case it would refer to hormone imbalances. Occasionally, when the Devil also appears in the spread where illness has already been indicated, it can mean cancer of the reproductive system, or a gland.

If the Moon falls adjacent to Temperance, it does not always mean illness, though. Near the High Priestess or Hierophant, it can mean an individual who is, or is studying to be, a psychologist. And Moon/Temperance near any card representing work could mean that your client works in the health field healing women. (Throw the Empress in for good measure, and perhaps he's a gynecologist-obstetrician).

Special Note: *The Moon is one of the most important cards in the deck, representing as it does all that is receptive and feminine. Sleeping on this card and meditating upon it can aid you in strengthening your connection to your feminine side, and will enhance your intuition. Many of the mysteries of this card can be revealed only through your own inner searching.*

Personal Notes

_____

_____

_____

_____

_____

_____

_____

_____

_____

_____

_____

Simplified Meanings:

Upright – Reunion, rebirth, marriage, birth of a son, joy, happiness, the Higher Self, summer, warmth, the life-force, completion, light. Freedom to be who you are.

Inverted – Divorce, separation, despondency, lack of vitality, choosing not to follow a path begun. Darkness. Losing your connection to your Higher Self.

Number – The number 19 is actually a number 1 (1 + 9 = 10 and 1 + 0 = 1). The number 19 is a new beginning again, but this time on a still higher level. Remembering that 9 is the number of spiritual completion, it is when we reach the number 19 that our journey is completed and that we may return to unity in the 1. In the I Ching it is regarded as "Promotion."

In-Depth Meanings:

The Sun is the life giver of our solar system – where it shines there is light and warmth. It is masculine and generative in its nature, and when it combines with the cool receptivity of the feminine Moon that rules the waters, the combination of life giving solar energy and nurturing water creates the perfect environment for all living things to grow and flourish.

As the Moon rules the night, so the Sun rules the day. It is generative and wants to act on the world, not being content to let the world come to it. Like Leo, the astrological sign it rules, the Sun is outer directed; it is impetuous, vibrant and energetic; it wants to be the leader, and to be recognized for its leadership and accomplishments.

The Sun represents the ultimate male force, the God force, if you will, in our world. It also represents the Higher Self within each of us. The Moon represents the gateway to the Higher Self, but the Sun is the Higher Self as represented by the Tarot.

When I occasionally turn this card up in a reading as the indicator card, I know that the person I am reading has a stronger connection to his (or her) Higher Self than the average person. Whether the client is aware of the connection is unimportant. What is important, is that he is following the guidance of higher consciousness in whatever it is he is doing. Because the client is following that higher guidance, he is happy, has lots of energy, seems to be in the right place at the right time for each major step in life. He attracts people like moths are attracted to a flame because although other people may not understand what they are attracted to, the Sun individuals personalities are so vibrant and pure, so strong and directed, that it acts as a beacon to those less directed personalities around them.

The Tarot depicts the journey of the soul, not only from birth to death, but also in its process of evolution spiritually through many successive lifetimes. When the Sun occurs in a reading, from a spiritual point of view the soul's long journey is at an end; reunion with the God force, or with the Divine within is near at hand. The Path begun with the Fool, which became conscious with the Moon, is fulfilled in the Sun.

But most times when you see the Sun in a reading, even though these more spiritual meanings may also have a bearing on your client, you will be looking at more mundane meanings.

Mundanely, the Sun upright always gives the reading a positive, up feeling. Emotionally and materially things are looking up when the Sun appears. The client is happy, he is in the right place at the right time in life, he has family and friends around who are supportive. The client feels the warm glow of acceptance from others and pride inwardly.

Often the Sun means that a marriage or engagement is about to take place (look at its placement in the spread for timing), or that the client will be reuniting with someone he has positive emotions for. Remember, a marriage or reunion shown by the Sun upright will be a good one.

The Sun can also represent birth. When applied to the client, see it as a rebirth, or opportunity to get re-in-touch with himself. Seen in this light, if the Sun fell upright near a card representing work, you could assume that the new job the client is taking is exactly what he should be doing, and perhaps will allow greater self-expression. Indeed, the client may feel like he is coming home to this job. Surrounded by Pentacles, the Sun upright may mean that the client has arrived where he wants to be financially, and can relax and enjoy it for a time. Or perhaps, it means that your client has made a good marriage to someone with money.

The Sun upright may also represent the actual birth of a boy child, but remember to consider this meaning only if other pregnancy or birth cards such as the Empress, Ace of Swords or Wands, and/or a Page falls near it in the reading.

Many times I have also seen the Sun fall near the Ace of Wands or the Four of Cups to indicate a change of residence – and each time it has meant that the client was moving south or to a warmer climate. Remember, the Sun is warmth. Since it also represents happiness, invariably those moves where it is involved will be happy ones.

But what about the Sun inverted? Well, you might think of a light going out. Remember that the upright and inverted meanings are always both inherently contained in any card. So the Sun upright is like a beacon, a bright light shining outward, uplifting to any who move into its aura. Inverted, it's like the light just went out, leaving darkness, debilitation, and emptiness.

Inverted, the Sun shows your client's lack of energy and vitality. He may be subject to many illnesses (especially if Temperance and some Wands are nearby) and/or have poor recuperative abilities. When the Sun is inverted in a reading it means that the person it refers to in the reading is separated from his goals, from himself personally, and from his Higher Self.

Inverted near work cards like the Three of Pentacles or Ace of Pentacles it would mean that your clients are leaving the present job for a new one. Emotionally it feels like they are divorcing the company they worked for. Inverted in position 8, or the home position, would mean that they or someone closely connected to them is divorcing a marriage partner. Inverted, the Sun is divorce and separation; just remember, divorces aren't always marital ones. Your client could be the child moving out of his parent's home for the first time, or the person leaving a home he has lived in for many years, or even two friends going their separate ways. The key is that no matter what is being divorced, the client feels the keen sense of loss and emptiness that accompanies any permanent loss. He knows he can't go back. The light of that particular period or area of his life has gone out.

It's important as you council clients who are experiencing an inverted Sun in their readings that you point out to them the areas in their lives where the Sun still shines, so that they relearn to focus on the positives as opposed to the negatives in their lives. If they continue in dwelling on the negatives, eventually a true spiritual emptiness will take up residence in their hearts.

__Special Note__: Inverted, the Sun will never represent a birth of any kind. Since its primary meaning when inverted is separation, a reunion or marriage planned when it's inverted will not take place or will not last. The life or spiritual path started on will not be continued. There is a certain sadness inherent in the inverted Sun, as in a special opportunity lost, or the sun disappearing behind clouds on a sunny day. We don't quite know what we've lost, yet we feel something special has been taken away. We feel less than whole.

Personal Notes

_____

_____

_____

_____

_____

_____

_____

_____

_____

_____

_____

_____

_____

_____

_____

XX – Judgement

JUDGEMENT.

Simplified Meanings:

Upright – Death and rebirth onto a higher plane; Divorce from something or someone you no longer need; Freedom; A legal judgment; A judgment you need to make. Seeing clearly by means of the intuition.

Inverted – Your rebirth or divorce or a death has already occurred, or you have decided to stay where you are, as you are. Judgment has been passed.

Number – The number 20 is really a 2 (2+0 = 2). But this time the 2, meaning duality, is raised to a higher level. It is only by working together, and by seeing that all truths are one truth, that we can ultimately attain wholeness. In the I Ching it is regarded as "Contemplating."

In-Depth Meanings:

A long time ago, I had 'dreams' about the Tarot cards in which I received instruction. Those of you reading this who have tried sleeping with a card under your pillow, or even the whole deck, may have had similar experiences. I consider them to be real, and feel the information dispensed in such dreams is often invaluable. In one of these dreams I was given to understand that the last two cards of the Major Arcana, Judgement and the World, were not part of the original theme of the Tarot, but were added on later, probably sometime during the middle ages. They may have replaced two cards that had been lost, or simply been added, I do not know which. However, one thing is clear – Judgement breaks with the flowing evolutionary path outlined by the previous cards. Its many meanings still work well in readings, though, so do continue to use it, as most other readers do.

On the face of it, this card depicts a picture of 'judgment day,' as shown by all of the people in the card rising up from their coffins, having been called by the Archangel Gabriel, who according to the Christian Bible guards the gates of heaven. Note also that the coffins float on the waters of the unconscious, which reminds us of the water in the Moon, that the crayfish was crawling out of, or awakening from. The judgment day depicted in the card is a day of reckoning, a day mentioned in the Hebrew and Christian Bible, and thrown up by ministers for centuries to induce fear in parishioners. It is the day, supposedly, when all souls, from the very beginning of time, must rise up and be accountable to God for their sins. The artistic rendering of the card clearly is a result of the Christian epoch and does not date back to the early rendering of the preceding cards. But in spite of the fact that this card has been 'Christianized,' it still gives valuable insight in readings, especially regarding the issues of accountability and awareness.

The very image of someone rising up from a coffin floating on the sea of the unconscious tells us that as long as we move through life unaware of a higher purpose we are essentially dead. We truly only begin to live when we become aware.

Judgement is likely to turn up in any reading in which a client is waking up to reality, and recognizing that it is time to move on to new pastures, that the old one is now empty. Essentially, Judgement could turn up in any situation where you might see an inverted Sun, but when Judgement appears the emotional feeling is entirely different. Separations shown by the inverted Sun are accompanied by feelings of loss and despair, whereas separations shown by Judgement are accompanied by feelings of joy and freedom. You don't look back at what you no longer need. You are leaving the past behind because it is dead – you no longer want it.

Occasionally, Judgement may come up when someone dies physically. When it does, there is a feeling of the soul being released from a body, or a life, that had become a prison. There is joy and freedom expressed in this card when such a death occurs. Remember, this card alone will not mean a physical death, but if it turns up near Death, the Tower, or the Ten of Swords, there is a good chance it does. I once saw it turn up next to the Chariot, representing a funeral procession.

And yet, next to the Chariot, near the Hierophant as well, it means a legal judgment of some kind is being decided. Needless to say, this is a common card to turn up when issues surrounding a Will are in a client's life. But even here, like the Death card, Judgement only occurs in a reading when a change of consciousness is in process. So, for example, if a judgment is being awaited concerning the Will of a relative, it is likely that by the time the Will is resolved, the client will no longer feel the same way about the resolution, or about the other people involved, or even about the person who has died.

Judgement changes our consciousness by showing us the reality of our lives and making us face it. If we choose to live in a dead world, it is by our choice we do so. Judgement forces us to see the reality of and to be accountable for it, but making any changes is up to us. In this way, Judgement is a lot like the planet Neptune, which I associate with this card, along with the sign Pisces.

The judgment day depicted in this card also indicates that we will all be judged at the same time – this is somewhat in line with Jane Roberts' *Seth* material, which tells us that souls travel in groups and that they help each other to grow and evolve, and move on, together, to succeeding levels of awareness.

Whatever your own belief system is, understand that this card tells us that wherever we are going, and however we are growing, we cannot do it alone. We must help others along the way, and in turn, accept help as well.

Gabriel blowing the horn in this card may be looked at as the wake-up call your Higher Self gives you when it's time to make some necessary changes in your life.

When Judgement is inverted in a reading I do not read it any differently. It may mean that the death, rebirth, separation, divorce, etc., is already in the past. Or it may mean that some event occurred that caused your client to look more closely at his or her life, to face the reality of it, but chose, for his or her own reasons, to make no changes. In such an instance I would also expect to see an inverted Fool somewhere in the reading.

__Special Note__: In a spread this card may be read much like an inverted Sun, only with positive connotations, or like Justice, inasmuch as it pertains to legal issues and situations. If it's inverted, and you're reading it as a legal card, there may be delays and obstacles, or a judgment the client will not like.

Personal Notes

_____

_____

_____

_____

_____

_____

_____

_____

_____

XXI – The World

THE WORLD.

Simplified Meanings:

Upright – Freedom; Growing beyond restraints; A long-distance trip or move; All options are available; "The world is your oyster."

Inverted – Staying where you are; A trip or move delayed or completed.

Number – The number 21 is really a 3 (2+1 = 3), but again, this 3 is on a still higher level than the 2 previous ones (3 and 12, the Empress and the Hanged Man). Here, the 1 of unity and spirit combines with the 2 of duality to expand the self, or the couple, or the group, beyond its individual capabilities or limitations. In the I Ching it is regarded as "Reform."

In-Depth Meanings:

The World is a fitting last card for the Major Arcana. It is through this card that we grow beyond all of our earthly limitations to true attainment. In layman's terms, when the World appears upright in a reading, it always has the positive connotation of the realization of one's dreams. In essence, this card says an entire world of possibilities lies at your feet, and any dream may come true.

I often see this card appearing in the readings of young people who have just completed their education and look forward now to a rewarding career in the field of their choice. In these readings the World usually falls near the Ace, Three or Six of Pentacles. Or it may turn up in the reading of a youth going off to college. Then I expect to see it near the Hermit or the Hierophant, or perhaps even the Three of Pentacles.

The World does, of course, insinuate that your client is moving on, leaving behind an area of life that he (or she) has grown beyond. With the Ace or Four of Wands he is moving into a new home, perhaps a home in a far away place. Or perhaps the World is showing us that he is moving from a small apartment to a first true home of his own. The World always shows expansion – a leap to something larger, greater, or farther away. The World with the Ace of Pentacles may mean your client is stepping upward into a position at work that gives greater freedom, money, and possibility for growth. Or, it may mean he is leaving a job to start a self-owned business.

When the World appears in a reading its very presence insinuates that the client has grown beyond the present situation, and that a major change, involving some form of expansion, is imminent.

When the World appears in a reading with other travel cards, such as the Chariot, the Eight of Wands, or the Six of Swords, you can be sure that your client is planning a trip. In this case, The World tells you that the trip is a major one – it could be to another state or country, or it could have a major impact on the life of your client, or both. The mode of travel will be shown by the card it appears near (i.e., the Eight of Wands means airplane, the Chariot means car or bus or other road vehicle, while the Six of Swords means boat or ship).

When both travel cards and residence cards like the Four of Wands and the Ace of Wands appear in the spread, you know that you have a change of residence that will either be to a far away place, or result in major changes and growth for your client.

Remember also, that the World always carries with it the feeling of freedom. The changes, trips, moves, and so on that your client experiences when The World appears are accompanied by a feeling of freedom and often even exhilaration, as the old drops away and new growth and opportunity becomes available.

When inverted, the World may mean that your client had the opportunity to move on, but chose not to. Check the surrounding cards to see if this is the case. Usually most of them will be inverted, and there will be a general feeling of loss or depression to the reading.

Sometimes when inverted the World means that the trip, move, or whatever it brought is in the past. This is often the case when it occurs in position 1 or 2 in the spread, or in the position of the immediate past (6), foundation (5) or home (8) position.

And then again, the inverted World may mean that your client's travel or move plans will be delayed or changed. If you see other travel cards in the reading, this may indeed be the case.

Special Note: *This card cannot truly be associated with any one sign, unless it be Sagittarius, the sign usually associated with travel. The four fixed signs of the zodiac, Taurus, Leo, Scorpio, and Aquarius are shown in each corner of the card, probably because they represent the four fixed magnetic points and esoterically are responsible for maintaining the structure of the physical plane we live on which, of course, is the world.*

Personal Notes

_____

_____

_____

_____

_____

_____

_____

_____

_____

_____

You've now learned all of the Major Arcana cards, and all of the Court cards of the Minor Arcana. Armed with this knowledge, there is no reason that you can't do a complete Tarot reading for anyone. Remember, the Major Arcana cover all of the possibilities contained in life's journey. The Court cards are the people in your clients' lives. When, in the next several chapters, you learn the meanings of the Minor Arcana cards, you will only be filling in the 'nitty gritty' events and circumstances of your clients' lives. The Major Arcana cover all of the major life issues and circumstances that will affect them. Keep practicing with only the cards you've learned so far, until you don't have to look up the meanings any more. Then move on to the next chapter to begin learning about the Minor Arcana.

End of Chapter Exercise

Let's do another sample reading to get you started, this time using all of the Majors and all of the Court cards in the complex Celtic Cross that we learned in the last chapter.

Our sample reading is for an 83-year-old gentleman. Here's what the spread looks like. Go ahead and read it on your own (no guiding questions from me this time – if you need them, refer back to the exercise at the end of the last chapter, and the lines of force that help you to tie the cards into one another). When you're done, read on to see what I had to say about it.

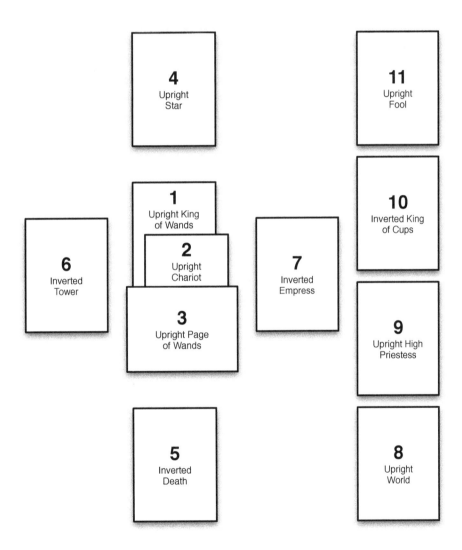

Figure 6: A Sample Reading from a Client Using a Complex Celtic Cross Spread

Well, let's see how your rendition compares with mine, and with what's actually going on in this client's life:

1. I first interpreted the King of Wands to be my client. He is actually an Aquarian, but since the King of Wands had turned up as the indicator card, apparently he is feeling fiery, physical, idealistic and is anticipating changes in his life. Since he's upright, my client is healthy and probably in good spirits. This King of Wands probably also represents one or more other men he is thinking about. It may be that the man on his mind is also physically active and may be involved in some of the changing events he is anticipating. Let's see.

2. The Chariot in the situation position (2) is interesting because it tells me that my client has something going on with his car (buying one, selling one, fixing one, I don't have enough information at this point to be more specific), or that he's taking a trip by car, bus or train (I doubt we'll find him on a bicycle at 83). Maybe he's doing both! It also says, since it's upright, that he's feeling in charge and capable at this time in his life, especially relative to the situation he's in.

3. The Page of Wands comes up in the next three months position (3). It indicates, first, that good news relative to a change he wants to make is coming. The news may be pertinent to his beliefs and ideals, or to a project or physical action he wants to undertake. Secondly, this Page is the one who (upright) acts like an adjective to tell you that you can trust the people, especially men, that he falls near – so the King of Wands that appears in the spread is someone whom he can, and probably does, trust. Lastly, the Page of Wands may represent a young child, possibly a grandchild (in view of his age, maybe even a great grandchild) that he may have close involvement with in the near future.

4. The Star in the distant future (4) is really nice to see because it allows me to tell him that the action he's taking now (King of Wands and Page of Wands in positions 1 and 3) will result in material wealth and happiness. If he does indeed sell his car, he'll be well rewarded. If he buys a car, it's a good car. If he travels, he'll enjoy his trip. You get the idea. The Star here also tells me that by and large, between one and three years from now he's in for a wonderful life.

5. The inverted Death card in the foundation position (5) talks about a change of consciousness that he's undergone. As a matter of fact, it's that change that has given rise to the events in this reading. After all, it's the foundation card. He may have experienced a loss, or the death of something. If I look toward the other cards from the past I may get some idea of what 'died.' The Empress is inverted in position 7, the immediate past. Perhaps an important woman that he related to in a mother sense either died, or left, or else he changed how he felt about her. Also, if I look at the World in position 8, the home, inverted Death relative to this card may indicate that he no longer feels the same way about his home and family as he did in the past.

6. The inverted Tower in the next six months position (6) shows that the turmoil and change that he's probably going through right now will be just about completed

by the time six months has gone by. He will be free, but he also will have given up a great deal to obtain that freedom.

7. The inverted Empress in the immediate past (7) shows us a woman he relates to in a motherly fashion (at his age it's unlikely to be his mother) who either has not been feeling well, or whom he has been having trouble with during the last six months. Also, since she's inverted in the past, it's possible that she is no longer in his life. Relating her to the three central cards and the immediate future (position 6) shows that she may in some way be responsible for much of the transition he's going through.

8. The World in the home position (8) is interesting. This is probably the one position where you could read it as a likely major change of residence, without even looking at any other cards. But since the Chariot also appears in the spread, it's likely he's changing his residence to somewhere he may visit first, and within driving distance. The World also has a warm connotation of freedom and growth, so the move will benefit him.

9. The High Priestess showing in the next 10 days (9) says there may be some hidden things he will have to be dealing with during that time. She can also be a person, so he may have a secretive yet supportive woman giving him advice or help (she's upright) during the next 10 days. She's often the ideal woman in a man's reading, so she might even be a special lady he's about to meet. Since she also falls in alignment with the central three cards and the next six months position, she, or something arising out of his involvement with her, will have a bearing on how he handles his trip (the Chariot), his various changes (the Tower), and the man he's going to trust (the King of Wands and the Page of Wands). She will even have some affect on his move or home expansion, since her card position follows the home position.

10. His concerns (10) seem to involve his own happiness (the first way to read any King would be as him), and how his dealings with a man the cards show as a King of Cups will proceed. Apparently, since the King is inverted, he's either worried about the man or afraid he will cause some kind of difficulty. It's possible this King and the King in position 1 are the same. But whether they are the same or different, the upright Page of Wands says to go ahead and trust them. The situation he's concerned about shows in the three central cards and the immediate future. It's even possible that the inverted King of Cups is another man who's talking against the upright King of Wands. It may be difficult, in this case, for him to know who to believe because the upright Page says both are honest.

11. The outcome of the present situation (11) shows the Fool. He has a choice to make. He will probably make a choice that he'll be happy with, and this will occur within a year from now or around the turn of the year because of the card's position in the spread. He will be protected during his transition, which we know

he will make because the Fool says he's stepping forward into the unknown. We also know he'll be happy since the Star, in the distant future, arises out of the Fool.

Of course, in an actual reading with clients sitting in front of you, you will be able to go into much greater detail, both because they'll be asking questions and because you're also able to read them in addition to your cards. As you gain experience this will happen more and more often. Let's look at how your own reading, and my abbreviated one above, compare with what's actually going on in this elderly gentleman's life.

Mr. X lost his wife some three years ago, hence the Death card, inverted, in the foundation. He related to his wife like a mother – she took care of all the bills, and him. It's taken him nearly three years to get over her loss, hence the inverted Empress in the immediate past. He's finally letting her go! His stepson (the King of Wands) wants him to move out of his house, which he can no longer care for, and into an assisted living condominium. The stepson, we see, has his best interest in mind and can be trusted. His stepson-in-law, shown as the inverted King of Cups, is upset that he's moving because he and his wife (Mr. X's step-daughter) have been taking care of him while he's nearby. The step-daughter (shown again as the care-taking mother) is upset that she will no longer be able to help him. Mr. X is concerned that she and her husband will stay angry with him if he moves. The Page of Wands is also Mr. X's grand-nephew who lives in another state and has offered space for him to come and live. (Note, the Page follows the Chariot.) Mr. X wants to move, but he's not sure whether to move where the stepson says, in with the grand-nephew or to stay where he is to keep the step-daughter and her husband happy. Incidentally, he has just sold his car to his step-daughter. The reading shows that he will get some news within the next three months that will help him to make his decision, and that he will move. Judging from the fact that we see the High Priestess, an unknown woman and the Fool, a step into the new in this reading, I believe he will decide to move into the assisted living condominium and be very happy there. He may even meet a new lady friend, but it's still hard to tell – remember, he hasn't made his choice yet.

Chapter 6

The Minor Arcana

The Minor Arcana cards comprise the four suits of the Tarot, which have evolved into our modern day playing cards (minus the four Pages). The playing card suit of clubs corresponds to the Tarot Wands, the hearts to the Cups, the diamonds to the Pentacles, and the spades to the Swords. The similarity of appearance makes it easy to remember these correspondences. When I teach my students the Minor Arcana cards I always emphasize that it's important to remember each card by number and suit because by doing so you can easily transfer your knowledge to reading the playing cards and to reading any other standard 78 card Tarot deck. This is important because although most Tarot decks have Major Arcanas with similar illustrations, the Minor Arcana pictures can differ radically from deck to deck, with some decks having no illustrations at all, just a number. Remembering the meanings by number and suit therefore gives you a good starting point when you're trying to learn a new deck. For beginners learning from this book, I recommend that you begin reading with the Rider-Waite deck or one of its close clones, as those Minor Arcana illustrations will correspond most closely to the meanings I use (Rider-Waite, Albano-Waite, Morgan Greer, Aquarian, Hanson-Roberts, Sacred Rose, Connolly, Robin Wood, Cosmic Tarot, etc.). Once you have been reading the Tarot for awhile the cards will begin to talk to you, offering you new meanings of your own. Be open to them. They are what will give you a unique reading style. If you choose at some point to learn a new deck whose illustrations differ radically from the Rider-Waite, the meanings you've learned here will give you a base to build on, while the new deck's illustrations will suggest still new meanings to add to your repertoire. Do not be afraid to use them. Remember, though, try to stick to decks based on research into universal symbolism as opposed to an artist's intuitive design. The former ties your consciousness into the universal mind, the latter into the artist. Which would you rather have aiding your psychic reading?

In Chapter 1 you learned the meanings of the four suits, and even learned to do broad readings based solely on the interaction of the suit energies. Before continuing with this chapter it would be a good idea to go back and review the ways in which each suit manifests, as I will not be reviewing that material here. You also may wish to review Chapter 2, *The Court Cards*, because even though they are a part of the Minor Arcana, we will not be reviewing them again.

Remember as you read through the following chapter, that each of the cards reviewed represents only one quarter of the total energy of that number. It is for this reason that the Minor Arcana cards usually show us the minor issues in life, or the details of a situation, as opposed to the Major Arcana's broad, sweeping look at life and its major issues.

For example, the four Aces, each a number I, correspond to the Magician, also a number I. But the Magician represents the unity of the four elements working together in the card, whereas the Aces each manifest only one of those elements. So the Ace of Wands represents the fiery, action oriented aspect of the Magician, the Ace of Cups the watery, emotional, and enthusiastic aspect, the Ace of Pentacles the earthy, productive, and materialistic aspect, and the Ace of Swords the airy, mental, communicative, and thoughtful aspect. It is the same with all of the Minor Arcana cards. Because of this, in presenting them to you I will cover the cards 1 through 10, in order, dealing with each of the four suits of a single number before moving on to the next. In doing this, I hope to present a whole picture of each. If you would like to separate out your cards in the order in which we'll be doing them, we'll cover Wands first, then Cups, then Pentacles, and lastly Swords, of each number in turn.

The Aces

All of the Aces represent new beginnings in the life of your client. This is the case whether the Ace appears upright or inverted. Many readers believe that an inverted Ace means the new beginning will not happen. As far as I'm concerned, it only means the new beginning will manifest slowly, or will not have quite the impact or fullness of the upright Ace. Likewise, some readers believe that inverted Aces are bad, possibly because they are focusing on what must be left behind in order to begin something new. I feel that all new beginnings are good, since they represent growth and evolution – therefore, to me, Aces are always a positive influence in a reading.

The Ace of Wands

Simplified Meanings:

Upright – A new beginning physically; a new home, or change in an existing one; a new romance; a new baby; artistic and creative abilities; high energy; a new way of using your energies and abilities.

Inverted – Same as the above, but whatever is beginning will come slowly.

In-Depth Meanings:

The Ace of Wands is the most purely generative and creative of the Aces. It is action oriented and forceful. Usually when it appears upright, things are happening, and quickly, in your client's life. Upright, the client is usually following his (or her) dreams, desires, and ideals, which are leading him to make big changes and take major steps forward in life. Inverted, its meanings are essentially the same, but the client is overcoming either internal or external resistance, so the changes happen more slowly.

Often those changes reflect a new way of looking at or interacting with home or family. Since this Ace is so physically oriented, it can literally mean buying a home if it falls near some Pentacles (especially the Six of Pentacles), or getting a mortgage for a home if it falls near the Devil (the card that represents contracts). It may mean building a home if it falls near other Wands, or even making a long distance move if it falls near travel cards such as the World, the Chariot, the Eight of Wands, or the Six of Swords. Whatever the Ace of Wands is doing in the reading, you can be sure that it will bring changes of a physical nature into your client's life.

I've even seen this Ace, on occasion falling near the Three of Pentacles (the club, group, team, school, or career card) and other Wands to indicate joining an athletic team. On the other hand, if instead of other Wands nearby, you find an Ace of Swords or Ace of Pentacles, you would see your client going to school for art (with the Ace of Swords) or getting a new job in an artistic field (with the Ace of Pentacles). Get it?

Three out of the four Aces in the deck can also mean the birth of a real child, not just a child of your dreams, and this is one of them. But this Ace doesn't tell you the sex of the child. It does tell you that if it's a boy, he will be artistic and sensitive, in addition to his more boyish qualities. This Ace softens him. If it's a girl though, she will be a tomboy. The Ace of Wands toughens her.

It's true that whenever you see an Ace something is being born, but that something is not always a physical child. You'll know it's a real child if you also see the Empress, the Sun, or maybe a Page and either the Ace of Cups or the Ace of Swords in the same spread of cards.

The Ace of Wands also has a great deal to do with sex and romance. If your client is already in a romance and you see the Ace of Wands, it is likely that it is already or will soon be sexual in nature. If the Ace is inverted, the two people are likely very attracted to each other, but nothing has happened yet. If the Ace of Wands is upright in a future position, it's possible the romance hasn't yet begun, or that it will become sexual in the future. Inverted in the same position, may mean it will never become sexual. Know that this Ace represents romance when you see the person of your client's opposite sex in the reading near this Ace, surrounded by Cups.

The Ace of Wands also figures prominently in issues where there is sexual disfunction. If you see this Ace inverted next to an inverted King in the reading, his masculinity is in some way threatened. It may be merely that his creativity is being blocked, or that he has suffered some physical disability (for that, look to see if Temperance is also present). More often, though, this indicates he has no avenue for sexual release. This could occur for many reasons; perhaps he's not in a relationship; perhaps his wife or girlfriend is unavailable for some reason; perhaps he has some physical or emotional problem that blocks his sexual function. Try to find out from the surrounding cards what the problem may be, so that you may advise him. Do remember to treat this subject subtly!

Special Note: *In the Rider-Waite version of this card, a castle appears in the background, surrounded by lots of open land. I often find that if I am drawn to this image during a reading it means that my client is moving to a place in the country.*

Personal Notes

_____

_____

_____

_____

The Ace of Cups

Simplified Meanings:

Upright – The birth of love; something new relative to family or friends that brings joy; a baby girl; an opportunity to be happy; happiness.

Inverted – All of the same meanings as above, but slower to reach fulfillment. joy and happiness are not as complete; the baby girl is not yet conceived.

In-Depth Meanings:

The Ace of Cups is truly one of the most beautiful cards in the deck, in that its presence in your client's reading foretells great happiness and fulfillment in his (or her) life, especially when it is upright. This is the Ace that denotes a positive new beginning in all things having to do with the emotions.

This Ace will appear any time your client is making a change in his life which he is looking forward to, or hopeful about. You will see this Ace in readings where a new love has entered your client's life, when it will probably turn up near the person who is the love interest. You will see it in readings where your client buys a house or other major thing that he has wanted badly and will center much of his life around. In this case you will see it near some Pentacles, and perhaps the Ace of Wands or the Four of Wands if it's a home being bought, or near the Chariot if it's a car, and so on. Your client might even be getting a pet – the Ace of Cups near the Queen of Wands or Strength could be a cat, near the Fool a dog, near the Queen of Pentacles a rabbit, or near the Nine of Pentacles a bird, if you're using the Rider-Waite deck where these creatures appear in the cards noted.

This card always means an emotional birth of some kind is occurring. And sometimes that birth can be an actual child. But remember before announcing to your client that she is about to give birth, look for some obvious things – is she 60 years old, for instance? If she is, there could still be a birth somewhere around her – but it's not likely to be her who is the mother. If a baby is being born and this card turns up, it will be a girl. Look for the Empress, the Fool, a Page, and perhaps another Ace to be present before you tell your client she's pregnant, unless you have a strong feeling about it that compensates for the lack of back-up cards. When the Sun turns up with the Ace of

Cups, the Sun, being a Major Arcana card will take precedence, and the child will be a boy – but, with the softness and joy that the Ace of Cups brings. Inverted, the Ace of Cups usually means that the child has not yet been conceived, but soon will be.

When this Ace is inverted it can also mean that the client has suffered some kind of a loss or deep hurt in the past, and even though all of the best new beginnings are available, he is having trouble opening up and trusting to move into that happy new future. He is doing so, slowly, but does not quite achieve the depth of joy and fulfillment that he would if he could fully let go and trust again. An emotional healing is going on, slowly, but surely.

__Special Note__: The water that streams out of the cup in the Rider-Waite version of the card fills the ocean beneath, on which lilies bloom. In turn, life-force flows back into the cup from the ocean. This symbolism shows the fullness of joy and happiness this card brings – so much in fact, that it overflows to everyone and everything around it, and is replenished by happiness being reflected back. This is truly the cup that is never empty, and is a particularly good symbol for meditation. The dove holding the cross above the cup to me shows that when this balance of joy with the world is attained the God or Higher Self consciousness of the individual is able to be heard.

Personal Notes

_____

_____

_____

_____

_____

_____

_____

_____

The Ace of Pentacles

Simplified Meanings:

Upright – New beginnings spiritually or materially; a new job; a new career or business; an offer or idea involving money, business, or material goods; self-employment; school aimed towards an affluent career; the journey into the afterlife begins.

Inverted – All of the above meanings remain the same, but their realization is slower. There may be things that must be taken care of before the new beginning can occur.

In-Depth Meanings:

The Ace of Pentacles, like all of the Aces, heralds new beginnings. In its case, the new beginnings it talks about are either beginnings in mundane and material matters like money and business, or beginnings in the realm of spirit. This Ace is the only one of the aces that does not concern itself with childbirth.

Usually when you see this Ace the mundane and material meanings will be the ones you'll use. Financial, job related, or material issues begun under the Ace of Pentacles will usually be very successful. Interestingly, both the Ace of Pentacles and the Ace of Swords deal with employment and school issues – but the Ace of Pentacles looks at them from a 'what will make the most money' point of view, whereas the Ace of Swords takes the 'what will I learn the most from and enjoy the most' point of view.

The Ace of Pentacles near the Three of Pentacles in a reading means your client is beginning a new job in a new profession. Sine the Ace is singular by its nature, the new job may be self-employment, or at least working in a very independent atmosphere. Surrounded by other Pentacles, the Ace of Pentacles can mean your client is considering a new means of handling his (or her) finances. Near the Ace of Wands or Four of Wands he may be buying a home or real estate for an investment. With the Four of Pentacles he is saving money for something, or perhaps will be investing his money in a new business. Near the Ten of Pentacles it may mean money is coming from a family member. Since this ace sometimes also marks the transition from life into death, when it falls near the Ten of Pentacles it could also imply an inheritance, especially if you see other cards in the layout that indicate illness or loss.

In its spiritual mode the Ace of Pentacles may indeed signify death, when it occurs near other cards that support that meaning (Death, Judgement, Five of Cups, Ten of Swords, etc.) – but remember, if the Ace of Pentacles has appeared, even the death it shows is seen as a spiritual beginning for the person who is dying; this Ace is not a card of loss, it's a card of hope and beginnings, of growth and transcendence. If you see it in this context in a reading, make sure you pass that understanding on to your client – it will help him to understand and deal with his own loss better. When it's inverted, someone in the client's life may have already passed on, yet the same quality of that passing still applies.

The Ace of Pentacles also can mark the beginning of other spiritual pursuits. Certain indicator cards, such as the Hanged Man, the Fool, the Star, the Eight of Cups and the inverted Five of Pentacles, will tell you that your client is embarking upon a spiritual journey of some sort, as opposed to the typical outer directed materialistic new beginning this Ace usually implies. If any of these cards appear with it, assume your client's journey is at least partly spiritual. In this case, if it also falls near the Hermit, or the Hierophant, your client may be entering a religious or seminary college. Near the High Priestess or inverted Hierophant, they may be studying some more occult knowledge. Near the Three of Pentacles, they might be joining a group whose aim is the pursuit of spiritual goals.

But of course one man's (or woman's) spiritual pursuit is not another's. For some, the pursuit of independence through financial security is the spiritual goal. For others, it's the attainment of wealth, or status, or position. Don't be judgmental. Just look for the apparent goal or focus this Ace is leading your client toward, and if you see those spiritual indicator cards with it – that is his or her spiritual goal!

__Special Note__: If in your reading you find yourself focusing on the archway (Rider-Waite Deck) and the mountains behind, this Ace probably marks a spiritual beginning for your client, and they are definitely undergoing some form of transition, as passing through any gateway implies.

Personal Notes

_____

_____

_____

_____

The Ace of Swords

Simplified Meanings:

Upright – A new idea or plan; a new way of thinking; a new business involving communications; school or new educational pursuits; a new baby boy, mentally crossing to other planes; release of the spirit from matter.

Inverted – Same meanings as above, but slower to manifest.

In-Depth Meanings:

All of the Swords operate best in the realm of thought, ideas, and communication – and the Ace of Swords is foremost among these. When this card turns up in a reading new ideas and plans are afoot. Often you'll see the Ace of Swords in your client's reading when he (or she) has a new idea for a business, educational, or financial endeavor, and then see the Ace of Pentacles at a later date when the client begins to implement the idea. But if the business or educational pursuit is in the realm of communication, it is the sole province of the Ace of Swords. This Ace deals with all forms of communication – from the spoken word to computers, telephones, television, and even travel. And if it turns up as the indicator card in a reading, you can be sure your client is both involved with the communications field, and also very good at it. He will likely be beginning a new endeavor in that area as well.

This Ace also may represent the birth of a male child, if you see other 'pregnancy' cards in the spread (the Empress or the Sun plus a Page or the Fool). Additionally, since the Ace of Swords represents a new beginning or a change in one's thought patterns, the child that is coming, in this case, will probably have a major affect on the ideas and attitudes of at least one of his parents.

Often when you see the Ace of Swords in a spread it shows an idea or offer that has come, seemingly out of the blue, to your client. It will always represent a new beginning with great promise, whether upright or inverted. It's just that if inverted there may be more preparatory work involved, or the timing may be wrong for the idea right now, but in the future it could work. The Ace of Swords permits one to enter into higher realms of thought, to mentally cross barriers of time and space, to reach true inspiration. When inverted, it may be that it is time to manifest some of that inspiration.

Like the Ace of Pentacles, which this Ace so often subtly mirrors, the Ace of Swords often appears in a spread when someone is crossing over into death. You should only use this meaning if you clearly see other death cards in the spread – such as Death, Judgement, the Five of Cups, or the Ten of Cups. And even in these cases, this Ace represents an expansion of the mind beyond the gates of death – not a termination of life.

You may even see this card in readings where your client is having out-of-body experiences, and you should expect to see the Nine of Swords or the Four of Swords to be somewhere near it. People experiencing the Ace of Swords often embark upon spiritual pursuits, just as the people experiencing the Ace of Pentacles did. But those using the Ace of Swords pursue their spiritual quest mentally, by reading and studying, whereas for those using the Ace of Pentacles the experience is usually more direct. When the spiritual side of this card is active, you will see one of those spiritual indicator cards in the spread to point this out to you – either the Hanged Man, the Star, the Fool, the Eight of Cups, or the inverted Five of Pentacles.

__Special Note__: Like the Ace of Cups, the Ace of Swords has the fiery 'yods,' the stuff of the life force showing us the constant flow of energy into matter and back again. This is truly a card of birth, and as with the Ace of Cups, both male and female energies are shown, showing the capability of true creative power in this card.

Personal Notes

_____

_____

_____

_____

_____

_____

_____

The Twos

In the Major Arcana the number 2 is represented first as the High Priestess, and later as Justice (11 = 1+1 = 2). You'll recall that when these cards were discussed the number 2 was given to represent all polar opposites, and those forces that unify them, separate them, or balance them. Right and wrong, black and white, male and female, up and down, and so on — all are principles understood only through the presence of their opposites. In some religions it is said that when the universe began, "God separated from himself, in order to see and comprehend himself," and hence you have the far distant beginnings of our material world. And it is certainly true that you can never fully understand anything until you have experienced both it and its opposite — this continued swinging from pole to pole eventually brings understanding, balance, and harmony.

All of the twos represent this to some degree, each from the viewpoint of their own representative suit.

The Two of Wands

Simplified Meanings:

Upright – Long distance plans that will meet with success; organization and planning are needed to accomplish a goal; seeing things from an objective or higher viewpoint.

Inverted – Plans will be altered, or will not meet with success; poor planning; lack of objectivity.

In-Depth Meanings:

Eden Gray has defined this card as "the employment of the scientific method," which certainly gives some overall good insight into it. But when you look closely at the Rider-Waite version of the card, you are immediately struck by the central figure's contemplation of the globe in his hand, as well as his posture of looking out over hills, valleys and water that seem ready and waiting to be explored. The Two of Wands creates a forward-looking feeling of excitement and enthusiasm that might very well be present at the beginning of any project or journey. It's as if the new beginning initiated in the Ace of Wands is to be planned and carried out by the Two of Wands.

It is always at the beginning of any undertaking that we have the ability to see clearly the path before us, if we but take the time. It is also at this time that we may sometimes be overwhelmed by the sheer magnitude of what lies before us. But from our position of clarity, this card, when upright, assures us that our careful planning and organizing will result in the attainment of our objective. Conversely, if inverted, that objective will either fail, or perhaps our path to it will not be as we have planned – we may need greater flexibility in order to finally arrive at our scheduled destination.

When the Two of Wands falls near Pentacles, the plans will involve money and material things. Near the Ace of Pentacles, the Three of Pentacles, or the Eight of Pentacles they probably involve a new business or business dealings. Near travel cards such as the Chariot, Eight of Wands, or Six of Swords the plans would involve a trip. If to those you add either an Ace of Swords or Four of Swords, which refer to the home, the plans might surround a change in residence. The possibilities are limitless.

As an indicator or significator card (the first card down in your spread), this card would tell you that your client has an observant personality and a fine mind for details, as well as that he is laying plans for something. What that something is, the rest of the spread will tell you. If inverted, he may not be using that fine mind at the moment.

__Special Note__: In some readings when a trip or residence change is planned, if I find myself drawn to the water in this card, I know the client will be near or on water. If I'm drawn to the mountains, it will take him into a mountainous area. If I'm drawn to the valley, it will be to a valley at the foot of mountains. And if I'm drawn to the palisade the figure in the forefront stands on, I know he will be high up overlooking something, possibly in a tall building. This is what I mean by the cards talking to you!

Personal Notes

_____

_____

_____

_____

_____

_____

_____

_____

_____

_____

The Two of Cups

Simplified Meanings:

Upright – Your soul mate; a perfect relationship; a situation that fits you perfectly; perfect harmony and balance in a relationship

Inverted – A good relationship, but it's not your soul mate. A romance, sexual and strong, but not perfect.

In-Depth Meanings:

When I hear people call the Two of Cups the 'soul mate' card, I usually shrug and ask, "So what do you mean by that?" Unfortunately, we have yet to all agree on just what a "soul mate" is. Everyone reads this card as the soul mate card, but no two readers seem to have exactly the same meaning. And when this card turns up in your client's spread, and you happily announce, "You've met your soul mate!" your client may be hearing something very different than what you mean. Perhaps we'd better spend a few moments looking at this soul mate issue. To some readers, a soul mate is someone you've had a loving relationship with in a previous life. To other readers, it's someone you travel with on your soul's journey from life to life. To others still, it's someone that you can relate to perfectly, without tension or misunderstanding. And to some, it's the person you were born to meet and spend your life with. There really is no wrong definition of what a soul mate is, but I do feel we need to define to others just what we're referring to when we call someone a soul mate, since most of our definitions, though they contain similarities, differ.

For example, I do not feel that soul mates are necessarily born to spend their lives together. In my definition, soul mates have been together in so many lives that they've already played out every possible scenario of relating and literally have nothing left to learn from one another through the relating process. They understand each other too well. They've been mother and son, father and daughter, father and son, mother and daughter, brothers, sisters, best friends; they've been lovers, they've been enemies, they've murdered each other, fought together as comrades, taught each other, married and raised children together. Many times. So why do they come together in this life if they've nothing to learn from each other?

The answer to that is both simple and complex. The emotional tie forged between soul mates over centuries is a strong psychic connection. They cannot come into one another's space without feeling the recognition and the pull, even if they are both married to other people. Sometimes this pull can create real problems in the lives of everyone concerned. But more often, your soul mate comes into your life specifically to exert that pull because there is something in your life you are not doing that you should be. It's as if your soul cries out, and wherever your soul mates (you can have more than one) are on the planet, they must hear and respond. I have seen so many cases where soul mates specifically enter each other's lives to be catalysts to change that it's almost a foregone conclusion to me that the Two of Cups not only brings a soul mate into your life, but catalyzes a change in your life, and theirs, at the same time. Once the change is completed, there is no need for them to stay. In fact, usually if the relationship does continue the partners need to find many interests outside of each other in order to continue to grow. It's hard to grow when the relationship presents no challenge.

In some cases, you may see the Two of Cups reverse in clients' readings, when they stop relating to their soul mates at the soul level where there is perfect unity of body, mind, and spirit, so that they can drop into the personality level and continue to relate on that lower level, where mutual personality 'problems' may be worked through. Either way, though, inverted or upright, the Two of Cups is a nice card to find in a reading.

Most often, when inverted, it describes a relationship with someone your client has known in other lives, but is not yet a soul mate. There will still be strong attraction, sexual as well as emotional. There is potential for the two people involved to develop a soul mate quality relationship in this life.

The Two of Cups is not an indicator of longevity in a relationship, just quality. Most often it shows up between people of different sexes, since sexual attraction is a part of the card, but you may often find it in gay or lesbian relationships – and sometimes it may be the reason why an otherwise straight person finds himself drawn to a member of his own sex. Of course, the Two of Cups doesn't say if he is doing anything about the attraction – only that it's there.

*Special Note: The Two of Cups usually deals with relationships, but it's not unusual for it to appear in a reading where your client is entering a job or life situation that he (or she) is perfectly suited to. It's as if the client was born to do or be that person the job or situation will require him to be. In this case, you'll usually see a lot of Swords or Pentacles surrounding the Two of Cups.

Personal Notes

The Two of Pentacles

Simplified Meanings:

Upright – Juggling two or more people or things at the same time.

Inverted – Unable to deal with all of the things you must; being spread to thin.

In-Depth Meanings:

The Two of Pentacles in the Rider-Waite Tarot pack shows a person with a slightly worried expression on his face juggling two pentacles wrapped by an infinity sign. Ships are riding waves and swells in the background. Remembering this card is easy because its meaning exactly reflects the picture.

When the Two of Pentacles appears upright in a reading your client (or the Court card that appears closest to it) is attempting to balance two or more different things in which he (or she) is engaged. Think of this card as the Juggler.

You don't know from this card alone what those things being juggled are; surrounding cards will tell you. It could be two relationships (you'll see the two Court cards nearby); or two jobs (it'll be surrounded by Pentacles, the Ace of Pentacles, Three of Pentacles, or Seven of Pentacles); or maybe even two families (look for the Ten of Cups or Ten of Pentacles in the same spread).

As long as the Two of Pentacles is upright your client is successfully doing a balancing act. The worried expression of the figure on the card says he may be a bit stressed out by the situation, and the waves in the background indicate that there will be ups and downs in handling it, but the infinity sign surrounding all shows that it could go on almost indefinitely. As the figure on the card shifts his balance from foot to foot you can imagine your client constantly shifting his emotional balance to continue dealing with constantly changing situations.

When the Two of Pentacles appears inverted in your reading your client is no longer capable of dealing with the multiple issues in his life. The water is now on top of the card, showing his emotional inadequacy to meet the situation. In fact, the longer the client continues to try to handle everything, the more likely it is that he will make a mess of it. Your advice in this situation, should the card appear in the present, should be for your client to see what it is in life that he can eliminate – the client is simply spreading himself too thin. If the Two of Pentacles appears inverted in a future position, you can warn the client that the present juggling of affairs will soon have to stop.

*__Special Note__: When the Two of Pentacles turns up near the Seven of Swords, you can be sure that the thing that's causing the juggling is being hidden. Is it another woman, or another man? Look at the surrounding cards to find out.

Personal Notes

_____

_____

_____

_____

_____

_____

_____

_____

_____

_____

_____

The Two of Swords

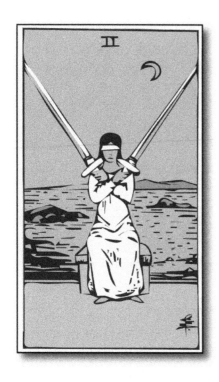

Simplified Meanings:

Upright – Sitting on the fence; trying to make a choice; over-thinking; stalemate; blind to the emotions.

Inverted – Decision made; following the intuition; getting off the fence; in touch with emotions.

In-Depth Meanings:

When the Two of Swords appears upright in a reading it means that the client or person represented by the nearest Court card needs to make a decision about something. Surrounding cards should tell you what the issue is; the Two of Swords only refers to the process of choice.

So long as it is upright there is an attempt to make the decision solely based upon the mental processes. The person is researching his (or her) options, talking to as many knowledgeable people as possible, asking others about their opinions, and spending inordinate amounts of time mentally processing all of this information. When done processing each bit of information, the person still feels unable to make the choice and go out to seek more information, which he will again put through an agonizing thinking and weighing process. The result is that the person is stalemated, unable to get off the fence that his own mental approach to the problem has put him on. All of us have been in this position at some time in our lives, and we know how uncomfortable, and sometimes even painful, sitting on that fence can be.

The truth is, that even though data and information are imperative to properly making any decision, the actual decision has to come from gut level, from the intuitive side of the self that alone is capable of assimilating and weighing all of the accumulated information. This can only happen when we push the brain out of the way, when we get in touch with our emotions. As long as the Two of Swords is upright this cannot happen. The figure on the card is blindfolded, meaning the person looks only inward at the information he is processing.

When the Two of Swords appears inverted in a reading, it tells you that your client, or the person represented by the Court card nearest to it, has made his decision. This does not mean the decision was right; it only means that the deliberation process is at an end. It also doesn't mean that the person has acted on the choice yet. Other cards in the spread will have to tell you that. But you know that a choice was made, the person this card refers to has gotten off of that fence; he has made the connection to his emotional and intuitive self in order to do so, attention is again directed outward, toward action.

*__Special Note__: Since the Rider-Waite deck pictures a woman on this card, many readers will feel the decision maker is female. This is not always true; it's the process of decision that involves the feminine principle, the intuition, that this card is representing. *When the Two of Swords falls near Temperance and Wands, it can signify eye trouble as a physiological problem.*

Personal Notes

_____

_____

_____

_____

_____

_____

_____

_____

_____

_____

The Threes

The four threes each represent some type of expansion or growth, each relative to their element. With only one exception, they are uplifting and happy cards, that reflect spiritual, as well as physical world, issues.

The number 3 is the number of expansion, of growth. It is the trinity in all things, that in itself is innately spiritual. The number 3 is literally the building blocks from the spirit world on which the material world is built. In a reading threes may bring expansion in the form of travel, education, social expression, planning, or emotional issues.

The Three of Wands

Simplified Meanings:

Upright – Waiting for plans already set in motion to manifest; distance (time or geographical) is involved with the issue; a good partnership.

Inverted – Disappointment; the plans will not manifest; beware of a bad partnership.

In-Depth Meanings:

The Three of Wands in the Rider-Waite Tarot shows a figure standing on a hilltop looking out to sea, where several ships sail. Land appears along the distant horizon. This is one of those Minor Arcana cards whose picture speaks for it. In one of her books, Eden Gray defines this card as "...waiting for your ship to come in." This definition is well suited as the primary meaning of the card, and certainly is easy to remember as well.

If you take a moment to look back at the Two of Wands, the card in which long distance plans were being laid, and then look at the Three of Wands again, you'll note that this card naturally picks up where the Two of Wands left off. In the Two of Wands the plans were laid, and in the Three of Wands your client is waiting for them to manifest. Whatever needed to be set in motion has been. The project has been launched. Now he waits to see what the results will be. Like the Two of Wands, this card implies long-term goals or physical distance.

As long as the Three of Wands is upright in the reading, the results of the endeavor, whatever it is, will be positive. But if it is inverted in the reading, either the results will not manifest at all, or they will not be what the client is wanting and expecting.

This is also the partnership card in the deck. The number 3 is comprised of 2 + 1, and when two (2) people come together to create a single entity (1), you have a true partnership. When the Three of Wands is surrounded by Cups in a reading, the partnership implied could be a marriage or two people living together in a sharing, partnership kind of way. Or if it is surrounded by Pentacles, it would imply a business partnership. When surrounded by Swords, the partnership is a meeting of minds, or perhaps is in the planning stages. Whatever the surrounding cards are, they will tell you the type of partnership, and the things the partnership will be engaged in. If it falls in position 1 or 2 (frame of mind or situation), it probably suggests that a partnership is being offered or considered. If it falls in a future position, a partnership will become available. But if it is inverted in the reading, either the partnership is undesirable, or for some reason your client will turn it down.

I have also seen this card in readings where my client was planning a cruise, next to a travel card. If a change of residence is evident in the spread, this card would imply that it is a long-distance move. Surrounded by Swords or other cards that emphasize communication, it could indicate a long-distance partnership with someone who is out of the area, with a lot of inter-communication. It's not uncommon to see this card in the readings of people who are involved in mail-order business, or whose business is inter-state and involves lots of contacts with people in other areas.

__Special Note__: In some cases, when a client has asked me to describe where he (or she) might move to, this card has turned up. I have replied alternately (and it seems with accuracy) that he might move to some place that is on high ground overlooking either a valley or an expanse of water, or that he might move to a desert or valley surrounded by mountains. Which to use? Well, what part of the card do you find yourself looking at? Remember to always go with your first feelings.

Personal Notes

_____

_____

_____

_____

_____

_____

_____

The Three of Cups

Simplified Meanings:

Upright – A party or celebration; a reunion of three friends; joy and happiness; over indulgence in food, drink or drugs.

Inverted – Hiding your unhappiness; a party you want to avoid; unhappy reunion; break up of a friendship; diet or abstinence.

In-Depth Meanings:

The upright Three of Cups is one of the happier cards in the deck. It generally signifies a celebration or reunion (or both) that the client is looking forward to, and that will be a very happy and joyous affair. Commonly it may be a wedding the client is attending, or a family celebration, or a school reunion and so on. Because of the full (upright) cups, you also know that the client will really be living it up and may even over-do it in the eating or drinking department. But he (or she) is sure to have fun, and to be glad he attended.

If, however, the Three of Cups is inverted, it means that your client either does not want to go, or will probably not have a very good time if he does go. You should pass that information on to your client, but he is probably already aware of this, or at the least is having misgivings. Inverted, it may also mean that your client has recently suffered an emotional loss of some sort and is going out to give the appearance that he is healed while still hurting inside. When the Three of Cups turns upright in readings with you again, you will know the client is feeling better for sure.

I also have often seen this card reflecting a friendship between three women. When upright, the friendship is happy and balanced, but when inverted, either there is trouble between the friends, or one member will cease to be a part of the group. Surrounding cards should supply this information.

The Three of Cups also is one of the cards you will often find appearing in the cards of someone dealing with addictive issues. When upright, the cups are full, so the addicted person is imbibing in food, drink, drugs, cigarettes, etc. When inverted, the cups are empty, so the person is on the wagon. Note that the Devil usually appears in spreads where an addiction is present, and that Temperance is also often present to represent both the health problems the addiction may be causing, as well as the control level the addicted person has over the addiction. Go back and read through the meanings of both Temperance and the Devil to get a clearer understanding of this.

__Special Note__: The Three of Cups is a harvest card. The fullness it brings is being reaped as a result of old efforts and friendships. It may also signify the fall of the year. Some Pagan sources see the Goddess in her three forms – maiden, matron, and crone – celebrating the joys of the full circle of life in this card.

Personal Notes

_____

_____

_____

_____

_____

_____

_____

_____

_____

_____

_____

_____

_____

The Three of Pentacles

Simplified Meanings:

Upright – Career change; career goals set; higher education; a group or club; a professional organization or group; the Mason; the artisan; the professional; a Christening; good medical or legal advice.

Inverted – Leaving a career; school ending; leaving a club or organization; bad artisan or tradesman; bad legal or medical council.

In-Depth Meanings:

For many of my students this is a difficult card to learn because of the many diversified meanings. And yet, studying the Rider-Waite version of the card, you can easily see how all of the meanings are derived. They're apparent in the card.

Firstly, this is the card of the master tradesman. The origin of this meaning was in medieval Europe describing the Masonic fraternity, a metaphysical yet main-stream organization originally composed of master tradesman and still very much active in today's world. From this root, the Three of Pentacles gains both its master tradesman meaning as well as its secret organization meaning. This card can describe any profession, so long as it is seen as a profession in which one can gain mastery of one's trade. It also may describe any organization, from a witch's coven to the local yacht club.

Usually if this card turns up relative to a job or field of employment your client is looking into, it signifies that this is an area that may be developed into a promising profession, with room for upward mobility. If inverted, however, it would mean the opposite, or that your client is actually leaving an old profession, or changing his (or her) mind about something he thought about doing. Likewise, if pertinent to a club or organization, upright it shows great promise both for the organization, as well as your client's position in it, while inverted it shows that the client will probably leave it because he is unhappy with it. Surrounding cards would tell you what type of organization it is – surrounded by Pentacles, it's probably a professional group, by Swords or Cups, a social group, and by Wands, a volunteer group. If the Seven of Swords is nearby it may even be a secret organization, and if the High Priestess or Magician is present, maybe a magical fraternity.

Relative to its professional meanings, the Three of Pentacles may also be the doctor whose professional group is treating you, or the lawyer whose law office is handling your case. Look for Temperance (medical) or Justice (legal) to be present to get a handle on which of these you're looking. Wands may also be present in either case. If the Three of Pentacles is upright, your client (or the person who is the subject of the problem as indicated by the nearest Court card) is getting good advice and service from the medical or legal professional. But if this card is inverted, you should recommend that he gets a second, or even a third, opinion. With the help of this card I have saved many clients over the years from some very potentially bad situations.

On a more pleasant note, the Three of Pentacles is also the card of higher education. It can describe anything from a vocational certification, to on-the-job professional training, to college. But upright, it always leads to mastery of one's chosen field, and is an excellent card to see in a reading. Inverted, it generally means that the education will be disrupted or maybe not completed at all. In fact, very often it means that your client will change his mind in mid-stream, and go into something else.

Last, but surely not least, this card will often appear when a baby is being Christened. This is probably because the picture on the Rider-Waite version is suggestive of a baby being held wrapped in blankets, and a Friar of the Church is present. Remember, often the cards can be very graphic. If the card is inverted, I do not apply this meaning at all. Usually if there will be a Christening, I see family cards such as the Ten of Cups or Ten of Pentacles, or at least the Ace of Cups, in the spread along with the Three of Pentacles.

__Special Note__: Many students have asked me which meaning they should use, when there are so many. My answer is always the same: use the first meaning that comes to you. And then, when you're done, go back and try the others. You may be surprised to find that they also fit your client's life.

Personal Notes

_____

_____

_____

_____

The Three of Swords

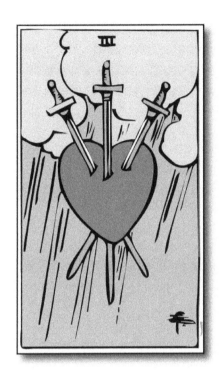

Simplified Meanings:

Upright – Emotional pain; mental anguish; despair; a medical condition involving the heart, blood, circulation, or chest area.

Inverted – Getting over emotional pain or mental anguish; a past medical problem involving heart, blood, circulation, or chest.

In-Depth Meanings:

The Three of Swords is one of the most difficult cards in the deck. I've often asked my students what happens when they keep thinking about and dwelling on an emotional issue. The answer is always the same – they blow whatever it is out of all proportion, and end up making themselves sick over it! That is basically the way the Three of Swords functions.

I do not mean to imply that the anguish the Three of Swords is showing you is not real; only that the presence of the Three of Swords in the reading shows you that your client's dwelling on the issue is making it a lot worse than it has to be.

Let me give you an example here. Suppose that I am in a long term relationship that suddenly breaks up. Because my love is rejected I will feel hurt, lost, sad, and probably fearful. These are all normal emotions in such a situation. If I allow myself to fully feel these things, I will quickly work through the negative emotions, and before long I am facing life with a positive attitude, looking toward the future, and probably a new relationship. It is amazing just how resilient the human spirit is. But supposing instead of allowing myself to fully feel what I am experiencing, I try to process it mentally. I go back over and over the argument that ended the relationship. I talk to all of my friends and my partner's friends trying to figure out what happened. I dwell on all of the bad, and good times we had. In short, by trying to work through an emotional issue with my mind instead of my emotions, I get locked into it and end up re-experiencing the hurt over and over and over again.

When the Three of Swords turns up upright in your client's cards, this is exactly what he (or she) is doing. The client has experienced a loss, a hurt that is quite valid; but by thinking about it too much he is holding on to it and blowing it up into something that causes him to be living with the hurt long after it should have been done. We are all guilty of this at some time in our lives. Spend a little more time with this client, helping him to work through the hurt, so that he can let it go and move on.

You'll see the Three of Swords upright in any situation where loss and hurt have happened; when a loved one dies or leaves, when an important job is lost, when someone has slandered your client, and so on. Surrounding cards should define the situation for you.

Inverted, the Three of Swords tells you that your client did go through that hurt and anguish, did dwell on the emotional pain, but has finally just about worked through it. I say 'just about' because if he was finished dealing with it, this card would not be in the reading at all.

Now, on an entirely different note, this card that generally shows a heart pierced by three Swords can literally mean the heart. Some older books say it means you're heart-broken, which meaning is fairly accurate in simplified terms. Yet it also can apply to the physical heart.

If you see the medical indicator card, Temperance, in the same spread, and especially if several Wands are present (or if your intuition yells at you to apply a medical interpretation), this card appearing upright can indicate physical heart, blood, circulation, or chest area problems.

In particular, if it falls near the Ten of Swords (in addition to the above mentioned cards), it could mean open heart surgery; near the Devil it could mean a chronic heart condition; near the Eight of Swords it could mean lung problems; near the Moon it could mean blood-hormone problems; and near the Five of Wands it could mean circulation problems in the extremities.

Remember, if the Three of Swords turns up inverted in the reading, and the above cards appear, it would mean that the problem is in the past. However, pay close attention to whether Temperance is upright or inverted. If it is inverted, the problem could reoccur.

It is no surprise to me that the same card that deals with holding on to emotional hurts also deals with physical heart conditions. Evidently, one rises out of the other. In certain readings where you are seeing a focus on spiritual growth the Three of Swords falling next to the Sun can mean an opening or expansion of the client's Heart Center, one of the seven major chakras, or psychic energy centers of the body.

__Special Note__: I have noted that in cases where a heart problem will lead to death, the Ace of Swords, Ace of Pentacles, Five of Cups, Judgement, or Death, will be present in *addition to the above cards. Even then, I never see Death as an inevitability. Armed with the foreknowledge you have given, your client can freely take the necessary steps to heal himself, or pass it on to whoever needs it.*

Personal Notes

_____

_____

_____

_____

_____

_____

_____

_____

_____

_____

_____

_____

_____

_____

The Fours

The number 4 is the number of the physical plane that we live on, and so the fours in the deck deal primarily with physical plane issues, like money, and jobs, and everyday life things. They deal with issues where a foundation for something is being created. The 4 is a totally stable number. It is used for support and for holding and protecting and creating security in one's life. Fours are slow; they build by adding to what they have, not by changing or throwing out their old in favor of new. The four Minor Arcana fours also depict the four elements, fire, water, earth, and air (Wands, Cups, Pentacles, and Swords, respectively), the four cardinal points, South (Wands), West (Cups), North (Pentacles) and East (Swords), and the four fixed signs of the zodiac, Leo (Wands), Scorpio (Cups), Taurus (Pentacles) and Aquarius (Swords).

The Four of Wands

Simplified Meanings:

Upright – Foundation for home and family; a new home; a happy social gathering; a wedding; a new romance with marriage potential.

Inverted – Changes in the home; a romance begins; a marriage unfulfilling or ending; a social gathering you don't want to attend.

In-Depth Meanings:

The Four of Wands represents the physical (Wands) establishment of a foundation (the number 4). Most commonly in our present culture the foundation being referred to is that of marriage, since most people will marry before establishing home and family. When this card turns up representing a marriage, you know that the marriage will be traditional and will be a strong foundation on which the two people involved may build their lives. If a marriage is indeed what is being referred to, expect to see a lot of Cups in the same spread, and maybe one or more of the other marriage cards (the Sun, the Hierophant, or the Three of Cups).

Most often this card refers to foundations that involve the home and family, since it is Wands, but I have seen instances when the foundation being built was for a business. In this case expect to see a lot of Pentacles in the same spread, and perhaps the partnership card, the Three of Wands, and maybe even the Ace of Pentacles or Ace of Swords as well. This combination would be particularly appropriate if the business is being run from the home.

The other foundation we find people creating in our society is that of having a home, or a base of operations from which to work. If you see no marriage cards in the reading, but you do see some travel cards, such as the Chariot or the World and perhaps a Pentacle or two to show money going out, and especially if you also see the Ace of Wands in the same spread, you're probably looking at a new home. But if this card turns up with a lot of Wands around it, it may just be renovation work being done in the home.

If it is inverted and a marriage is planned, it probably will be delayed, or perhaps may not happen at all. When inverted, any move to a new home will also be delayed, or perhaps the client will choose to remain where he (or she) is and renovate. The implication, though, would be that the client had first planned to move, or it would not be inverted.

This is also a wonderful card for romance, either upright or inverted, the only difference being that when upright the romance may lead to a marriage, but when inverted it is likely that it is just for fun and neither party has marriage on the mind.

__Special Note__: This is one of my favorite cards, since most of its meanings are so positive and the foundation that your client is establishing in his or her life when this card turns up is always positive and leads to a time of plenty and abundance.

Personal Notes

_____

_____

_____

_____

_____

_____

_____

_____

_____

_____

The Four of Cups

Simplified Meanings:

Upright – Meditation; deep thinking; an offer or opportunity; emotional stability; a message from your higher self.

Inverted – An offer or opportunity turned down; emotional instability; not listening to higher guidance; not meditating.

In-Depth Meanings:

Above and beyond all other meanings, this card represents total emotional stability. What is the only time that your emotions are totally stable and still? No, it is not when you are sleeping. The number of times you have awakened in the night with anxiety over something you cannot name should tell you that sleep is no escape from the emotional roller coaster most of us ride through life.

The average person experiences that complete emotional stability, that feeling of being still inside, only once in a great while, when there are no major anxieties to deal with, no major decisions to make, and no external obligations to deal with. But we have all experienced that moment, so we know what it feels like. And in that moment, because we are still and that inner voice that jabbers at us constantly is for the moment silent, we can hear a softer voice, one that comes from the very depths of our beings, that many call a gut feeling, or higher intuition, or the Higher Self, or guides or angels gifting us with inspiration. Whatever you want to call it, it is an inner guidance that is only available to us when we are in complete emotional balance, when we are still enough to hear.

Through meditation the mind can be taught to remain still, the emotions to remain calm, so this card is also a card of meditation.

Usually when the Four of Cups turns up upright in a reading I know that my client is either a person who practices meditation regularly or has recently experienced that stillness I mentioned above. Either way, he (or she) is in a perfect mode to receive guidance in whatever life activity. If, in such a case, I see the Four of Cups inverted, it is probable that the client is receiving the necessary information, but is refusing to listen.

But remember, the number 4 is also the number of the physical plane, and in a purely mundane reading this card shows the client, or Court card nearest to it, waiting for the right offer or opportunity. And as long as it is upright, the person will get it! But even here, it's important that you tell the client to listen to that inner voice – after all, how else is he to know the right one when it comes?

Inverted, the Four of Cups not only means that the client or person represented by the nearest Court card is not listening to what he should be, but will probably either turn down an offer or opportunity, or perhaps what the person is waiting for will not be offered.

The crossed arms on the Rider-Waite version of this card indicate that whether the advice/offer/opportunity will be received is up to the client; is he willing to reach out? The Four of Cups upright only shows the person contemplating it. Other cards will have to tell you if he takes it or not. If inverted, he probably won't.

__Special Note__: I often find that when upright the offer or opportunity presented by this card is a good one, whether the client accepts it or not. If inverted, it's usually not what the client is looking for anyway.

Personal Notes

_____

_____

_____

_____

_____

_____

_____

_____

The Four of Pentacles

Simplified Meanings:

Upright – Greed; the miser; not letting go; saving money; the pack-rat; a weight problem.

Inverted – Letting go; spending or losing a lot of money; losing weight.

In-Depth Meanings:

In a reading it is important to get a handle on who the Four of Pentacles is referring to before you try to interpret it because its meaning will differ depending on whether it refers to the client or to someone else in the client's life.

For example, the upright Four of Pentacles is the card of the miser; but when that miserliness pertains to the client it is actually advice to the client to watch his (or her) pocketbook carefully. Perhaps some unforeseen expense is coming (when it falls near the Seven of Swords or the High Priestess), or someone will ask the client to loan money that he can't really afford to (when it falls near the Six of Pentacles). However, when it pertains to someone else in the client's reading (usually a nearby Court card) it describes that person as unbending, self-centered, opinionated, and so miserly that he wouldn't part with a dime to help his own mother! Your client will certainly not receive any generosity from this person!

As a general rule, when you read the Four of Cups as pertaining to the client, read it positively; when it applies to someone else, read it negatively.

Upright the Four of Pentacles may also mean that the client or someone in the reading is holding on to something he needs to let go of. That something could be money, a relationship, a job... let the surrounding cards fill in the proper scenario.

Likewise, when upright, this card shows a weight problem, probably obesity, that someone is dealing with (if it falls near Temperance, and especially if Temperance is inverted). If the Moon is also in the same spread a hormone problem is involved; if the Three of Cups or the Devil is in the spread, it may be a bingeing or addictive problem, perhaps even bulimia.

But if the Four of Pentacles occurs inverted in the spread, it could mean that your client (or nearest Court card indicating another person) is losing weight. Near an upright Temperance the weight loss will be controlled, as in a good diet, but if Temperance is inverted, it could be an unhealthy weight loss caused by nerves or improper dieting.

Also, when inverted it could show a lot of money going out all at once, either to pay bills or as a loan (Six of Pentacles), or to make a major purchase. Surrounding cards should show you what is being bought. Lastly, you will see the inverted Four of Pentacles in any spread where the client is letting go of something, or sacrificing something. Perhaps he is going to take less money for the house than it is worth, or he is letting go of an old love. Again, fill out your meaning by looking to the surrounding cards.

__Special Note__: I often find the Four of Pentacles and the Ten of Pentacles in the same reading, when money is being loaned to or borrowed from a family member. The upright or inverted positions of both cards will define the scenario for you: Ten inverted and Four upright means the family won't loan money, because they can't afford it; Ten and Four both upright means the family won't give the loan, yet they could afford to; Ten upright and Four inverted means that they will give a loan or money; and Ten and Four both inverted means that they will give the money even though they can't afford it. I think you get the idea!

Personal Notes

_____

_____

_____

_____

_____

_____

_____

_____

The Four of Swords

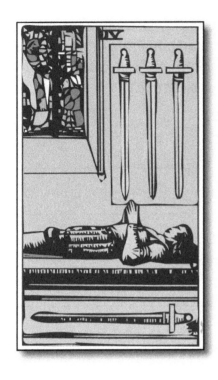

Simplified Meanings:

Upright – Waiting; inner stillness; peacefulness; observing; rest.

Inverted – Returning to action; mental activity; plans underway.

In-Depth Meanings:

In the Four of Swords the mind (Swords) is concerned with foundation, work, balance, and stability (the number 4). Usually when the Four of Swords turns up upright in a reading the client is moving through a time in his (or her) life when there is stability and balance and are dealing with the mundane and humdrum things of everyday life. There are, at the moment, no major crises, no exciting events, no heavy emotions of any kind, good or bad. This card tells you that the client is in-between those major life ups and downs. At the moment the client is moving through uneventful times, doing uneventful things. The best part of this card is that when it shows up there are no immediate crises to be resolved; the worst part is that the client might be bored.

I personally like this card a great deal because I feel that we all occasionally need that break from life's challenges. I see this card as a much needed period of rest during which we may recuperate from our last challenges and prepare for our next ones.

Very often this card signifies a period of waiting that a client is going through, and if you feel drawn to the number on the card, it may mean that the total period of waiting is four (4) months, days, or years. Or another card nearby may supply you with the correct number if it ties into this one. The waiting may be for an offer or opportunity, or to put plans into action. Nearby cards will tell you what those plans or offers are. But those things can never happen so long as this card is upright, because the client is frozen in stillness.

When the Four of Swords turns up inverted in a reading it means that there is a return to action in the client's life. Whatever he has been waiting for or planning is now about to occur; or, if there have been no plans or conscious waiting for something to occur, it will merely mean that life's roller coaster ride is about to begin again and the much needed (but perhaps boring) time of peace is at an end.

__Special Note__: You might bring the inherent stability and peace contained in this card to your client's attention when it occurs upright in his or her reading because it is during such times that we have time to work on ourselves. Take advantage of this time of seeming boredom to get your physical, emotional, and spiritual self into shape, when there are not so many outer distractions to interfere with your progress.

Personal Notes

_____

_____

_____

_____

_____

_____

_____

_____

_____

_____

_____

The Fives

In the Major Arcana the Hierophant, who represents the extremes of conformity and non-conformity is the number 5. He represents the root of evolution through either of those extremes, as the number 5 itself is the number of evolution and change. Later on in the Major Arcana we see Temperance, the number 14, which reduces to a 5, bringing back balance after the change has occurred.

In the Minor Arcana the number 5 is broken down into the four suits, each dealing with a major aspect of life, and again we see the number 5 acting through each to bring change and evolution into the life of the client. Largely the fives are looked at as negative cards in the Minor Arcana because anytime you have a major change or shift in life, you must give something up. It is a fact that true change and evolution may not occur unless that which was holding you back is taken away. Most readers perceive the fives as cards of loss or conflict; I prefer to see them as the necessary upheaval leading to soul growth.

The Five of Wands

Simplified Meanings:

Upright – Struggle; conflict; battle; the client has the upper hand in each of these.

Inverted – Same as upright, but the client is in the weaker position and will lose provided nothing changes.

In-Depth Meanings:

This card is very easy to remember and to read because it means exactly what it seems to. Whether upright or inverted it means that the client or person represented by the nearest Court card is in a battle over something. If it appears upright in the reading, the person has the upper hand in the situation, and will win the battle provided he (or she) changes nothing in the approach, whereas if it is inverted, he doesn't have a good position and will lose the battle.

But what is the battle all about? Look at the surrounding cards. If the Five of Wands is surrounded by other Wands, the battle is physical. The meanings of the individual cards will tell you more about the particulars involved. For example, if it has to do with a sporting event, the Six of Wands may appear. If there is physical fighting, there will be more Wands (look for an inverted Court card or two to represent the contenders). If Temperance is present in the reading, the physical battle may be an illness. If the Five of Wands is surrounded by Cups, the battle is emotional, but will have its roots in a physical crisis. Again, the inverted Court cards will tell you who the 'problem' people are. When it's surrounded by Pentacles the conflict has to do with money, business, or things. If Swords are the closest cards, the fight is probably verbal, and may involve slander or mental manipulation and maneuvering.

As I explained earlier, all of the fives involve change, and when the Five of Wands is involved the change will be fast and furious, and is often accompanied by some major upheaval. If the Five of Wands appears inverted in the reading, it may be that the client is resisting the coming change.

Remember, when the Five of Wands is upright, the client is fighting a winning battle. But when it is inverted, he will lose. Often the inverted Five of Wands is accompanied by feelings of fear, depression, and loss because of this.

Special Note: *Since the Five of Wands actually shows five (5) contenders (in the Rider-Waite deck) the conflict the card depicts in your client's life may have many different roots, or there may be more than one source of opposition.*

Personal Notes

_____

_____

_____

_____

_____

_____

_____

_____

_____

_____

_____

_____

_____

The Five of Cups

Simplified Meanings:

Upright – Separation, loss, divorce. Depression.

Inverted – Same as above, but the loss or separation is past.

In-Depth Meanings:

When the Five of Cups turns up upright in a reading you may very well want to spend a little extra time with the client to help him (or her) to understand and to better deal with whatever it is in life that he has lost, or are losing. Sometimes this card may herald only a minor loss, like having to let go of a friend you've outgrown; but other times the loss may be deep and profound, like the death of a loved one, or the break-up of a home and family. As usual, the surrounding cards in the reading will give you the particulars.

The surrounding layout will tell you if someone has died, moved away, or let your client down. It will tell you if your client has just moved to a new area, and misses home, or if he just lost a job. The layout will tell you if the client, or someone close to him, is getting a divorce. But the Five of Wands itself tells you the client's state of mind over this issue, whatever it may be. That state of mind is depressed, bereaved, unhappy, and lost, if the Five of Wands is upright. If it is inverted, it means he is just beginning to get over it. And either way, this card is a signal to you as the reader, that you can help.

The figure on the Rider-Waite deck has its back to you and to the future. It looks back toward the past, toward what it has lost. On this card what has been lost is represented as a castle, which doesn't just signify home and family; it symbolizes the security of what is known. A river separates the figure (who is your client, or the person in the reading who has or is experiencing the loss) from the castle. This signifies many things. It is your client's rampant emotion. It shows that the client can't go back, can't cross over, even though he might try. It shows that in truth, an ending has occurred in the client's life, but since he keeps looking back, he hasn't yet made the new beginning that should naturally follow out of any ending. In the card, the river runs toward a rising, or setting, sphere beyond the two towers that brings back the Kabbalistic symbolism in the deck once again. The 'river of life' is leading clients toward a future they do not have the courage to pursue. Yet it is the very emotion that is being experienced when this card turns up that will lead clients to transformation and growth. All that is necessary is their understanding. That is why you, the reader, can be so helpful at this juncture. You can help them to understand, so that, in their understanding, they can let go.

This card speaks of pain, and as long as the client holds on to the past that is gone, he will remain in pain. The client, like the figure in the card, is fixated on the three spilled cups; he has forgotten, in fact, that there are two more perfectly good cups available. It is your job as a reader to remind your client of this, help to open the door back up to future possibilities, and to stimulate his curiosity enough to get him to start looking forward again. It is only at that point that healing can begin.

As soon as the client has reached this point you will see the Five of Cups turn up inverted in the clients' cards the next time you read them. This by no means indicates that their healing is complete, or that they have forgotten their loss. Rather, they have awoken to the fact that life goes on, they do have a future, and it is time to let go of the past – even though they may still be inwardly wrestling with it. You will know that the healing is complete when the Five of Cups no longer turns up in regular clients' readings.

This is a very difficult card, reflecting a difficult time in your client's life, whether it is upright or inverted. But for you as a reader, it is giving you an opportunity to step in and do a special little healing for your client – by extending to him a combination of understanding and anticipation.

__Special Note__: When the Five of Cups falls next to the Ace of Pentacles or Swords, Judgement, an inverted Ten of Pentacles, the Ten of Swords, or Death, it could indicate a death. Look for a medical or accidental cause to be sure. Next to the Sun, Judgement, the Hierophant, the Three of Cups, or the Four of Wands, especially if any of these are inverted, it could be a divorce. With the Three of Pentacles or the Seven of Pentacles it's a job that was lost. I think you get the idea!

Personal Notes

_____

_____

_____

_____

_____

The Fives of Pentacles

Simplified Meanings:

Upright – Being at the bottom, financially, emotionally, physically, and spiritually.

Inverted – Things are getting better, financially, emotionally, physically, and spiritually.

In-Depth Meanings:

Eden Gray called the Five of Pentacles "Dark Night of the Soul," which to me is a truly fitting catch phrase for this card when it is upright in a reading. The Five of Pentacles, upright, shows the extreme of human suffering on all levels of being, physical, emotional, financial, and spiritual. This card appears upright in readings when the people it represents have tried everything they know or can imagine to get themselves out of debt, only to find themselves in deeper still. It shows up when someone is feeling totally shut out of his (or her) circle of family and friends – having no one to lean on, no one to care for him, and no one to care about. He even feels locked out of his belief system, whatever it may be – it feels like even God has deserted him. Physically, he may be hurting or infirm and have no one to turn to. If Temperance, our medical indicator card, turns up nearby, there could be a physical infirmity involving the head (note the bandage around the head of one of the characters) or the bones (note the crutches). Since one of the characters in the Rider-Waite version that I use has his leg bent up, I have found this card sometimes appears to represent a person who is an amputee.

This card, upright, is definitely the bottom. The people it represents have reached the bottom of their downward spiral, which is perhaps the best thing that can be said for it, since once you're at the bottom, there can be nothing worse. In fact, from here, the only way to go is up. That's what the bell around the neck of one of the characters in the card is all about. It's a wake-up bell. This card, in fact, is the wake-up call that you've been on the wrong track, and that the only way to get back on the right one is to let go of whatever it is you've been trying so hard to hold on to that you've lost everything important to you in the trying. Unfortunately, most of us need to hit bottom before we recognize this.

Next to the Three of Cups, or the Nine of Cups and the Devil, this card would indicate an alcoholic or drug-addicted person that has lost everything because of his habit. It's the wake-up call. Near the inverted Sun, the High Priestess, and the Seven of Swords, it's the man whose wife is divorcing him because of the other woman. Too late, he hears the call. These are rather extreme examples, and this card does not always indicate such extremes – but it does mean that we have lost the thing(s) we most want or cherish because we held on too hard to those things that are of lesser value. Usually when we hear the wake-up bell is when this card reverses.

Inverted in a spread, it means your client, or the person it talks about if not the client, has already hit rock bottom. He has heard the call, done an enormous amount of letting go of something, and is on the way back up. Perhaps the person let that extra big house with the extra big mortgage go for less money than he could afford – but now he is free of it and can begin to build a fortune again. Perhaps the person let go of the marriage or the lover he had sacrificed everything for, but still failed to find happiness with. Perhaps the person has accepted his physical infirmity, and decided to look forward and live life again, in spite of it, even though handicapped.

No matter what it was the person let go of, it represented a change in values that had to happen before he could make the change required to begin living again, to begin to come back up from the bottom. Because of this, when inverted, the Five of Pentacles is considered to be one of the most spiritual cards in the deck. Some say it represents a spiritual rebirth. One thing is certain; most of us who have experienced the whole journey of this card have found something within ourselves and our world that we didn't dream was there before the experience. This card teaches us to let go and to trust a higher power. It's only when this has occurred that our upward journey begins.

Upright this card is indicative of a lack of faith and deep mistrust; the person it represents is locked in himself. But inverted it is a restoration of faith in a higher power, and a renewal and re-adjustment of values.

__Special Note__: The cards are often very graphic. If this card appears when a client has asked a question relative to timing, the answer could be 'in the winter' because of the snow in the card. I also have seen this card come up to represent the artist or artisan dealing in stained glass.

Personal Notes

_____

_____

_____

The Five of Swords

Simplified Meanings:

Upright – Walking away from a battle you cannot win; a triangle situation you are leaving behind.

Inverted – Returning to renew the battle, though you know you cannot win it.

In-Depth Meanings:

To my way of thinking, this is one of the most karmic and most spiritually important cards in the deck. Upright it means that your client, or the person it represents in the reading, is walking away from a situation that he (or she) cannot win. Just think of the ramifications of this. It means the individual has understood the futility of his battle, and has also understood that it can go on and on forever with the same futility unless he walks away. At the end of the movie *War Games* the computer voiced this very succinctly: "Strange game... the only way to win is not to play!" When people have recognized this about important situations or battles in their lives, they take an enormous step forward in spiritual growth. By extracting themselves from the situation they free up all of the energies they had tied up in that futile cause, and now can use that energy for more worthwhile pursuits.

On a deeper level still, this card often indicates the resolution of a karmic situation the client is walking away from. Suppose, for example, that this card turns up for a client who is going through a divorce. It means that the present situation is only the most recent development in a series of relationship problems that may have gone on between the client and his partner for many lifetimes. In fact, he may have been fighting the same battle for centuries, and it is only in this current lifetime that the client has concluded that he cannot resolve these conflicts and must simply walk away. Of course, the karmic situation isn't always a relationship – it could have to do with work or money or any other aspect of life where unhealthy patterns have developed. Look for the surrounding cards to show you what area of life the battle concerns.

Because the Rider-Waite version of the card contains three characters, a triangle situation is sometimes implied. If the problem has to do with a relationship, one partner could be cheating, or there could be a third party that is constantly interfering with the relationship. Or a third party could be the key to resolving the situation and walking away! If the problem is a more everyday issue, such as work, the third party could be a job offer from another company, or several people interfering with your ability to perform your job properly.

What is interesting about this card is that only the client or person the card refers to in the reading will experience the growth, enlightenment, and sense of freedom obtained by walking away from whatever karmic situation is implied. The other people or groups involved may quite happily go on fighting, barely missing the one who has walked away, since they weren't ready yet to outgrow the pattern they were in. Take, for example the woman married to an alcoholic man who fights a long-term battle with him over his alcoholism, only to have him divorce her and walk away when he finally recovers. All too often she will marry another alcoholic and begin the battle all over again. What happened here? He outgrew his pattern and his need of her to support it. She didn't. Still needing the same battle, she found someone else with which to work through it. If you spend some time thinking about this, there are some very deep revelations about human nature and the process of spiritual growth here.

In our karmic growth through a pattern that may last lifetimes, we tend to push ourselves gradually toward an extreme of behavior, only to whiplash back into the opposite extreme, and then gradually narrow that pendulum swing back down, lifetime to lifetime, until finally we achieve balance once again. We then recognize any extreme of behavior relevant to the situation as being futile and not worth our effort. We have outgrown the pattern. Upright, the Five of Swords shows this as the end result. It is, as I said, one of the most spiritual cards in the deck.

Inverted, it is not so pleasant though. In order for it to appear in the reading at all, the client must have seen the futility of his battle. But if the Five of Wands is inverted, even after having recognized the futility of it, he returned to the battle for another round, even knowing that he cannot win. It is a sad card. An opportunity to resolve a lifetime's old karmic pattern or debt is lost.

But don't form negative conclusions about your clients too quickly. For some, I am sure, the lure of the battle and the desire for 'last licks' made them pass up their chance. But for others, there may be deeper reasons that we must not pass judgment on. Take for example the following situation, experienced by an actual client of mine. An older woman, she took her son and daughter-in-law to court to try to take custody of her grandchildren from them. She had proof, you see, that both parents were sexually abusing her grandchildren. For whatever reason, the court sided with the parents and denied her custody. The court also moved to deny her the right to see her grandchildren again. In her reading with me at that time the Five of Swords turned up upright. She knew the situation was futile, and she could do nothing about it except let go and move on with her own life, thereby resolving a centuries-long karmic battle involving her son and daughter-in-law. Certainly, no one would have faulted her for this. She had given it her best try. Even she knew it was time to quit. But she also had deep compassion for the two little girls. And even though she knew their battle would go on as long as she lived, she couldn't bring herself to let them face it alone. She begged her son and daughter-in-law to let her interact with the children again, and promised never to interfere again. And she hasn't. But the Five of Swords now shows inverted in her readings – you see, she doesn't interfere; but she does everything she can to show those little girls honest love. She's still fighting that battle, even though she knows it's already lost.

__Special Note__: The figure in the forefront of the Rider-Waite card is gathering up the weapons as others leave the field of battle. This both implies that the client has been made stronger by the battle, and also that the client may be in a position to disarm his or her opponent.

Personal Notes

_____

_____

_____

_____

_____

_____

_____

_____

_____

_____

Now, let's learn to answer questions using the cards and then we'll do a sample reading using all of the cards we've learned so far. Practice with these until you feel comfortable with them. Some people like to work only with the cards they're actually learning, until they are fully proficient with them. When you're ready, move on to the last chapter for the last of the Minor Arcana.

If you're only looking for a direct yes or no answer, feel free to ask questions for yourself at any time. But if you can't help reading deeper into the card meanings, don't do it! You'll only confuse yourself.

How to Answer Questions with the Cards

1. This first technique is the simplest. Merely take the deck of cards and shuffle it, or have your client shuffle it. One of you lay the deck of cards face down on the table. You, as the reader, spread the cards out by brushing your hand across them. One of you is going to draw one card to answer a question (first decide who). Now, have your client focus on the question, and tell it to you. You voice the question, and one of you should immediately draw a card from anywhere in the deck, and lay it face up on the table, so that you, the reader, will be able to read it. If it appears upright (as you, the reader are looking at it) the answer is yes. If it appears inverted, the answer is no. If you are reading for yourself, go no further. But if you're reading for a client, after you give him (or her) the yes or no answer, you may also interpret the card relative to the question to give him a more complete answer.

2. The second technique involves drawing two cards, this time right off the top of the deck after it has been shuffled or, if you like, you may have your client divide the deck into three or four piles first. Now, you slide the top card toward you, but leave it partially over the second card. Take both cards together and flip them over sideways onto the table. The card that was second in the pack is now your top card, with the card that was on top in the pack now being the bottom card. The card now on top is your primary indicator of yes or no. If it is upright, the answer to the question is yes. If it is inverted, the answer to the question is no. The bottom card only qualifies this answer. If it and the top card are both upright, the answer is a definite yes with no reservations. But if the bottom card is inverted while the top is upright, the answer is still yes, but there are reservations, possibly some potential problems. When the top and bottom card are both inverted it is a definite and very vehement no. When the top card is inverted but the bottom is upright, the answer is still no, but it will be for the best. Now again, if you're reading for yourself, this is as far as you should take it. But if

reading for a client, feel free to interpret the cards relative to the question for more information.

3. This last technique should only be used with a client, since you will be reading the cards for your answer. If you practice on yourself, do so lightly. This is a three-card spread that gives insight into a situation, but does not give direct yes or no answers.

Shuffle and divide the cards, or work directly from the top. Or, spread the cards out like a fan and let your client select three. Lay the cards down in a row, from left to right. The first card down is the past, the center card is the present, and the third is the future relative to the question. The center card will most closely describe the nature of the problem or situation, and describes the client's position in the situation as well.

A Practice Reading

Lay your own cards out to mirror this reading and see what you come up with on your own. When you're done, take a look at how I read it and note that cards with '@' next to the position number represent a second layer.

Note that I'm adding in a second layer in this sample spread. When using a Celtic Cross spread a second layer can give added insight by acting as an adjective layer to the first layer. As I lay each card in the second layer down next to the corresponding card in the first layer, the new card adds depth to what the first card has already told me. Occasionally, cards in the second layer may tell their own story; but that story will be of secondary importance to the one told in the original spread. Always read the original spread first before even adding the second layer, and remember, it's less overwhelming to lay them down and interpret them one by one, tying them back as you go along. Don't add more than one layer when using a Celtic Cross spread, or it simply becomes redundant, and hard to read.

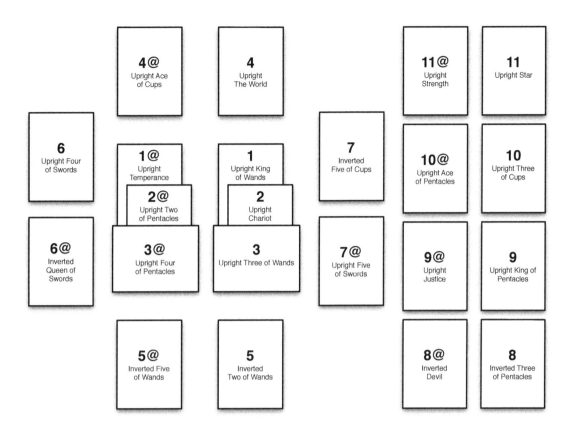

Figure 7: A Sample Reading from a Client Using Two Layers of the Complex Celtic Cross Spread

Now let's take a look at this reading for an elderly woman.

1. I first interpreted the inverted Queen of Wands, in the frame of mind position (1) to be my client. As a Wand I know her natural character to be physically active, assertive, and perhaps even aggressive. Yet since she is inverted I feel that she may have some physical or emotional problems. Next, I read this card as another woman in my client's life. This woman is either a friend who has some problems, or a woman she knows and is currently thinking about who is actively antagonistic toward her, and whose morals and/or values seem questionable. Perhaps it's all of these.

2. The upright Ace of Wands is exciting to see here in the current situation position (2). It tells of physical changes coming into her life that lead her to a new beginning. Perhaps these might include a return to a healthier state emotionally or physically, or a change of residence, or even changes in her current home decor or layout. Even given her age, there might be some romantic interest brewing here, so I'll keep a lookout as I read further.

3. The Three of Wands in the next three months position (3) tells us of long-distance plans being laid during this next three months that will affect my client's

future. Since the Ace of Wands appeared in position 2, I'm going to assume that a change of residence is intended, but may take some time to occur. But, since this position is read upright, it appears that the plans are well laid, and that they will come about as intended. Additionally, this card may denote a partnership of some kind that may be discussed within the next "period of 3" – either weeks or months.

4. The World, upright in position 4, assures me that her move will be made within one to three years, and that it will be a big move – either to a place geographically distant from where she currently resides, or to a place much bigger or more upscale than she is now in. The World in this position may also discuss some major trip she will take during that same time frame. The trip may also be in the planning stages now, and she may have a partner (see position 3) that she is planning it with.

5. The inverted Two of Wands in the foundation position (4) says that past plans she made didn't work out the way she intended, or, that she had to alter plans she had hoped to achieve. Since this is the foundation of the reading, it is quite possible that those failed plans have landed her in the current position she desires to move from, and are responsible, in part, for her (the Queen of Wands) being inverted in position 1.

6. In the next six months position (6) we find the Four of Swords, upright. Apparently, the next six months will be relatively uneventful, and will be a time of waiting for her. Since from the rest of the reading it looks like a move is in process but won't be completed for some time, this is exactly what is expected.

7. The past six months position (7) shows a difficult time for her emotionally, depicted by the inverted Five of Cups. This card shows that she has gone through some sort of loss or separation, and during the past six months she began to recover from it – maybe another reason for the inverted Queen of Pentacles in position 1? Perhaps the inverted Queen shows her continued emotional depression, and perhaps it shows that the person she feels separated from is a woman – a Queen of Wands?

8. The home position (8) shows concern about money in the form of an inverted Three of Pentacles. Looking further into the deeper meanings of this card we see my client leaving a group she's no longer happy with that is in some way connected to home and family, and we also see her getting poor advice from a counselor who is either in the legal or medical profession.

9. The King of Pentacles turning up in the next 10 days position (9) lets me know that soon a man with strong money-handling abilities will be involved with her. He's upright, so he's going to be a good influence. Perhaps he's someone who will give her better advice than she's been getting from her doctor or lawyer, or he

might be a new one. Since he's falling in line horizontally with the Ace of Wands, there might even be some romantic attraction, or he could be involved with her plans to move.

10. In the hopes and fears position (10) the upright Three of Cups shows her desire for happiness and friends to celebrate with.

11. The outcome position (11) is the upright Star, which gives strong indication that her desires for happiness in position 10 will be achieved, and probably within the year. It looks like she'll be financially stable as well.

All in all, this first layer of the Celtic Cross looks like she's making changes in her life for the better and that she's in the process of correcting some past mistakes. The large number of Wands (4) in this 11-card spread emphasize the qualities of change and activity that predominate the spread. Let's add our second layer:

1. Temperance appears upright in the frame of mind position (1) adjacent to the inverted Queen of Wands. This indicates that even though my client may be emotionally or physically (or both) ill now, her problem is under control. Of course, I know there are lots of other Wands in the spread, so I will assume there is a physical illness or infirmity of some kind. With all of the Wands, and the Five of Cups, the infirmity probably is relative to the bones or head. Also, the woman whom she is worried about is probably doing alright, although the inverted posture of the card tells us she's not terribly happy, and the woman she is having the problem with may still be a problem, but my client, at least, has come to terms with it.

2. In the current situation position (2) the Two of Pentacles appears. My client is juggling two things – two sources of income, two friends, perhaps two homes. Since it falls next to the Ace of Wands, she's either just beginning this juggling act, or is changing it to something new. And since the Two of Pentacles is upright, she's being successful at it.

3. In the next three months (3) the Four of Pentacles shows up. She's going to be saving money, or perhaps just being very careful about where it goes. Since it falls next to the Three of Wands, this is probably money being saved toward her long-distance plans.

4. Next to the World in the distant future position (4) is the Ace of Cups, upright. It looks like her move will be a happy one, and that she may be happy traveling.

5. The Five of Wands is in the foundation position (5) next to the inverted Two of Wands. It looks like her plans from the past that didn't work out correctly resulted in a lot of strife. Looking back up the vertical line formed by this card in the second layer of the spread, a lot of that strife was financial. (Note the two Pentacles in positions 2@ and 3@.)

6. In the next three months position (6) the inverted Queen of Swords could be my client, who will be mentally (Swords) aggravated by the necessity of waiting (Four of Swords in the first layer) for her plans (Three of Wands, first layer – position 3) to manifest. It also could be a mentally- and socially-oriented woman whom she hasn't met yet, but will have a communicative type of relationship with. And it could also be a verbally vicious woman whom she knows, and will have to put up with (Four of Swords in the first layer again – waiting) for the next six months.

7. The Five of Swords, upright in the last six months position (7) tells that she's walked away from some person or situation – probably a triangle situation. Falling next to the inverted Five of Cups in the first layer as it does, this shows up like a divorce of sorts. By walking away, we know she's resolved a karmic pattern with the people or situation involved.

8. The Devil, inverted, shows up in her home position (8) next to the inverted Three of Pentacles in the first layer. Apparently, she's freeing herself from some form of bondage having to do with her home and/or family by making the move she is planning. Additionally, the bad legal or medical advice she's received she'll no longer be listening to.

9. In the next 10 days (position 9) Justice turns up upright next to the upright King of Pentacles from the first layer. There will definitely be some good legal advice coming, and help from a competent professional as well. Remember, the King could be several people. A lawyer, a friend, a relative – all of whom are now giving her some good advice.

10. Position 10, her hopes and fears, holds the Ace of Pentacles next to the Three of Cups from the first layer. She's hoping to have more money to socialize and have fun. Apparently, she's looking at her potential move as an improved financial situation.

11. In the outcome position (10) is Strength. The changes she is making now should lead her to greater strength both physically and emotionally. Falling next to the Star in the first layer this is especially nice; it seems there's a restoration of confidence in herself that's accompanying her move. The Strength card here could also mean that she's going to make a younger friend who'll be a good travel companion (note the World and the Ace of Cups in the adjoining distant future position).

Let's compare our readings to what this woman later told me is actually going on in her life.

This is an elderly, unmarried woman who moved to Florida some time ago with a girlfriend, to be near a third married girlfriend and her husband. The husband had been the legal advisor and realtor at the time. The condominium she ended up buying was far too expensive, with expensive upkeep. In the ensuing years, there were falling outs between her and the two girlfriends, one of whom she no longer speaks to, the other of whom she worries about, but doesn't see because of the other one. Her health began to deteriorate, as she developed both osteoporosis and Parkinson's disease. Before long, her only friends were people from a local club she joined. Some of these recently have looked into moving into an assisted living facility that is far less expensive than where she is, and has exciting social activities and travel opportunities. Three of them are planning on moving there, and they want her to join them. She's already talked to some knowledgeable people in her family who are supportive, especially because of the good medical facilities that will be available to her, and she will consult an attorney in the next week. The only drawback is that there is a waiting list of up to two years. She wants to do it and I told her from her reading that it looked very good. She believes her two former friends will be envious and will slander her, and again, from the spread of cards she's probably right. But it looks like it won't stop her from being happy.

In the above reading, there were many more Major Arcana cards than normally appear in a 22-card spread. This means that the events transpiring in her life now are broad and sweeping, and that as things progress, she will feel like she is being carried along by them. Also, the large number of threes in the reading (Three of Wands, Three of Pentacles, Three of Cups) shows an emphasis on that number in her life right now – lots of expansion, growth, and spiritual awareness. It's also interesting that the number 3 is following her – she made her first move as one of three friends and she's been invited to make the next move by three friends.

Chapter 7

The Minor Arcana Continued

The Sixes

In the Major Arcana the number 6 was found in the Lovers, Key VI, and the Devil, Key XV. From these, we know that the number 6 is always a number of choice, and of the success that comes through the ability to sacrifice and to master crisis. It is in the number 6 that the spirit undergoes the necessary change and evolution to do these things. The number 6 incorporates into it all of the numbers that have come before. It may be derived from the 1 + the 5, or from the 4 + the 2, or from the 3 x the 2. It's important to remember these numbers behind the 6, because they add insight. The 1 – spirit, unity, undergoes change, the 5. The structure and foundation, 4, is created and maintained by balance, by opposing forces working together, and by constant decision and correction, the number 2. Ultimately the stubble to maintain the balance of opposites, 2 is lost, and expansion, 3, becomes inevitable. All of these contribute to the energy of the 6, which I see ultimately as a number of success gained through hard work and sacrifice.

The Six of Wands

Simplified Meanings:

Upright – Success; reward following hard work; winning; promotion.

Inverted – Failure; rewards are delayed; passed over for promotion or recognition.

In-Depth Meanings:

In the Rider-Waite deck (and most others) the main figure in the card is depicted riding a horse in a parade-like atmosphere, surrounded by apparent supporters and wearing the laurel-leaf crown of the winner. When upright the symbolism of winning and of success is readily apparent. The upward pointing wands almost seem to be raised in cheers.

This card will appear upright in any situation in which the client is winning, being promoted, getting recognition, or getting or receiving something for which he (or she) has been struggling or waiting a long time. There is an implication in the card that a struggle has been won, making the success all the sweeter. I often turn the Six of Wands up when someone has overcome a physical stubble as well, since Wands usually imply physical change. So don't be surprised to find this card in a reading when your client has been pronounced cancer-free following a long struggle with the disease, or when you see him winning a sports competition. As a matter of fact, if your client is engaged in horseback riding competitions, this card will come up fairly frequently in his readings, either upright or inverted, depending on whether he is showing well! As usual, the surrounding suits that predominate will tell you whether what's being won or lost (upright or inverted) is a physical competition (Wands), an emotional issue (Cups), a financial or job-related situation (Pentacles) or an educational, verbal, or mental struggle (Swords).

As noted above, if this card is inverted in the reading, your client will either be losing his struggle, or the attainment of his goal will be delayed. When I find this card inverted in a spread I usually tell my client that it is unlikely to receive what it is he is hoping for right now, but that does not mean he should give up the struggle – just because you don't win this round, doesn't mean you won't win the next. In fact, you have a better chance next time around, since you're now armed with experience!

Special Note: *One of the things I especially like about the Rider-Waite version of this card, is that it shows you all of the facial expressions on the people who are in the crowd around the main figure – these are the people who are supposed to be happy for your client at his (or her) success. Note the worried looks, and the outright frowns on some of those faces. Note also that there are some who are entirely hidden, we don't know how they really feel. I generally feel it wise to advise the client, keeping these so-called supporters in mind, that not all the world loves a winner, and that it might not be wise to shout his success too loudly, or to inadvertently rub it into the wrong person. Today's friend could be tomorrow's enemy! Also, the people attracted to your client, because of his success, may be fair-weather friends at best. Note that when this card is inverted, the friends all fall away. The client feels lost, alone, and embarrassed at his 'failure.'*

Personal Notes

_____

_____

_____

_____

_____

_____

_____

_____

_____

_____

_____

The Six of Cups

Simplified Meanings:

Upright — Good fortune arising from past actions, situations, relationships; a sibling or close friend; twins; a karmic relationship wherein the other person feels like a sister or brother to your client.

Inverted — Situations or relationships from the past return, but no good will come of them, they have no future; problems with a sibling or close friend; a karmic relationship is not good for your client; termination of a karmic relationship.

In-Depth Meanings:

This is one of the more karmic cards in the deck in that it denotes situations and people coming from the past, both in this and other lives that affect the client now. Generally speaking, upright the affect is good, inverted it is bad. The first way to read this card in a Tarot layout is that an old relationship or situation is returning. When it's upright, you can tell your client that future possibilities may arise out of it, but if it is inverted, he (or she) should either avoid it, or at least hold no hopes for a positive result. Inverted it's merely dwelling in the past on a relationship or situation that will not change and cannot grow and must ultimately be left behind.

New relationships, as well as old ones, may be shown by this card. When it's in its upright position they will be good for your client, and have an old-shoe kind of feeling to him. The client feels comfortable with the other person, he feels as if they've known each other forever, and there is a mutual sense of responsibility to each other and commitment to the relationship, whatever its nature. Obviously, even new relationships are karmic. The people involved have known each other in other lives. If the Six of Cups is inverted, however, the same sense of having known the person before, and being responsible and committed may be there, but the person is not good for the client. He or she may use or otherwise take advantage of the client, and should be avoided. Often in these cases the client finds himself in the role of the older sibling, perpetually taking care of the irresponsible younger sibling. I have regressed several clients to a past life following such a reading and discovered, indeed, the habit from that previous life was to take care of a totally dependent younger sibling who seemed suspiciously like the problem person in the current life.

I often find this card representing the spouses in clients' readings, if the relationship between the clients and their spouses is karmic, but they are not 'yet' soul mates, just working on it. Interestingly, in these types of spousal relationships, the partners often develop a very close and supportive friendship and sometimes relate in a brotherly/ sisterly way as well. If the Six of Cups turns up inverted though, the above negative sense of responsibility and obligation may prevail and the relationship will not be a good one, but will be hard for your clients to terminate because of their unconscious feelings toward their partners. The inverted position of this card, though, informs you that the client has really outgrown the partner, and is ready to move on.

If a pregnancy shows in the reading and this card turns up upright, it's possible that the woman will bear twins, or that another child will be born very close to this one who is a 'twin-soul' to this child (and not necessarily to the same woman). I generally make a habit of asking if twins run in the family when I see this card relative to a pregnancy in a reading. It's amazing how many times it turns out just that way! I remember one especially unusual situation. I was reading for a woman who had no interest in having children, and was definitely not pregnant at the time of the reading. I saw the Empress upright next to the upright Six of Cups, and with them was the upright Five of Wands and the upright Devil. I predicted a twin pregnancy for her. I told her there would be struggle around the pregnancy, but that she would have the children; that the children were bound together as twins because they both wanted to be born to her, not because they were twin souls. They were fighting each other to come in to life, and the only solution was to come in together. At the time she did not believe me, and told me twins did not run in her family. I wondered a bit myself just where this 'way-out' information had come from. But several years later she returned to me and told me she did indeed have those twins. They were identical, where the egg itself splits – the kind anyone can have. She did struggle, both in deciding to have the twins, and then in carrying the pregnancy of both girls to term. It seems that while still in the womb, one was stealing the other's blood supply and almost killed her. Their struggle continued after birth, and today those twin girls are still locked in a struggle for their mother's love and attention.

I have also seen this card representing two children who had something in common, setting them aside from the rest of the family. For example: these children were both toddlers, while the third was a teen; or everyone in the family was dark, but these two children were light; or these were the only two girls. Often you can count the children in a family by the Pages that appear in a reading, plus two for this card and two for the Ten of Cups (we'll be getting to that later in the chapter).

If you see this card upright surrounded by other cards that indicate family, it could represent an actual sibling to the client. Add a travel card such as the Chariot, and it may be that a sister or brother is coming to visit your client, or that the client is traveling to visit a sibling. If the sibling is getting married, buying a home, or changing jobs, surrounding cards will give you that information as well. If the Six of Cups representing a sibling is inverted, the sibling is either having trouble in his or her life (surrounding cards should show you what the trouble is) or is a problem to the client. Again, surrounding cards should tell the story.

__Special Note__: Perhaps it's the old buildings shown in the background of the Rider-Waite version of the card, but I often find this card popping up in readings for clients who are traveling to the Old World – England, France, Belgium, Germany, and so on. Upright, it's also encouragement to anyone who needs to revisit the past (actually or figuratively) to work something out, or perhaps regain something he or she has left behind.

Personal Notes

_____

_____

_____

_____

_____

_____

_____

_____

_____

_____

The Six of Pentacles

Simplified Meanings:

Upright – Budgeting funds; balancing finances; distributing or lending money; enough money is available.

Inverted – Being overdrawn; finances out of balance; improper handling of funds; bad financial situation.

In-Depth Meanings:

The Six of Pentacles is one of the easiest in the deck to remember because the picture, similar on most decks, is very descriptive of its meaning. When it appears in a reading upright, the client is concerned about money and finance (otherwise it wouldn't be in the reading at all), but appears to be doing fine in that department. Upright, this card means that an adequate amount of capitol is coming in to cover the living or other expenses that the client has, and that he (or she) is budgeting expenses fairly well. This means, for example, if the client has a question about whether his finances will adequately cover the purchase of a new home, that yes, they will.

Often this card will appear upright in a reading when a client is either asking for a loan, or is floating one for someone else. Either way, as long as it appears upright, there should be no problem with either the lender or the borrower.

When inverted, however, the Six of Pentacles shows that whomever it aspects in the reading has poor spending habits, which may have greatly overextended this person financially. Essentially, this shows debts. If there is a question about a loan, this card would either tell you that the client or whoever is looking for the loan will not get it due to his financial situation, or that the client should not lend money to someone who wants it for the same reason. Whenever this card turns up inverted you should warn the client about spending frivolously, perhaps even recommend that he go to see a financial counselor or someone who could explain loan consolidation.

Special Note: If you should see this card inverted in a future position, be sure to counsel your client to put some money aside now because you see more money going out in future than he will have coming in. Perhaps the surrounding cards will show you why. If it's upright in a future position, it may be a subtle way of telling you that the client is in poor financial shape now, but that things will be improving. Remember, that a card's inverted and upright meanings are always present, just that one or the other is dominating at the moment.

Personal Notes

The Six of Swords

Simplified Meanings:

Upright – A trip or move, near water; a boat trip; moving away from one's problems.

Inverted – A trip or move near water is completed or will not be taken. Returning to problems.

In-Depth Meanings:

When upright the Rider-Waite version of the Six of Swords shows a boat moving away from the rough water in the foreground, heading toward calm water and a peaceful, if somewhat hilly, distant shore. The symbolism is simple. Upright, this card shows the client turning his (or her) back on a difficult situation or time period and moving into a calmer, more peaceful one. Notice that the card shows the backs of the people in the boat.

Often this is the card that comes up when someone is taking a vacation. In this case it promises a needed time of peace and relaxation. When this card comes up relative to a change of residence, or job, or relationship (surrounding cards may tell you which), it also promises that the future will be more peaceful and calm. What is implied, though, is that where the client is coming from is a time or place filled with chaos and strife. That is, what he is turning his back on is what he is moving away from. The smooth water in the background that the clients are moving toward promises that their decision to move on is the right one; the distant shore promises dry land, not just a boat, to hold them above the emotional issues of the moment. Trees on that land promise future growth and expansion. The present is a time of transition, the client is located between discord and harmony, has not quite finished the one, not quite fully entered the other. But the boat has a person poling it through the water, which tells you that the client has help in making the transition, and the boat has two passengers, which also tells you that he is not making this transition alone. He goes with a friend, or his family, or a colleague.

Near Wands, especially the Ace of Wands, this is a change of residence. Surrounded by Pentacles, a change of job. By Swords, it's unlikely an actual move will take place, but the change will be to eliminate mental anguish. Surrounded by Cups, it's a move away from the family, or out of an emotionally trying situation. In all cases, the move described by the Six of Swords upright will be a good one. Often the move will place the client on or near the water.

The Six of Swords is also the boat card in the deck. So, if someone owns a boat and spends a lot of time on it, you'll be sure to see this card. If it's surrounded by Pentacles, the person may be buying a boat. Likewise, if the client is taking a cruise, this is the card you'll turn up, usually accompanied by another travel card, so that you can be sure it's a trip.

When the Six of Swords is inverted in the reading, it implies that the person had left the difficult situation at hand, but now has decided to return back into it. So, maybe this person has just returned from vacation. Or perhaps he planned on moving, but decided to stick it out for now and has put off the move. Look at the surrounding cards to determine just what the card is referring to – a trip, a move, a job change. Then assume that because it's inverted the move either was considered and the idea discarded, or it was put off to a later date, or it's already happened and the client has returned to his former situation. Usually, when the inverted Six of Swords is in the present it means the client has just returned or has decided not to go. In a past position, it probably means a trip or move was completed. In a future position, it will mean the client will return back to a former situation in the future, or is planning a trip he will not take.

Inverted, if it applies to the client's boat, it could mean there will be some problems with it. Surrounding cards will describe the problems. If it applies to a cruise, the client probably will not go, or will experience some difficulties along the way.

__Special Note__: The Swords all point down in this card, and the figures in the boat are all slumped. I always feel a sense of exhaustion from this card, both mentally and physically. The need to escape the current difficulties is great. Encourage your client to take that trip, make that move, take that step forward.

Personal Notes

_____

_____

_____

_____

_____

The Sevens

The number 7 is the number of mastery. Not mastery of the self, but mastery of the world that we live in, which teaches mastery of the self. In the Major Arcana we first learned about the number 7 through the Chariot, Key VII, in which we gained self control, and learned to deal with our own, and outside authority. Through this first 7 we learned the importance of directing our will properly so as to have the best control over our material environment. Then in the Tower, Key XVI, we learned that nothing is permanent, that to truly be in control we must be able to give up that which we control. To do less says that we accept that our material world controls us, instead of the reverse. Each one of the Minor Arcana sevens shows the means by which we obtain mastery relative to its suit.

The Seven of Wands

Simplified Meanings:

Upright – You have the advantage in a physical battle; high energy; mastering a physical problem; competition.

Inverted – Losing a battle; being at a disadvantage in a fight; lack of confidence.

In-Depth Meanings:

The upright Seven of Wands is a wonderful card to turn up in a reading in which your client is dealing with any physical situation because it gives him (or her) the advantage in dealing with it and all but ensures a win. Note, that in the Rider-Waite version of the card the main figure in the card has the high ground, the wands raised against him occupy a lower, less easily defensible position. Note that this card does not tell the client he will win, only that he has the advantage.

For example, if you are doing the cards for clients who are dealing with medical problems, this card upright in the reading shows that the treatment they are getting is aggressive and that they will return to health if they continue to follow their present course of action. You will probably see Temperance, and perhaps a card denoting the medical condition in this spread. Likewise, if the client is dealing with a legal situation it is probable that Justice would turn up in the same spread. The presence of the upright Seven of Wands would give the client the advantage in settling the case to his own best interests. This card deals with any and all physical issues, and with any physical changes the client might be making in his life.

Inverted, the Seven of Wands warns the client not to proceed with his plans for a physical change, or conflict. It may be that the timing is off, or that he is not properly prepared to proceed. The client does not have a good position to initiate a law suit, for example, if you see Justice with this card. Even if Justice appeared upright, it would mean the law suit was settled fairly – but not in the client's favor. Relative to a medical condition, it means that the present means of treatment will not be as effective as the client wants and needs it to be. Here, if you see Temperance upright, the client will still get well, it'll just take a longer time; but if Temperance is inverted, the client may not get well unless some major changes in treatment are made. If the conflict is already in progress, and the client refuses to or cannot back off at this time, he is certain to lose.

__Special Note__: This is a card of dynamic action. When it appears in a reading, expect to see your client going through a lot of changes and either adopting an aggressive 'I can do it' attitude (upright) or a 'poor me, the world has me beaten' attitude if it's inverted. If it's the latter, take a moment to show your client how, through letting go of the battle, or changing his focus, he can regain control in his life.

Personal Notes

_____

_____

_____

_____

_____

_____

_____

_____

_____

_____

_____

_____

_____

The Seven of Cups

Simplified Meanings:

Upright – Choice; multiple options; confronting your desires; confusion.

Inverted – Choice made; regrets; looking back at desires passed up.

In-Depth Meanings:

As with all the sevens, the Seven of Cups is quite straightforward and easy to remember. Upright its meaning is that a choice is to be made. Inverted, the choice has been made. The Seven of Cups helps you to master your emotions through the process of making the choice.

When you attempt to make a choice based on your intellect, you hunt information, you talk to people, you research the situation, and generally speaking, the more information you uncover, the more difficult it becomes to make a clear choice. But when you attempt to make the same choice based on your emotional desire you also become confused, usually being caught between what you desire and what you feel are the desires of others. And regardless of whether you make your choice with your head or your heart, you always feel like you're making the choice blind, and find yourself looking back at what might have been had you made the choice differently.

Your advice to your client, when the Seven of Cups appears upright in his (or her) reading, is to make the choice from the gut – to follow his intuition. It is only when a choice is made on that level that we feel that measure of certainty, that inner feeling of 'this is right.' Choices made through intuition aren't regretted – they are trusted.

The Seven of Cups teaches us to be responsible for our choices. As we move through life there really are no wrong choices; just shorter or longer routes to the same ultimate destination. This card tells us to accept the choices we make, the routes we choose.

It's also teaching us that we can't satisfy all of our desires here on the physical plane. As soon as we make a choice to obtain or follow one desire, we may open possibilities that many more may be obtained, but we also firmly close the door on others that might have been.

The Seven of Cups doesn't offer a choice between two things, people, or situations; rather, it offers many opportunities, suggests many choices, it confuses us with half-seen or half-understood possibilities. A choice that looks good on the surface may have negative aspects we can't yet see, or a choice that looks bad at first may have unexpected benefits. When the Seven of Cups turns up in readings upright, your clients are confused. They think they know what they want, and want it very badly, but they aren't sure because they can't see the whole picture. They will want you to make their decision for them, for you to tell them the part they can't see. But you can't do that because if you do, you will interfere with the lesson they are learning by making the choice. You must tell them to trust to their intuition.

Many people don't know how to listen to their inner voices. I often tell my clients to put all thoughts of their questions out of their heads, go to the beach or some other place of relaxation where they can immerse themselves in something else that lets them totally forget the decisions they need to make. At the end of the day, just before they return home, I instruct them to let their minds return to the problems – the correct thing to do will be the first thing that enters their minds, before they have time to think about it. Usually the answer is also accompanied by a feeling of lightness and rightness.

When it's inverted, the Seven of Cups tells us, depending upon where it falls in the readings, that the choice has already been made (past position), or that there is a danger of making a choice the clients will regret (present position), or that an action they are taking now will result in the need to make a future choice. All of the emotional confusion and stripping down to the core one's real desires will be a part of that choice, as noted above. Sometimes, through questions and answers, or a separate spread, you will be able to show the client the direction his life will take depending upon which choice he makes. This may help the client to make the choice – but be careful; it may also deprive him of the experience of really getting in touch with his own desires.

__Special Note__: I have always felt this card has a strong affinity for the planet Neptune. That should help you astrologers who are reading this. Remember to tell your clients that the most important thing of all is that a choice is made. This card will not allow them to sit on the fence. If they try, they will lose it all.

Personal Notes

_____

_____

_____

The Seven of Pentacles

Simplified Meanings:

Upright – Reaping what you sow; whatever has been set in motion must be completed; the end is in sight; karma; waiting; love of the out of doors; the green thumb; resting, laziness.

Inverted – What has been set in motion must be completed, but it takes longer than expected; a karmic journey slowly finishes; not getting enough fresh air; the black thumb, indolence, boredom.

In-Depth Meanings:

The basic meaning of the upright Seven of Pentacles is that whatever has been set in motion must finish; this, of course, is the root definition of karma. In many books it has been described as 'reaping what you sow,' another way of describing this card's karmic attributes. Most of us have been trained to think of karma as something that follows us from life to life; but in the Seven of Pentacles we are seeing the results of our actions in this life being reaped in this same life. It better falls into the category of instant karma.

When the Seven of Pentacles appears in a reading, whether upright or inverted, you will know that whatever the clients' original intentions or plans of action were relative to the situation, that is exactly what will be occurring, even if they think they have changed their mind or altered things through their actions. If the card is upright, the situation is coming to its conclusion in a timely fashion, but if it is inverted, things may be drawn out before the ultimate result is reaped.

This card shows the gardener during the period in which he is watching the seed he has planted grow. The fruits of his labor are not yet ready for harvest, so he waits and watches, knowing he has done all he can do give it a good start, and hoping for a good harvest. But there is little to do at the moment except wait. If he moves to another field, or forgets he has planted the seed and ignores it, or even if he nurtures it, it will ultimately make little difference. The seed will survive, it will mature, it will bear fruit. His actions will only determine how good, or poor, the ultimate fruits of his labor will be.

This means that if your client considered divorce six months back, but decided to give the marriage another try, and you see this card in a present or future position, the couple will still get that divorce. Likewise, if a job change or move was planned, but was delayed, the appearance of this card in the spread promises it will occur. When the Seven of Pentacles is inverted it means the same thing, but just takes a bit longer. I do believe that some people need to take that extra time to get used to the idea of change.

This card also has some more rudimentary meanings attached to it, as noted above. When upright it may denote a person who loves the out of doors, or spends a lot of time outside. This is definitely the card of the gardener or farmer. It tells you the person it describes is good with plants and animals, and is inherently patient. His (or her) presence may be calming and restful to others. He may be a bit on the lazy side. When it is inverted, though, the person it describes doesn't spend enough time out of doors, tends toward impatience, is generally not good with plants or animals, and may be so lazy that he tries to get others to do work for him.

__Special Note__: When the Seven of Pentacles is in readings, it's a good idea to assure your clients that whatever they are working toward will come to pass, they only need be patient. The need for patience is especially important if it's inverted. The clients may also be feeling uncomfortable at doing nothing at the moment toward their goals – if so, you may assure them that they have already done whatever is necessary to set the wheels in motion, and more work lies ahead as they begin to harvest the results of their actions. They should be enjoying this temporary rest.

Personal Notes

_____

_____

_____

_____

_____

_____

_____

The Seven of Swords

Simplified Meanings:

Upright – The sneak; disarming one's opponents; the need to move cautiously; caught between factions.

Inverted – The sneak gets caught; unscrupulous behavior disclosed; cast out or disbarred from participation.

In-Depth Meanings:

The Seven of Swords upright or inverted is a card of clandestine activity. You'll find it with Cups in a reading where someone is cheating on his or her spouse or lover, with Pentacles to indicate theft of money or material goods, with other Swords to indicate verbal communications and secret plans of an undermining nature, and with Wands when someone is attempting to hide or cover up physical actions he or she has taken.

It is very important that you are able to determine whether this card pertains to the clients or to the people around them. If it pertains to the client, and it's upright, you know that he (or she) is, or should be, hiding something, and that it is in the best interest to continue to do so. If it's inverted pertaining to the client, advise him to take extreme care because he is about to get caught. (Or maybe, if it's in a past position, he already has been.)

If, however, it pertains to someone around the client, you will read it almost exactly the opposite way. Upright, someone is doing something in secret (which may or may not cause your client harm – check the surrounding cards) and he or she is getting away with it. Often the surrounding cards will tell you what the thing is, and even who is doing it. If the Seven of Swords is inverted, it says the culprit will be caught.

I have also seen this card in numerous readings of clients who are carefully disarming their opposition or competition in a family (surrounded by Cups) or work (surrounded by Pentacles or Swords) situation. In this case, as long as it's upright they're successful in their endeavor, but if it's inverted, the situation is probably going to blow up and they will be the loser.

Very commonly this card is indicative of a situation in which your client is caught between two people or groups that represent opposing factions, and is confided by both sides without the other knowing about it. As long as it remains upright, your client is able to continue his involvement with both sides, although that position is precarious and you should advise the client to be careful not to carry tales back and forth. If it is reversed, the client will get into trouble with one or both sides for his involvement with the other. He may very well lose all of his friends, or the job, or whatever group the factions represented in the reading.

This card, incidentally, is one of the few that contains tents in the Rider-Waite deck, and would be the card to represent camping, or a circus, or an army bivouac. In fact, during the Desert Storm War I kept seeing this in clients' cards who had sons or daughters stationed in the middle east fighting zone. Remember, the cards can be very graphic at times, and this card contains both the tents of the temporary encampment, and the traditional fez hat worn by middle-easterners. Of course, you'd expect to see Swords involved in any military action anyway.

__Special Note__: If you should determine that the Seven of Swords falling next to the King that represents your client's husband means that he is cheating with the High Priestess on the other side of him in the spread, use some common sense before dropping this on your client. If the Seven of Swords is inverted, she probably already knows, or at least suspects, but if it is upright, she may not know, and may never find out unless you tell her. I generally inquire casually if the client has ever been concerned about her husband cheating, and base what I do or don't tell her on her reaction. If the Seven of Swords is inverted, I have to discuss the possibility with her because he will be caught, if he hasn't been already. But I will do so gently, letting her know she needs to pay closer attention, just in case I'm right, but that I could be misinterpreting the symbols. I hate to sow seeds of discord in a marriage. If I see the Seven of Swords upright, I'll be even more careful. If in response to my question, she says, "No, of course not!" I'll probably drop the subject altogether. If she suspects, I will explore it with her, but again, gently. Oddly enough, in some marriages the other woman or other man has been known to save the marriage by draining off excess tensions that would otherwise destroy the marriage. Not every marriage in which one or both partners cheat fails. But if the cheating comes out in the open the pride of the other partner usually prevents the marriage from continuing, or remaining healthy if it does. There is no right or wrong way to handle this because every client and every situation calls for a different approach. I can only advise you to tread carefully here, and let your own feelings relative to the situation be your guide.

Personal Notes

The Eights

The eights in the Major Arcana consist of Strength and the Star; remember, all four of the Minor Arcana eights will reflect some of the meanings of these two cards, each according to its own nature and element. The number 8 is always a very karmic number, bringing to completion physical plane issues and actions. Eight is known as the 'pay-back' number, but it is also the number where we may reap the benefits of our good deeds. Eights deal with power, with money and material things, with tug-of-war conflicts, with work, with communication, and with spiritual strength. Eight is the number of Scorpio.

The Eight of Wands

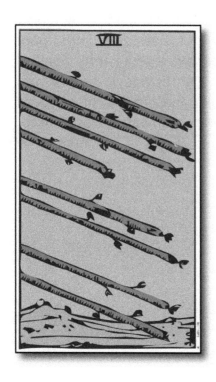

Simplified Meanings:

Upright – Long distance communication; air travel; the communications industry and fields within it; active communication, fast action, mental telepathy.

Inverted – Misunderstandings; Incomplete or lack of communication; jealousy; delayed or cancelled air travel.

In-Depth Meanings:

The Eight of Wands is primarily a card of communication. Those of my readers who are astrologers may be asking themselves now, "What does communication have to do with Scorpio, the astrological sign associated with the eights?" The answer is simple. In spiritual astrology, the planet of communication, Mercury, is assigned to be the esoteric ruler of Scorpio. This means that on its higher level Scorpio has a lot to do with communication. This is the card of communication in all of its forms. Talking, listening, mental telepathy, radio, television, telegraph, satellite communication, internet, and any other form of communication that you can think of are ruled by this card. It rules job fields related to these areas, as well as computer, sales, and counseling. When it is upright, things relative to any form of communication indicated in the reading are going well, when it is inverted they are either struggling or totally blocked from happening. Since air travel is essentially a form of long-distance communication, it falls under this card as well. You'll find these meanings easy to remember if you're using the Rider-Waite deck or one of its clones, since not only are the wands in the card flying through the air, but they look suspiciously like telephone lines.

When the Eight of Wands is accompanied by an Ace of Wands, another card we associate with a change of residence, it could mean that the client is moving to another geographical area that would be more readily reached by plane than car. When it is surrounded by cards representing family activity it might mean that clients are visiting family or friends out of the area, by plane, or vice-versa. Or, they might simply be in long distance contact with a family member or friend. Surrounding cards should tell you which way to read this. When the Eight of Wands is surrounded by Pentacles the communication or travel indicated will have to do with work or money. For example, next to the Two of Pentacles and the Ace of Pentacles it would mean that the client is starting new employment that will have him working between two locations – perhaps just by phone, or perhaps he will be traveling. The locations will not be near each other. The Eight of Wands is implying long-distance travel or telephone correspondence.

When the Eight of Wands is inverted, problems will be evident in any communications-related area in the client's life. If an air trip or move is planned, it is delayed or not happening. Or, if this card is found in the past in the reading, it has already occurred. Surrounding cards will inform you if it was successful or not. More commonly, the inverted Eight of Wands tells you the client is experiencing a breakdown in his communications with someone. Perhaps the client is waiting for a phone call that's not coming, or there has been a falling out with a friend whom the client is no longer talking to. When I see this card in a reading where marital problems are evident, I know the two partners are not communicating, and I generally recommend counseling, if they are interested in trying to heal the breach. Often, the inverted position of this card in the spread tells you that there is jealousy at the root of the communications problem. The nearest Court card(s) should tell you who the jealous party is.

__Special Note__: Since this card can represent a field in the communications area, when it turns up in a client's reading who is working in that field, inverted, it will tell you that he or she is ready to be done with that line of work, having become disenchanted with it. Relative to health, if you see the Eight of Wands inverted in a reading with Temperance (the health indicator card) there could very well be physiological communication problems.

Personal Notes

_____

_____

_____

_____

_____

_____

The Eight of Cups

Simplified Meanings:

Upright – Looking for something greater than one already has; turning one's back on the material in favor of the spiritual; beginning a spiritual journey; leaving something one has found joyous and fulfilling, moving on.

Inverted – Returning to the material, following a spiritual retreat or journey; turning one's back on the spiritual path; staying where you are.

In-Depth Meanings:

The upright Eight of Cups probably pertains more closely to the spiritual side of Scorpio than any card in the deck. Scorpio is not only the 8th sign in the zodiac, but it also is a water sign (Cups). In the Rider-Waite version of this card, and its clones, we see a figure with its back to us, moving away from eight full cups. It follows a watery path winding between two rugged peaks, ultimately leading to the union of sun and moon, Higher Self and lower personality, which we see in the sky at the end of the path. It is obvious to anyone contemplating this symbolism that the figure, representative of the client, is moving away from something or someone, toward something unknown, yet compelling in its promise.

Once again, in this card we see the ancient Kabbalistic symbolism of the Middle Path leading between two pillars, or in this case, mountains. The watery path in this card represents the flow of the universal mind or higher intuition, which describes the path of evolution of the soul. This evolution may only occur when we voluntarily look for deeper meaning in our everyday lives, when we choose of our own volition to turn our attention from the acquisition of material goods, money, and power, toward something far less tangible, but internally more rewarding. This is one of the cards in the deck that may represent the birth of spirituality, or the beginnings of a spiritual path for your client, when it is upright.

Let's take a more mundane look. The client is leaving something in his (or her) life. The full cups indicate that whatever the client is moving away from, it is certainly not bad. In fact, at one time, those cups held all that the client held near and dear. But he has outgrown those old goals, old belongings, old pursuits and old loves. It's time to move on. Often the moving on is painful; after all, this is the suit of Cups. But as long as the card is upright, the client will follow his inner compulsion, will leave what is known and loved and understood, for that which challenges and compels his curiosity. This may imply a physical moving on, or just an emotional withdrawal from a situation.

I often see this card in the readings of people who are withdrawing emotionally from their family or spouse, to follow their own desires unhindered by non-supportive persons whose emotional toxicity has become a limitation. Sometimes these people eventually get a divorce, or move out, but that physical move would be shown by other cards and usually only occurs when the spouse or family actively blocks the client's attempts at personal growth. The Eight of Cups is the emotional divorce from the situation, which often occurs long before any physical divorce is even thought of. In fact, I have clients who are in marital and family situations that they wouldn't dream of leaving because they fulfill all of the emotional needs of family, yet who get this card all the time because they've had to turn from their family in certain areas, for example, to pursue their work as an astrologer, or to follow a spiritual belief system the family doesn't agree with. These people involve themselves with the family in every way, but block the family from any involvement with their own path. An aspect of them remains inviolate to others.

If you see this card upright in a reading accompanied by a card which could mean travel, the client is probably traveling relative to some special goal or spiritual search. If you see it upright near education cards such as the Hermit or the Hierophant, the client could be studying or taking classes relative to a goal that to him is spiritual.

Don't assume that the goal the client has is always outright spiritual. Many times we walk paths that represent spiritual growth in our own lives, but that others would not see as particularly so. For example, if this card fell upright near the Three of Pentacles, the Star, and the Ace of Pentacles, I might see my young client beginning a new career in the art field, which for him is a spiritual undertaking, whether he consciously realizes it or not! The rest of the world might just see him getting a new job.

When inverted, the Eight of Cups tells you that either the client's spiritual journey is completed and he is returning to apply the new found insights to life, or that he has chosen not to follow the spiritual path, even though it was tempting. If Wands also occur in the reading, the client may actually have moved or taken a trip, or left a job, only to return to the former situation.

This is one of the cards where the inverted and upright meanings are always changing back and forth, so it's very important to pay special attention to where the card appears in the layout. If it's in the past, upright, look at what is going on now. Does it appear that the client is still on the journey, still remains removed from what he has walked away from, or does it look like he has returned to it? Inverted in the past, does it imply that it is upright in the present, that the journey progresses now? Or if inverted in the future, does that imply also that the client is on the path, or leaving something, now? Let the surrounding cards help you to expand your interpretation.

__Special Note__: Many times the rest of the world simply does not understand your client when this card appears upright in the reading. To all appearances, the client is walking away from everything he or she could want, to something unstable, insecure, and not especially desirable. But to the client the choice is clear, and there is no contest.

Personal Notes

_____

_____

_____

_____

_____

_____

_____

_____

_____

_____

_____

_____

The Eight of Pentacles

Simplified Meanings:

Upright – Job change; new work; handiwork; blue-collar labor; working with one's hands; apprenticeship; beginning at the bottom of something one might work up the ladder in; working on or through some issue.

Inverted – Leaving work or job; failing to work through an issue; leaving a trade or profession; problems at work.

In-Depth Meanings:

The Three of Pentacles is the career; it is the placard on the door, the title you call yourself. But the Eight of Pentacles is the actual work you do behind the door, on a daily basis. It is your handicraft, whether you are a doctor or a carpenter. This card in a reading always talks about your employment, or about some issue you are attempting to work through. In earlier times, this was the blue-collar worker, the Three of Pentacles the white-collar worker, but nowadays there are many gray areas here; it is best to see the Three of Pentacles as the career, but the Eight of Pentacles the work. It is HOW you earn your money.

Relative to employment, this card will only appear in the reading at all if the client's work is an issue. Often this appears upright when clients are beginning new jobs. When it does, it is assurance that the jobs will be something they can learn well, and that they will give them adequate experience to move on to better jobs, either in the same company or elsewhere. The position the clients hold, when this card is in the reading, will not be permanent. It is a stepping stone to something better. However, you have to start at the bottom to work up. As long as the Eight of Wands is upright, the job will go well, and the client will probably like the work. He (or she) may, however, only see the job as a means to make money, not as a career.

When it turns up inverted in the spread, the Eight of Wands tells of problems the client is having with work. Perhaps the client just doesn't like the job and would like to leave (accompanied in the spread by Cups), or perhaps he is in the process of leaving or has even just left the job (accompanied by Wands). Either way, the surrounding cards will give the story of what's going on. When surrounded by Wands, Swords, and Cups, the client may have been fired or laid-off. The interesting thing about this card when inverted is that the client (or whomever the card is representing) not only leaves the job or task he is doing, but will not use those skills again or enter that particular line of work again.

Often this card appears in a reading where the client is trying to work through a major issue in his life. For example, the client is struggling to finish school, or is trying to keep his marriage together. When the Eight of Pentacles appears upright in this person's reading, it is a promise that he will succeed in working through the problem. When it is inverted, the client will fail. If you see it inverted in a client's cards in such an instance, you should tell your client to ask himself if the situation is worth all the effort required because it doesn't look like he will succeed, at least not using the present approach.

__Special Note__: Oddly enough, I often see this card in the readings of people who NEED to work with their hands in order to remain happy and whole in their lives. If your doctor client seems to get this card a lot, you might recommend that he take up woodworking or ceramics as a hobby.

Personal Notes

_____

_____

_____

_____

_____

_____

_____

_____

_____

_____

The Eight of Swords

Simplified Meanings:

Upright – Trapped; blind to your own situation; controlled by your own mental constructs; out of touch with your emotional needs and desires, perceptions, and feelings.

Inverted – Free; breaking one's bonds; getting in touch with one's physical perceptions, feelings, and emotions.

In-Depth Meanings:

The Eight of Swords is very close in meaning to the Devil. Upright it means bondage, and inverted it means breaking free of the bonds to obtain freedom.

The central figure in most decks is a woman, so most often we will see a woman in the client's life, or the female client, being indicated by this card. I have, however, seen it pertain to a man upon occasion, so don't be close-minded about this. This central figure is bound, blindfolded, and surrounded by swords. This symbolism definitely implies the person is trapped by her (or his) own mental expectations or limitations, (the swords) and that she is blind to this (the blindfold over the eyes). The bonds in this card do not allow the person the freedom to remove the blindfold with her hands; a change in her thinking is required in order to see the means to her freedom. In the Rider-Waite version, the figure stands amidst scattered puddles, giving us a sense of the extreme emotion the situation has generated, that has just about dried up as the person has come near to giving up. In the background is a stark image of a castle atop a craggy mountain, implying both that the object of one's deepest desires, home, family, security, is unobtainable, and that the person is bound and tied, out of reach of aid.

When the Eight of Swords appears upright in a reading, whomever it represents in the reading feels so trapped by her life situation that she has basically turned off all feeling and perception, living life almost like a mannequin going through the motions, not knowing how to change the situation, has given up trying, and the only way to continue is to turn off the perceptions that would give her constant pain otherwise.

When inverted, the clients, or whomever this card represents in the reading, have changed their mental attitude toward their situations, and in so doing, have broken free.

Note that in the Rider-Waite version, the puddles of water are now on top of the card. The person now follows her intuitions, and feels emotions again.

It is common to see this card in any reading where the client feels trapped or confined by tradition, or by certain aspects her life situation. In a worst-case scenario you might see this card representing the woman who believes her husband or lover is totally in control of her. I recall reading the cards of a woman married to a man who didn't work because he was supported by disability insurance (inverted King of Wands with upright Temperance and Justice). The man beat her regularly (upright Five of Wands, Devil and inverted Ten of Cups). She was mother to four little children and wasn't allowed to work. He had her under constant surveillance as he was always there, and kept the keys to the only car in his pocket at all times. He gave her no money except that used to buy groceries. She believed that he had the upper hand, that because he was officially disabled, no one would believe her story, and that if she left,she couldn't leave and take the children. She believed that the courts would award the children to him, and that he would see to it that she was left destitute, or worse. She feared for her life, and yet allowed him to beat her in front of the children because as long as she let him he would leave the children alone. You and I could immediately see her perception of the situation was in error, but, represented by the Eight of Swords, she could not. She came to me for readings for a long time, on the sly (when she was supposed to be grocery shopping), before she gradually altered her perception of her situation. She began to realize that he wasn't strong, but weak. She eventually realized her own strength, learning to read the Tarot, and, again on the sly, doing readings and saving all the money from them for a getaway. Today, this woman is finally divorced and lives on her own with the four children that she primarily supports, with minimal help from his disability. She was able to get a writ of protection against him for herself and the children. She has put herself through school and leads a very normal and promising life. The Eight of Swords no longer turns up in her readings at all, but a long time ago, when she first developed her plan to break free, it appeared inverted, and I celebrated with her. Freedom has to be in the mind before it can be manifested in life.

*Special Note: When this card appears in a reading near Temperance and Wands, a medical problem may be indicated. It could have to do with inhibited movement (i.e., the person has trouble walking or needs a wheel chair), or with the ability to see. For further tips on how to interpret these cards together, refer back to Temperance, Chapter 5.

Personal Notes

_____

_____

_____

The Nines

The number 9 is the last number in our numerological system, and as such, it symbolizes finality, the true end before the beginning. The number 8 completed the physical, manifested karma; the number 9 is the internalization of the lesson. It completes the karmic lesson on the spiritual level, where it is understood and assimilated. As such, nines in numerology are usually teachers – not teachers who go to school to learn their subject, but rather teachers who are born knowing or who teach the wisdom they have learned in the school of life. It is not until we are ready to teach it that the lesson is truly learned. The nines in the Major Arcana, as you might expect, are both cards of learning and spiritual growth and attainment. The first nine is the Hermit, the second is the eighteenth card, the Moon. The first has to do with learning and teaching relative to the mind, as we find our way through life's various lessons, and then disseminate them; the second has to do with learning and teaching relative to the spirit and the higher intuition, as we learn to listen and follow our inner voice. All of the nines in the Minor Arcana reflect these lessons to some degree.

The Nine of Wands

Simplified Meanings:

Upright – The lesson has been learned; ready to battle again; distrust; on the defensive.

Inverted – Incapable of withstanding another attack; lesson not learned; weakness.

In-Depth Meanings:

The figure in this card in most illustrated decks stands ready to do battle again, despite obvious wounds from the last foray. He fought for his cause, and won or at least defended himself adequately, though he was injured, physically or emotionally, in the battle. He looks like he's taking a rest, but is very much on the defensive, expecting and ready for the worst, if need be. This card is an active and physical version of the Hermit card in the Major Arcana.

The Nine of Wands usually turns up in someone's cards when he (or she) has experienced a life lesson having to do with trust that was misplaced. For example, if I am reading the cards of a man whose last girlfriend has cheated on him, this card represents him after his battle to find out about the situation, confront it, and resolve it. It doesn't tell how he did these things, only that he confronted what was for him a very difficult situation and worked through it. We see him now, represented by the Nine of Wands, no longer trusting and idealistic relative to this situation. In fact, it looks like he's expecting the worst, just in case, and is ready to beat in a few heads if he has to.

I am generally glad to see this card upright in my client's cards because it means he has come through the ordeal mostly intact, and has learned a valuable lesson from the experience. The only thing I generally warn the client against is the tendency to become overly suspicious. Sometimes people who have been through the events leading to this card develop a chip-on-the-shoulder attitude that has them ready to condemn innocents even before they've made the expected wrong move. For example, the man in the above scenario might assume that his next girlfriend is going to cheat, too, and so not trust her or open up to her enough to form a healthy relationship. In fact, his suspicion could even result in a continuation of the problem from the last relationship into the present one. It is important to assimilate the lesson, to know what you will and will not tolerate, and how to deal with it if it occurs; but it's just as important to be able to feel confident enough in yourself that you're capable of handling any situation that arises, that you don't need to move through the world with suspicion as your shield.

When the Nine of Wands is reversed, it means that the client has not yet developed the personal strength to deal with the situation unaided. For example, in the above situation, if the man's old girlfriend comes back, and the Nine of Wands is reversed in his reading, he will have no power to resist her, and she will do the same things to him again. It isn't that he hasn't learned the lesson; he has no problem understanding that she hurts him. It's that he cannot seem to gather the will power to apply the lesson, and turn his back on her. The only good thing we can say about this is that each time he gets hurt the same way, he gets a little bit better at 'taking the punch' and eventually he becomes immune to the pain and will be capable of taking action. Your client may go through the same scenario over and over again, but eventually he will develop the strength to deal with it. You may be able to help the client if you see this card inverted in the reading, by warning him about going back to the old situation, explaining that he is not yet ready to be able to handle it.

When this card appears with Cups the lesson is emotional, having to do with relationships or family issues. When it is with Pentacles it will have to do with money or job related issues, and when it is with Swords, it deals with gossip and slander, or perhaps educational issues. With other Wands, it tells us of physical changes or sports events. As always, look to the meanings of the surrounding cards to get more insight.

__Special Note__: The Nine of Wands, when near Temperance, may indicate an illness or injury involving the head.

Personal Notes

_____

_____

_____

_____

_____

_____

The Nine of Cups

Simplified Meanings:

Upright – Getting your wish; drinking or eating too much, overdoing something; weight gain or loss.

Inverted – Not getting what you want.

In-Depth Meanings:

Upright, I think of the Nine of Cups as the *bar-card* and the *wish-card*. The wish part is easy. When the Nine of Cups turns up upright in your reading, you are getting what you want (whether it's good for you is not a consideration). When it is inverted, you will not get what you want. Clients are always very interested in this aspect of the card, and it's a simple way of telling them whether their immediate desires will be satisfied. Just look for this card in the spread.

The bar-card part of the meaning is more difficult to be sure of, and requires more tender handling. Upright, this card always means that the client, or person it represents in the reading, is overdoing something. Usually the problem person will be represented by the nearest Court card. If there isn't one, it may be someone the client is thinking of, or it may even be the client. Ask him (or her) if someone close to him has a problem with something he is overdoing, that could potentially do the client, or others, harm. Surrounding cards will tell what that is. Surrounded by Pentacles, it might be work, or by Swords, it might be thinking or gossiping too much. By Wands it could be overexertion or sexual addiction. But by Cups it is overdoing something we consume. The person represented by the card either overeats, drinks too much, smokes too much, does some type of drug to excess, or is co-dependent. Some decks remind us of this secondary meaning by giving the little man a red nose.

When the Nine of Cups appears upright in a reading near upright Temperance, the person is still doing the thing he has a tendency to overdo, but is maintaining a sense of balance about the problem at the moment. If Temperance is reversed, he is way out of control. Likewise if the Devil appears upright in the reading near the upright Nine of Cups, he has a very bad addictive problem of some kind. If the Devil is inverted, but the Nine of Cups is upright, the cards are telling you the person does overdo it, but it is not an addiction – yet!

When the Nine of Cups is reversed it tells you the person with the problem is not getting what he wants (i.e., he is not eating, drinking, or otherwise consuming or doing the thing he has a tendency to overdo). Again, upright Temperance tells you the client is in balance because he is not doing it, inverted Temperance tells you the client is out of balance, probably because he is having trouble not doing it. The upright Devil near the Nine of Cups tells you the client is an addict, but is also on the wagon; the inverted Devil tells you there is no longer, or perhaps never was an addiction here, but the person is not doing that thing he has a tendency to overdo anyway.

This card also appears often in readings when the client is concerned with weight gain or weight loss. It could stand for either obesity and eating addictions or for malnutrition, anorexia and bulimia. Usually, Temperance and several Wands will appear with it since these represent health conditions. I also often find the Moon nearby when the health problem involves a glandular disfunction, such as diabetes. In such a case the eating problem indicated may not be overeating, but eating the wrong things.

__Special Note__: We live in an addictive society. Every one of us has something in our lives that we seem to not be able to survive without. It is very common to find this card in your client's readings, and gives you some strong hints as to where he (or she) needs help in life. But do be careful how you approach this. The client may be comfortable enough discussing Mom or Dad's addictive or compulsive behaviors, but when it comes to his own you may face an entirely different person – one not nearly as receptive to receiving your help.

Personal Notes

_____

_____

_____

_____

_____

_____

_____

The Nine of Pentacles

Simplified Meanings:

Upright – A woman alone, yet happy and independent; love of the out of doors; green thumb; financial independence; a bird.

Inverted – A woman losing her independence or her financial security; not spending enough time out of doors. Problems with the bird.

In-Depth Meanings:

One of the fun things about this card is that it is the only one in the Rider-Waite deck that shows a bird, so if you're reading with this deck and your client has a bird, this card is the bird. Some other decks, such as the Aquarian, have birds on other cards and some have no bird on this card, so use your discretion here. If your deck has it, use it! If not, ignore it. If it's upright, the bird is fine – perhaps it's in the reading because your client is about to get one (look for more Pentacles in this case). If it's inverted, the bird is sick, or perhaps the client has another problem with it. Before you use this meaning, inquire if she has a bird.

More commonly the Nine of Pentacles is read as a woman alone, but comfortably so. She is financially able to take care of herself; in fact, she is quite good at handling money. Whether or not she is well off, money is not a concern. The interesting thing about this card, though, is that the woman pictured in it is so comfortable being alone, that she is not seeking a mate, nor does she feel the lack. She likes her own space. She is not lonely, or fearful, or feeling like half a person. She is complete in herself.

I have seen this card come up representing a married woman, but in each case, the woman was so independent that she maintained her complete autonomy even while in the marriage.

Often this is a business woman, or an older woman left independent upon her husband's death or a divorce from him.

When the Nine of Pentacles appears inverted in the spread it tells a sad story. This independent woman is losing her independence, or her freedom, or the financial security that gives her independence. Look at the surrounding cards to learn the rest of the story. If you see Wands and Temperance in the spread, her health may be creating dependency. This is true of many older women who lose their independence when they can no longer take care of themselves, but could certainly affect a younger woman, too. If you see a lot of Cups in the spread, and perhaps a likely gentleman friend, she may be losing her independence due to a marriage, or a lover moving in. In this case you're likely to see a mixture of happy and sad cards, since she'll be happy about the relationship but unhappy and perhaps a bit frightened about losing her aloneness. Surrounded by Pentacles she could be suffering financial difficulty that forces her to take in a roommate or to become dependent upon other family members. With Swords, her independence and freedom of mind has been undermined by slander or gossip, or perhaps she's losing her professional position.

This card often turns up for women who like to spend time out of doors, camping, gardening, or just walking. This is the green thumb card just for women. When it's inverted she might not be getting as much time out of doors or in the garden as she would like, or needs. Her green thumb may also have turned into a black one.

Occasionally, you may see this card in a woman's reading when she is planning a change of residence. In this case, the move will be to a house with a lot of ground and open space around it, and she will have ample time and space to herself. As long as the Nine of Pentacles is upright, it should be a good move. Note that this card describes the place to which she would move; it in itself does not mean a move – other cards in the reading would have to tell you a move is planned.

__Special Note__: I have a special place in my heart for this card, since this is how many people see me.

Personal Notes

_____

_____

_____

_____

_____

_____

The Nine of Swords

Simplified Meanings:

Upright – Trouble sleeping; extreme nervous tension; danger on the astral plane; headaches.

Inverted – Sleeping problems diminishing; tension easing; headaches and anxiety in the past.

In-Depth Meanings:

Upright, the Nine of Swords is not a pleasant card. It generally means that the client, or other person it represents in the reading, is suffering from anxiety and hypertension and is probably having difficulty sleeping. Often the hypertension will lead to chronic headaches, in which case you would also see some Wands and probably Temperance in the reading. This would also be the card to describe other sleep disorders, such as snoring, in which case you'd also expect to see the Eight of Wands along with Temperance.

When, occasionally, the Nine of Swords appears in a reading near the Moon, the client has a very strong emotional tie to someone that is interfering with his (or her) sleep. The person may wake up tired, day after day, or may have trouble getting to sleep or staying asleep. Many people do not realize it, but when there are strong emotions between two people (good or bad, it doesn't really matter), a psychic link is created between those two people. One person's nervous tension and anxiety can travel the link to interfere with the other person's sleep, even though the two may be consciously unaware of the problem. This is the simplest way of traveling the astral plane because anyone can do it. And it can be just as serious a psychic attack as if the person doing it is fully aware of what he or she is doing! Find the Court card closest to the Moon and you will know who the psychic link is to. Once you pinpoint the person, the client can take steps to break the link, and begin to have normal sleep patterns again. Oddly enough, it doesn't seem to matter if the Moon is upright or inverted, either way the link that interferes with sleep may develop. If it's inverted, it may be a bit easier for the client to see it for himself because he will recognize the person doing it as currently having emotional problems.

Some of the simple things your client can do to break the link are as follows: First, tell the client to visualize putting the problem person in a strongbox and locking it before going to sleep. This may take a few tries, but if the client is vigilant he will eventually succeed. It is also the best method because it involves only his own mind. If the client is repeatedly unsuccessful with this, tell him to put a clockwise circle of either kosher or sea salt around the bed before going to sleep to seal the invading person out of the space. Finally, if the client needs more permanent help, tell him to select a small candle of a color reminiscent of the problem person, and inscribe on the candle the person's name using a sharp instrument, and that the person may no longer affect the client mentally, emotionally, physically or spiritually (it's okay to write over the words if there's not enough room on the candle). Then tell the client to wrap the candle in tin foil, shiny side in, to make it like a mirror. When the problem person reaches out toward the client, he will be reflected back to himself. Finally, store the wrapped candle in the freezer compartment of the refrigerator until this protection is no longer needed. I call this last technique 'putting someone on ice.' It's amazing how well it works. If the client is still bothered by a link to this other person even after all of this, he is generating the link himself, and needs to spend more time with the first technique I mentioned.

Very occasionally you will read for someone who is actually under a real, conscious psychic attack by someone. Such attacks will be made during the hours the client is asleep because that is when the psyche is most susceptible to suggestion. Note that this type of psychic attack is very hard to recognize because it usually will not cause the anxiety and sleeplessness that the psychic link would. The person conducting the attack would be much more subtle than that, his or her actions would go unnoticed, except by possibly you, the reader. In the cards the psychic attack would look much the same as the psychic link, with the Moon near the Nine of Swords, but there would also be a Magician, High Priestess, or Devil nearby. The client would protect against it in the same way as noted above. If he cannot figure out who the attacker is, rather than using a name, have him write on his candle, 'whomever is attacking me,' and it will serve the same purpose.

When the Nine of Swords is inverted in the reading it means that any headaches, anxieties, sleeplessness or other related problems are in the past. They may not be completely done (or the card wouldn't appear at all) but they're a lot better than they were.

__Special Note__: It is extremely rare to read for someone who is really being psychically attacked. Most people who ask you about this are merely being paranoid, and you will be able to assure this person there is nothing of the sort happening – it will not be anywhere in his cards. If you do see a real psychic attack in someone's cards, I suggest you approach the subject with care, unless he specifically asked you about it. Most people will be understandably hostile to this information because of the public outcry against psychic scams in which the client is set up by the reader to spend large amounts of money to have the reader remove the curse or protect the person from the *attack. I make a habit of never telling anyone I will do any such service, or even hinting at it. I have actually turned down money offered to me for this purpose. Let's work to give psychics a better reputation!*

Personal Notes

_____

_____

_____

_____

_____

_____

_____

_____

_____

_____

_____

_____

_____

The Tens

Ten is actually one on a higher level; ten is one and zero, which when added together is again one. In all of the tens the 'one' representative of the self and unity must reach to a higher level, to be concerned with the extensions of itself that it has created on the physical plane. So, the Tarot Minor Arcana tens deal with family issues, with responsibilities, and with issues beyond the experience of the one, yet which the one is a part of in the greater whole. Ten is the zero, the completed cycle, plus the one. It is to be expected that on this higher level the one approaches life with greater experience and insight. The karmic pattern continues on a higher level in which the self reaches beyond its own limitations to attain unity. The tens in the Major Arcana are the Wheel of Fortune and the Sun.

The Ten of Wands

<u>**Simplified Meanings:**</u>

Upright – Carrying a burden; heavy responsibility; resentful of obligation; heavy lifting; back problems.

Inverted – Laying down the burden; letting go; lifting and/or back problems are in the past.

<u>**In-Depth Meanings:**</u>

When the Ten of Wands appears upright in a reading, the person it refers to, usually the client, is carrying a heavy burden. The person's responsibilities are many and heavy, almost more than he (or she) can bear, yet this person will keep trudging along, one foot in front of the other, doing what he feels necessary. Surrounding cards will define for you what the burden is. Is the client caring for an invalid mother, or supporting one? Is he a single parent with six children? Working two jobs to pay off bills? This burden is not just emotional; it is an actual, physical thing the client must do day after day.

It's true, though, that usually when one's responsibilities become a burden it's really a matter of attitude. For example, if I volunteer to do an extra job that imposes upon my time, when I first volunteer I recognize the sacrifice I must make, but it feels unimportant when weighed against the extra income and recognition. I initially do it willingly, and often even eagerly. I barely feel it is a burden because I am happy to be doing it. But some months later, when I am always tired and no one is jumping up and down applauding me any more, I begin to wonder if the little bit of extra money is really worth it. Here begins the change in attitude that will ultimately lead to my feeling put upon and resentful, sorry for myself because I no longer want the burden I've assumed, yet don't know how to gracefully release it.

Often you may help the client when you see this card in his spread by reminding him that his assumption of the burden he is carrying was voluntary, was his choice in fact. You see, when he began to feel that he had no choice except to carry it, he forgot that he was the one who made the choice and agreed to carry the burden to begin with. It's amazing what kind of change I've seen come over clients who have been reminded of this. They walk into my office worn and bent, and they walk out tall and straight, ready to face the world another day. All I need do is to ask them how they came to be carrying this responsibility, whatever it is, to begin with. They usually answer me with something like, "Well, we were having trouble making the bills, so I needed to take the extra job." Instead of merely accepting this statement, I explore it a little. How long ago was that? Does he still need the extra money now? If he hadn't taken the extra job, what would have happened? By doing this, I gradually get him to put this responsibility he's carrying back into a proper perspective. He did voluntarily assume it, and for good reasons. If those reasons still exist, and he still feels they are valid, he can continue to carry it feeling better about himself and his life because he again knows he does so by choice. I've helped to put him back in charge of his own life again. If in evaluating the situation he realizes he no longer agrees with his reason for assuming the burden, or that it turned out to be much more responsibility than he expected, or even that he's actually completed what he set out to do already, his recognition that it was his choice to assume it to begin with gives him the freedom of choice to put the burden down now.

When the client has made the choice to put down the burden, or when circumstance has removed it for him, the Ten of Wands appears inverted in the reading. I've seen this in clients' cards representing their freedom from a marriage, or getting out of a job they didn't like, or even following the death of a loved one they took care of for a long time. There is always a strong sense of relief accompanying this card when it appears inverted in a reading.

When pertinent to a job, this card upright would mean that the client will be assuming a lot of responsibility, but it could also mean that the job requires a lot of heavy lifting. When inverted, it could mean that the reason the client left the job is because of the lifting required, that he could not, or would not, do.

When Temperance is also present in the spread, this could be an indication that the client, or person represented by the closest Court card to the Ten of Wands, has a back problem. If the Ten of Wands is upright and Temperance is inverted, an injury may be indicated. If the Ten of Wands is inverted, it generally means the problem is in the past. But even here, if Temperance is inverted there could be a re-injury of the back. If the Devil appears in the spread of cards, too, the problem is chronic.

__Special Note__: Anything in our lives may be a burden to us, if our attitude is that we 'have' to do it. This card's appearance upright in a reading tells you the client is presently approaching something in his (or her) life with this attitude. He may be generally very negative, too, because so much of life is focused on the burden he thinks must be carried. Sometimes people are afraid to put the burden down because it has become their identities!

Personal Notes

The Ten of Cups

<u>**Simplified Meanings:**</u>

Upright – Happy family; happy home; two children; the immediate family.

Inverted – Unhappy family situation; problems with children.

<u>**In-Depth Meanings:**</u>

Upright, this is one of the happiest cards in the deck. The immediate family (that's mom, dad, and the kids) are doing well, and fulfilled in their everyday experience of family life. Look at the surrounding cards to find out what everybody's so overjoyed about. Are friends or relatives coming to visit – if so, you will see some travel cards. Is the family buying a new home? The Ace of Wands or Four of Wands will appear in the spread. Is there a new baby on the way? Look for the Empress, or perhaps the Ace of Cups. This is always a nice card to see in your client's spread. It gives an up feeling that will permeate the whole reading, and will make the impact of any negative cards in the spread a lot less. Upright, this card tells you the client's family is fully with and supportive of him, and vice-versa.

Often, I see the two children in the Rider-Waite version of the deck as indicative of two children in the marriage. Often they represent the client's two children, or, sometimes a third child may be represented by a nearby Page. This arrangement tells me something about the family organization. Two children may be girls, the third a boy; or two may be toddlers, while a third is a teen.

When the Ten of Cups is inverted it brings unhappiness and pain into the family. Look at the surrounding cards to find out what the difficulty is. If a family member has died, or lost a job, or is in trouble with the law, this card will turn up inverted, and the appropriate cards to reveal these situations would appear in the spread. If you should ever see this card inverted near the upright Devil and the Five of Wands, you are probably looking at a family where the wife or children are being battered. Look at the arrangement of Court cards in the spread – they will tell the story of who the protagonist is and who the victim is. Approach this subject delicately; often the victim in such a situation is terrified and doesn't know how to reach out for help, or is in outright denial. If this person is in denial, there's not a lot you can do. But if he or she can be made to talk about it, this person has taken the first step out of the situation.

Remember, this card only deals with the immediate family, and its closest friends.

Special Note: *I have found over the years that it is a good idea to collect phone numbers of local agencies and professional services that are qualified to deal with all manner of family or personal problems – from financial advisors to psychologists. Often times, clients will open up first to us about their problems, since as psychics, they assume we know it all anyway, and automatically assign to us that sense of privacy usually obtained only in the confessional. This is all very nice, and flattering to our egos, but we are generally not equipped to really help the client, nor should we try, if the problem area requires professional attention. Don't hesitate to recommend your client with major family or personal problems to the proper professional.*

Personal Notes

_____

_____

_____

_____

_____

_____

_____

_____

_____

The Ten of Pentacles

Simplified Meanings:

Upright – Extended family members; family money or business; grandparents and older people in the family; family gathering.

Inverted – Problems in the extended family; financial problems for extended family members, especially old people; a family gathering you won't attend.

In-Depth Meanings:

The Ten of Pentacles is a card rich in symbolism. It pertains to the greater family, including aunts, uncles, cousins, grandparents, nieces, nephews, in-laws, and so on. Usually when this card turns up in an upright position there is a lot of interaction between the client and the extended family. As long as it is upright, that interaction is usually good, even though tensions may exist between certain family members, as is often the case in large family groups. But when it is inverted, you can be sure something major is wrong.

If, for example, you see Temperance near the upright Ten of Pentacles, and other cards that show an active illness, you know that there is an illness in the extended family, probably involving an old person. The fact that the Ten of Pentacles is upright tells you that the family is really pulling together at this time to help. Often an additional inverted Court card will actually show you the person who is ill. If, however, the Ten of Pentacles was inverted in this case, you would know that there are real problems in the way this situation is being handled by the extended family. Look carefully at the surrounding cards to determine what these might be. Is one member of the family preventing the rest of the family from seeing this ill person? That might be indicated by an inverted Four of Cups or another card telling you an offer is declined. Is there someone blocking the person from getting proper medical care? Look to see if an inverted Three of Pentacles is present. Is the family already squabbling over the money? Look for a lot of Pentacles in the surrounding cards; maybe Justice appearing in the spread as well adds legal issues to the problem.

Because this is a Pentacle, it often brings issues of money into the reading. If you see that your client is experiencing financial problems and the Ten of Pentacles is upright in the reading, he will be able to count on the family for help. If, however, it is inverted, he should look elsewhere, because the family will not be there for him.

Perhaps an extended family member has been arrested; look for an inverted Ten of Pentacles near the Chariot and Justice. If the person is going to jail, expect to see the Devil, upright, as well.

Sometimes the inverted Ten of Pentacles merely defines the fact that there's someone in the family the client would rather not associate with, but presently must. Surrounding cards should not only show you who that person is, but what he or she does or has done to draw the client's dislike, and create discord in the family. For example, one of my clients had gone into business with his brother, and his parents had put up the money. The brother ran up gambling debts and caused the business to fold. My client was left paying back a debt to his parents that his brother ran out on. This appeared in the reading as an inverted King of Wands (my unhappy client) falling next to the inverted Ten of Pentacles (his parents) with the inverted Knight of Swords (his brother). The reading contained lots of inverted Pentacles, mirroring my client's financial problems, among which were the inverted Three of Pentacles and Ace of Pentacles, showing the failed business.

I particularly like the Rider-Waite version of this card because the picture on this card really allows it to be adapted to fit many family situations. For example, the old person in the foreground may be read as the primary subject of the card, or as an old person who sets himself aside from family issues and therefore has greater objectivity, or as an old person who stirs up trouble and then sits back to watch what happens. When you look at this card, is this the first part of the card you look at? Which of those meanings is the first to pop into your head? Or did still another meaning suggest itself to you? If it did, use it!

In various readings over the years I have read this card as an older person with two dogs. I've read it as an old person having trouble with a daughter and son in-law, or with a son and daughter-in-law. I've seen a woman (note the female figure in the background) protecting her child from her husband or lover. I've read it as a woman using her child to control her husband and manipulate him against his mother, or parents. I've read it as a couple squabbling, and a parent who sees, but carefully avoids being drawn in. It's as if every time I look at this card, the figures take on lives of their own, and the card talks to me about the present family situation. Surrounding cards will further help to define it. It doesn't make any difference if the Ten of Pentacles is upright or inverted; you can still pick any of these meanings out of it. Just remember that if it's upright, these things may be a part of family politics, but it is still an overall happy family that 'hangs together.' If it's inverted, these problems are probably blown far out of everyday family politics into something very hurtful.

Special Note: *Often the inverted posture of this card merely means that your client chooses to have no involvement with the greater family. Perhaps this person has heard of a family gathering, and is not going because he or she has nothing in common with these people and doesn't want to waste the time! The one time you will see this card inverted, whether there are family squabbles or not, is when someone has died. Then you have to let the surrounding cards tell you whether there are additional problems involved, or if it's the death that's causing the family unhappiness.*

Personal Notes

_____

_____

_____

_____

_____

_____

_____

_____

_____

_____

_____

_____

The Ten of Swords

Simplified Meanings:

Upright – Extreme pain (either emotional or physical); being back-stabbed; surgery; acupuncture.

Inverted – Pain is in the past; surgery is either in the past, delayed, or will not be done.

In-Depth Meanings:

This card is one of the worst cards in the deck when read upright, as a state of being. The person described by this card is depressed and is in physical or emotional pain that is so deep that he (or she) is just going through the motions of living. This is as bad as it gets. Usually, relative to this meaning, if it turns up in the present in the client's cards, it is not the client, but rather someone close to him that he should be offering help and understanding to. The reason I say it is probably not your client, is that when things are this bad, a person has neither the time nor the inclination to get a reading. He is too busy just trying to survive. If it's in a future position, you might give your client some warning and look at the surrounding cards to see if you can find out what the problem will be – perhaps it's avoidable! If it's in the past, shake the client's hand. He has been through it and survived! When it's inverted relative to this meaning, it means the difficulty is in the past, the client is putting life back together, he is feeling better, although the wounds are still a little raw.

This card often means being stabbed in the back, figuratively. Look at the surrounding cards to determine if this is relative to home, family, or work, and who the back-stabber is. Remember, if it's in the future, perhaps your warning can alter the outcome to something more desirable. If it's inverted, the situation is past, though the client may still be dealing with the aftermath.

I often see this card in clients' readings pertaining to surgery. If it's upright, the surgery is definite, and the part of the body being operated on probably appears in the cards surrounding it. Usually the surgery will be successful, unless you see a lot of inverted Wands nearby. It's typical to see some Wands nearby to let you know it refers to the physical action of surgery, not the emotional state of despair. If Temperance appears in the reading with it, the surgery is probably for health reasons; if not, it's probably

Additional Products and Services

If you enjoyed this book, you may be interested in the many other products and services offered at www.SandyAnastasi.com.

Personal Readings With Sandy Anastasi

Are you interested in communicating with your Guides and Higher Self in order to obtain key messages that can help you overcome the challenges you will be facing in the future? Or would you like to revisit and learn important lessons from past lives you may have lived? Are you interested in finding out just how astrologically compatible you are with your friends, family, and significant others?

The benefits of having these insights are HUGE. Many people can live for decades without having access to such information, which can provide a critical insight in how to move on and move up in life. And there are many options to fit your specific needs, such as:

- Channeled Readings
- Past Life Reading Using Tarot and/or Astrology
- Death and Afterlife Charts
- Astrology
- Astrology Comparisons

For a limited time only, I am still willing, able, and excited to take on new clients. However, I can only handle so many one-on-one sessions in a given week and I'll always give scheduling preference to my loyal client base. So if you're interested, please book as soon as possible in order to get your spot! Rates and additional information can be found at www.SandyAnastasi.com.

Workshops and Classes

Many of my clients find that the workshop environment is an ideal way to make large gains in their skills and understanding of these topics. And I agree, because workshops provide many benefits and opportunities that cannot be wholly replicated in book format. These advantages include:

- In class demonstrations for hands-on experience.

- Immediate feedback from myself and other skilled instructors.

- The ability to meet with other highly motivated people that are interested in this area of learning and development.

- Question and answer sessions for those burning questions on your mind.

- An environment full of high energy from the instructors and other students.

- An affordable cost compared to one-on-one training.

For a current listing of available workshops, please visit www.SandyAnastasi.com.

Appearances, Interviews, and Lectures

I also am available for appearances, interviews, and lectures outside of the classes and workshops already listed. Please inquire for availability, topics, and (if applicable for the particular format) pricing.

Books and Audio CDs

If you're like a majority of my friends, colleagues, and clients, then I know that an interest in one genre will turn into an eager desire to explore them all... and that's a good thing! Often some your biggest insights and "ah ha" moments will come in areas you least expect it. So while your primary interest may be in spiritual channeling, experience in Tarot reading may be the key to unlocking your ability (or at least guiding you into the right direction).

In terms of topics, my 30+ years of experience and training has allowed me to create over 100+ books and CD sets covering the following:

- Crystal and Stones

- Divination

- Dowsing

- Energy Healing

- Healing

- Kabbala

- Meditation

- Numerology

- Philosophy

- Psychic Development

- Psychic Protection

- Channeling and Spirit Communication

- Radionics

- Tarot

So regardless of which genre you're on now, there is something for everybody and something to expand into to diversify your skills and talents.

Most Popular Products

- The Psychic Development Series (books and CDs). This six-part series will systematically teach you drills and techniques that will greatly improve your current psychic abilities, regardless of your current skill level. Topics covered include: energy balancing, how to send and receive information, remote viewing, radionics, channeling/mediumship, soul retrieval, and much more!

- Basic Tarot (books and CDs). Using the Rider Waite deck – The meanings of all the cards are discussed as well as their history and many uses. Students may use any deck utilizing 78 cards. The basic Celtic cross layout is used while finishing with students doing simple but accurate readings

- The Astrology Series (books and CDs). This series will teach you the many components of reading, creating, and interpreting astrological charts. Part 1 begins with learning the basic meanings of the symbols, planets, and houses while the advanced levels cover the nuances of lunar nodes, interceptions, decans, and other important topics that are often ignored or misunderstood.

- The Psychic Development Workshops (transcripts and CDs). These expand upon the book series listed above, particularly in the following topics: psychic self-defense, seeing and feeling the aura, using the pendulum, astral travel, crystal gazing, and psychometry.

- Kabbala Pathworking (books and CDs). A unique experience in exploring the 22 paths of the Kabbala; an ancient system that becomes a roadmap to delineating the soul path to enlightenment. A series of guided visualizations on each Path are designed to open the doors of your unconscious to the energies of the Higher Self and the God consciousness within.

Free Support Materials

In order to help you get the most out of the content of the books and tapes, many of the exercise sheets and other support materials are freely available for download online at www.SandyAnastasi.com (For example the crown chakra mandala and the Psychic Development Aptitude Test). There you will also find free gifts and bonuses, such as a downloadable chakra meditation audio that you can use to balance your body's energy system. You are allowed (and highly encouraged) to give and distribute these materials in whatever ethical manner you deem appropriate to others that have an interest in this type of journey.